Praise for Kit O'Toole's
Songs We Were Singing: Guided Tours through the Beatles' Lesser Known Tracks

"In Kit O'Toole's *Songs We Were Singing* (aptly subtitled *Guided Tours through the Beatles' Lesser Known Tracks*) the reader is taken on exactly that: an informative, interesting, worth-its-weight-in-gold journey through the music of John, Paul, George, and Ringo. O'Toole knows music criticism and could plumb its depth, but she restrains herself — offering commentaries that are thorough without being dull. I was nodding, learning, and turning pages as quickly as I would with a best-selling novel. This is no dull treatise; it is a magical mystery-solving tour!"

—Jude Southerland Kessler, *The John Lennon Series
(Shoulda Been There, Shivering Inside, She Loves You)*

"Back when the Fab Four were first conquering the pop music charts, there were a number of entry points to Beatlemania. Some liked the groundbreaking long hair. Most teenage girls swooned at John, Paul, George and Ringo's looks. But many of us became fans because of the music. And one thing that made The Beatles so different was that they filled their albums with quality work, rather than just packaging a couple of hits with filler tracks.

"By the time second-generation fans like Kit O'Toole were discovering the group, the vintage film and video of their 1960s appearances must have looked kind of quaint, and long hair was no big deal. Instead, their interest in The Beatles tended to be based primarily on the music itself. So, it's particularly apt that Kit, one of the main second-generation contributors to *Beatlefan*, a magazine founded by original fans, has become a leading analyst of the Fabs' lesser-known music and lyrics, including cover tunes, largely through her 'Deep Beatles' online columns.

"Now, many of those insightful, carefully researched pieces have been collected into a handy volume that can serve as a wonderful introduction to those Beatle songs beyond the hit singles, allowing a third and, yes, even a fourth generation of fans to discover the remarkable breadth and depth of the band's music. And Kit knows her Beatles music, as she shows in championing tracks like the oft-overlooked B-side 'I'll Get You.' All in all, *Songs We Were Singing* provides a valuable overview of those deep Beatles tracks that too often get overlooked."

—**Bill King, Publisher,** *Beatlefan*

"Kit O'Toole is the definitive 'go to girl' when it comes to all things Beatles. And that's why her *Songs We Were Singing* is such a fab and erudite addition to the Fab Four folklore. Read. Enjoy and be enlightened. Yeah. Yeah. And definitely Yeah."

—**Ivor Davis,** *The Beatles and Me on Tour*

"Kit O'Toole's *Songs We Were Singing* is a delightful guide to under-appreciated gems in the Beatles' treasure trove. Offering a reader-friendly combination of geek thoroughness and fan passion, the essays are loaded with interesting observations about the music, the lyrics, and the Lennon-McCartney process. Readers will be inspired to go back, listen again, and be amazed, again.

—**Candy Leonard,** *Beatleness: How the Beatles and Their Fans Remade the World*

"Kit knows how to split the atom!...YUP and take your breath away too. Her writing is exciting and fresh....she unfolds the story like opening a box of chocolate. Her work builds up to a crescendo by breaking down all the flavors in stunning forms. It's EAR EXTASY to be treated to Kit's fine authentic work."

—**Dave Morrell,** *Horse-Doggin': Dave Morrell Archives, Vol. 1*

Kit O'Toole brings deep knowledge and deep passion to a topic that is clearly very close to her heart: some of the more obscure recordings by John, Paul, George, and Ringo (as well as Pete), both collectively and as solo artists. In each case, detailing the inspirations and motivations behind the songs, O'Toole blends a fan's love with a musicologist's analysis of the subject, and the result is an informative, entertaining, sometimes thought-provoking guide to the back roads of The Beatles' career that will prompt you to reevaluate many of their lesser known tracks."

—**Richard Buskin,** *New York Times* **bestselling author and cohost of Something about the Beatles**

"Great writers show and tell, they reveal parts of their heart even as they illuminate the concrete facts that gird those emotions, they make us see but also excite the other senses. Kit O'Toole is that kind of writer, someone who creates with a technician's particularity but — and this is the tricky part — without losing an artist's flair for the perfect splash of color. That makes her perfect for the music commentary found here, all of which necessarily requires us to hear without actually hearing. No worries. Her words do the singing."

—**Nick DeRiso, Award-winning journalist and Co-Publisher and Managing Editor**, *Something Else Reviews*

"Kit O'Toole, known for her 'A Hard Day's Net' column in *Beatlefan* and her own 'Deep Beatles' column, brings a lifetime of Beatle lore, scholarship and interpretive skills to this book, chock full of information and viewpoints you won't find anywhere else. So many Beatle-related books concentrate on the big recordings, the songs that *everybody* knows. Kit brings that same level of attention to the lesser-known tracks, the non-hit 'deep cuts' which are just as compelling and informative in their own right. *Songs We Were Singing* brings out the undervalued and the undersung to show just how deeply the Beatles' musicianship and professionalism lay. Covers as well as Beatle and ex-Beatle originals are treated in loving detail, and the reader is sure to emerge with a well-rounded understanding of the complex wealth of different musical strands that are woven together in the rich tapestry that is the Beatles' sound."

—**Walter Everett, Professor of Music Theory, University of Michigan; author of** *The Beatles as Musicians: The Quarrymen through Rubber Soul* **and** *The Beatles as Musicians: Revolver through the Anthology*

"With *Songs We Were Singing*, Kit O'Toole takes readers on a journey down the roads less traveled in Beatledom, offering up examinations of an array of overlooked gems. To infuse possibly well-worn subjects with freshness would be a challenge for any Beatleologist, but so skilled is her research and writing, Kit manages to transcend any potential pitfalls, presenting pleasing, insightful prose that is as illuminating as it is entertaining."

—**Robert Rodriguez,** *Solo in the 70s; Revolver: How the Beatles Reimagined Rock 'N' Roll; Fab Four FAQ; Fab Four FAQ 2.0*

"Kit does a wonderful job of putting together individual essays on many of these great songs and walking us through the landscape in which they were recorded. Correctly placed in chronological order, the reader can jump around in time and pick different songs from different times to read about. Very well researched and written, a book any fan of any age can truly appreciate."

—**Mark Lapidos, Owner The Fest for Beatles Fans**

"For those who want to dig into the Beatles beyond the mega hits, Kit offers an alternative canon with a trove of juicy details that recast underrated cuts in a new light. Each chapter offers something to muse on, from wild performances in Hamburg, to Paul's bass playing, to unexpected interpretations of George's lyrics, to the songs the group gave away."

—**Andrew Grant Jackson,** *Still the Greatest: The Essential Songs of the Beatles' Solo Careers*

"In a world where the topic of the Beatles has been greatly examined and explained, it's always nice to read from somebody with a "new" perspective on the once in a lifetime mania that was created by four young men from Liverpool. Kit O'Toole manages to bring a unique perspective to the subject by combining straight facts about the well documented act, along with the feelings that they not only convey, but the ones that were received, by countless planet wide fans of the band. With a strong knowledge of the days before the Beatles, the Beatle years, as well as the solo days O'Toole paints a very complete picture of a monumental topic."

—**Gregory Alexander, "Professor Moptop," Breakfast with the Beatles, WXRT-FM**

SONGS WE WERE SINGING

GUIDED TOURS THROUGH THE
BEATLES' LESSER-KNOWN TRACKS

Kit O'Toole, Ed.D.

12 BAR PUBLISHING, LLC
Clarendon Hills, Illinois

Copyright © 2015 Kit O'Toole, Ed.D.
All Rights Reserved
ISBN-10: 0996577203
ISBN-13: 978-0-9965772-0-5
12 Bar Publishing, LLC

Cover art by Enoch Doyle Jeter
Title: "See Ya on the Other Side, Lads!"
Image Commissioned by Kit O'Toole

Cover and interior design by Sara Greene
Copyright © 2015 Kit O'Toole, Ed.D.

All rights reserved. No part of this publication may be reproduced, distributed, or transmitted in any form or by any means, including photocopying, recording, or other electronic or mechanical methods, without the prior written permission of the publisher, except in the case of brief quotations embodied in critical reviews and certain other noncommercial uses permitted by copyright law.

For permission requests, write to the publisher, addressed "Attention: Permissions Coordinator," at the address below:

12barpublishing@gmail.com

CONTENTS

INTRODUCTION i

FOREWORD
Kenneth Womack
*Dean of the Wayne D. McMurray School of Humanities
and Social Sciences at Monmouth University* v

PART ONE: 1962-1964
"Like Dreamers Do" 3
"Hello Little Girl" 6
"Three Cool Cats" 9
"Love of the Loved" 12
"Crying, Waiting, Hoping" 14
*The Beatles Live! At the Star-Club in
Hamburg, Germany 1962* 17
"Ask Me Why" 21
"The Hippy Hippy Shake" 23
"I Saw Her Standing There" 25
"Kansas City / Hey-Hey-Hey-Hey!" 28
"I'll Get You" 31
"Misery" 34
"There's A Place" 37

"Hold Me Tight" 40

"Don't Bother Me" 43

"All I've Got to Do" 46

"Honey Don't" 48

"Some Other Guy" 50

"Nothin' Shakin' (But the Leaves on the Trees)" 52

"I'll Be Back" 54

"When I Get Home" 57

"I'll Cry Instead" 60

"You Can't Do That" 63

"Any Time at All" 66

"Things We Said Today" 68

"I Call Your Name" 71

"Eight Days a Week" 75

"Baby's in Black" 76

"What You're Doing" 80

"Mr. Moonlight" 83

PART TWO: 1965-1970

"Tell Me What You See" 89

"I Need You" 92

"The Night Before" 95

"The Word" 98

"Wait" 101

"Run for Your Life" 104

"Rain" 107

"I Want to Tell You" 111

"Doctor Robert" 113

"I'm Only Sleeping" 116

"Good Morning Good Morning" 119

"Baby You're a Rich Man" 122

"Everybody's Got Something to Hide
 Except Me and My Monkey" 126

"Savoy Truffle" 130

"Cry Baby Cry" 133

"Hey Bulldog" 136

"Because" 139

"You Never Give Me Your Money" 142

"Sun King" 145

"Mean Mr. Mustard" 148

"Polythene Pam" 151

"She Came in Through the Bathroom Window' 154

"Golden Slumbers" 158

"Carry That Weight" 161

"The End" 163

"Her Majesty" 167

"Dig a Pony" 170

"I've Got a Feeling" 173

"For You Blue" 176

"Free as a Bird" 179

Who Has the Best Selling Album of the Decade? 183

PART THREE: SELECT SOLO ALBUMS AND TRACKS

"Flaming Pie" 189

"Coming Up" 192

"Bluebird" 195

"Little Willow" 197

Ringo Starr Plays Philosopher in 1992's
"Weight of the World" 200

Remembering John Lennon Lesser-Known Songs 203

Want to Hear Paul McCartney's
Most Adventurous Album? Just *Press to Play* 208

Giving George Harrison's *33 1/3* Another Spin................................ 211

PART FOUR: THE 2009 REMASTERS

Meet the Beatles Again through
Their Remastered Catalog 217

"Every Sound There Is": Comparing
the Beatles' 1987 CDs and Remasters 226

What Does "Remastering" Mean Anyway?...................................... 234

Controversies Surrounding the Beatles Remasters........................... 238

Bought the Beatles Remasters? Try These CDs
to Complete Your Beatles Library... 243

A Fantasy Beatles Compilation: "Beatles Deep Cuts" 246

PART FIVE: BONUS TRACK

Ten Underrated Ringo Starr Drumming Performances 253

ACKNOWLEDGEMENTS 259

SELECTED BIBLIOGRAPHY 263

ABOUT THE AUTHOR 273

ABOUT THE ARTIST 275

DEDICATION

I dedicate this book to all Beatles fans who love their music and have been profoundly influenced by the band throughout their lives. They live by one of the Beatles' greatest mottos: "The love you take is equal to the love you make."

INTRODUCTION

When I entered my eighth grade chorus class one Friday in 1985, I had no conception that my life would be forever altered. The teacher, Mr. Tantillo, allowed students to bring in their own albums (on cassette, of course) to play for the class. Looking back, Fridays must have been "break days" for the teacher, a time when he could take a brief rest from teaching us songs such as "Leader of the Pack," "The Rose," "Memory," and "Looking Through the Eyes of Love." On this particular day, a student brought in her copy of *The Beatles' 20 Greatest Hits*, a 1982 compilation. Initially not paying much attention, I sat with my best friend discussing pop music of the day by such 1980s stalwarts as Wham!, Duran Duran, and Madonna.

Suddenly, "Eight Days A Week" blasted over the stereo speakers, and my ears perked up. The sound was completely different from anything I had heard before — the tempo was slightly offbeat, the clapping irresistibly catchy, the harmonies tight, and the lyrics charming. I had heard of the Beatles prior to this moment — my father used to play "Let It Be," "Norwegian Wood," and "Michelle" on the guitar. But that was my *parents'* music, so like a typical teenager I dismissed bands such as the Beatles as "overrated" and "old."

Clearly I had a lot to learn.

After that day I searched out all the Beatles' albums, wanting to learn as much as I could about the group. Initially I responded more to their earlier songs and found *Sgt. Pepper's Lonely Hearts Club Band*, *Magical Mystery Tour*, and the *White Album* puzzling. As I read more books about them and saw documentaries such as *The Compleat Beatles* (1984), I discovered why the Beatles endured and how they contributed to modern music. I was officially hooked.

My earlier claim of my life being forever altered after first hearing "Eight Days A Week" in Mr. Tantillo's class may seem overly dramatic. However, that moment set my life on a course I never expected. Through high school and college I wrote several papers on the Beatles (I believe I earned "A's" on them), and even found a way to rhetorically analyze the *Hard Day's Night* film in a graduate level class. In college I was hired to write for *Showcase Chicago*, a free newspaper that covered local and national bands. While I did not write about the Beatles for the publication — I mainly wrote about rock and jazz — writing about the group gave me the courage to apply for the job.

My next big break came when I subscribed to *Beatlefan*, a publication made famous by their slogan "The Authoritative Publication of Record for Fans of The Beatles." I had subscribed to the magazine due to its stellar reputation, and dreamed of writing for *Beatlefan* someday. In 1996 the Internet began its path to ubiquity, leading to Beatles-related websites multiplying on the web. Thus the "Hard Day's Net" column was born, and the number of high-quality websites just keeps growing. Gradually I began writing features for the magazine, my favorites being articles on Apple artists, a Generation X member's perspective on *Sgt. Pepper's Lonely Hearts Club Band*, and a defense of the inventive Beatles/Jay Z mashup *The Grey Album*. After finishing my masters and doctorate degrees I decided to return music journalism, first writing for *Blogcritics* and eventually moving up to music editor. After a few years I moved on to *Something Else Reviews* and *Blinded by Sound*, two sites I still write for. The latter blog allows me to indulge in my other musical passion — soul and R&B — but the former gave me the opportunity to write a regular Beatles column, "Deep Beatles." Those articles, as well as previous pieces I wrote for Blogcritics, form the core of *Songs We Were Singing*.

This book will take you through some of the Beatles' lesser known songs — the tracks that were never released as A-sides or any kind of single. You may have forgotten about these unjustly overlooked songs, but they are important pieces of the Beatles' artistic legacy. They illustrate how the band grew artistically over a remarkably short period of time. *Songs We Were Singing* is a guidebook of sorts — it takes you on a tour of these songs, delving into the songwriting, recording, and place within Beatles and music history. By reading these essays, you may listen to the music in an entirely new way.

Part one addresses the formative years, 1962-1965, from the Star Club performances and Decca audition to the album that would mark phase two of the Beatles' career, *Rubber Soul*. After this discussion of their early compositions and live performances, part two covers Beatles 2.0, examining key songs from *Revolver* through *Let It Be*, with a "bonus track" from *Anthology 1*. Part three moves from the Beatles to the solo years, studying how select songs and albums by George Harrison, John Lennon, Paul McCartney, and Ringo Starr reflect their Beatles years yet demonstrate their individual identities. The fourth part consists of a series I wrote for *Blogcritics* commemorating the 2009 Beatles CD remasters. Learn about the remastering process, controversies surrounding the albums, and differences between the 1987 and 2009 CDs.

The final section consists of a "bonus track" exclusive to *Songs We Were Singing*, never before published. Too often Starr has been underestimated as a drummer and artist, so I pay tribute to a crucial member of the Beatles by highlighting ten overlooked drumming performances on Beatles songs.

For best results, read *Songs We Were Singing* as you listen to the tracks. Don your favorite pair of headphones, sit back with this book, and immerse yourself in the sounds of the Beatles' music. No matter how many times you listen to their albums, no matter how much you think you know the songs inside out, there is always something new to discover. Cherish the vocal, the guitar riff, the bass line, and drum fill you never noticed before. Excitement, surprise, discovery, and emotion: those elements are what make being a Beatles fan truly special.

—*Kit O'Toole, July 2015*

FOREWORD

Kenneth Womack

Dean of the Wayne D. McMurray School of Humanities and Social Sciences at Monmouth University

As we celebrate this unfolding decade of Beatles 50th anniversaries, music critics have appropriately marked the occasion by reflecting on the billions of recordings that the band has sold — an incredible feat unto itself — along with the virtual industry of merchandise that the Beatles phenomenon has spawned of nearly every possible size, shape, and vintage. Chief among this industry is the publication of more than 3,000 book-length volumes devoted to the lives and works of John, Paul, George, and Ringo — as a collective, as solo artists, and otherwise. From Beatlemania's earliest days, fans have enjoyed reading about those Four Lads from Liverpool, greedily consuming every possible morsel from the bandmates' earliest days through the present.

With *Songs We Were Singing: Guided Tours through the Beatles' Lesser-Known Tracks*, Kit O'Toole has achieved a truly rare accomplishment in Beatles studies. She has succeeded, quite simply, in traversing new and, in some cases, frequently unexplored ground. By concentrating on the nooks and crannies of the group's massive corpus, she has shed new light on tracks that some listeners — and, at times, even the Beatles themselves — might consider to be throwaways or, for lack of a better word, mere filler to round out their album-length forays.

For most readers, the greatness of songs like, say, "A Day in the Life" and "Hey Jude" has become uniformly self-evident, and, not surprisingly, they have received exhaustive critical treatment from nearly every possible perspective. To her great credit, O'Toole leads us into less well-trodden territory. Through her aptly-named "guided tours," she provides casual and more sophisticated fans alike with historical backgrounds and compositional contexts for each recording, while positing thoroughgoing and perceptive readings of the songs and their places in the Beatles' canon. In so doing, O'Toole's study highlights the incredible vastness and innumerable, often overlooked treasures evinced by the Beatles' wide-ranging catalogue.

As she progresses from the bandmates' incipient days as songwriters through the solo years and beyond, O'Toole peels back the layers of the Beatles' recording history and affords us with new readings of the group's more ephemeral works. The history of the Fab Four, and any nuanced understanding of their unparalleled contribution to twentieth-century Western culture, must first come to terms with the fact that the group's legacy is, almost without dispute, an embarrassment of riches. Looking beyond the touchstones of nearly 30 number-one singles and a raft of non-charting classic songs — not to mention such long-playing masterworks as *Rubber Soul*, *Revolver*, *Sgt. Pepper's Lonely Hearts Club Band*, *The Beatles (The White Album)*, and *Abbey Road* — O'Toole delineates the Beatles' stunning level of artistic depth beyond their most obvious aesthetic gems.

To inaugurate this much-needed journey, O'Toole deftly begins her study with an analysis of the band's failed Decca audition in January 1962. Rather than distancing her study from those early recordings, O'Toole highlights their place on the Beatles' road to artistic maturity, reading such songs as "Like Dreamers Do" and "Hello Little Girl" as precursors to the group's work on their first album *Please Please Me*. Even more impressively, she contextualizes recordings such as the Decca audition's tongue-in-cheek "Three Cool Cats" as being emblematic of the high-octane, anything-goes atmosphere of the band's Cavern Club performances and draws us into the sweaty confines of those early, rough-and-tumble lunchtime shows. Witness O'Toole's commentary on the band's BBC rendition of "Some Other Guy": "Listening to this performance," she writes, "one can imagine being packed into the Cavern Club like sardines, condensation dripping from the walls, watching the local boys just on the brink of stardom." O'Toole goes on to read "Three Cool Cats" as a kind of proto-feminist forerunner of later Beatles tunes like "Drive My Car" in which the female protagonist puts one over on her unwitting male counterpart.

In her reading of the Beatles' early years, O'Toole deftly, if not courageously takes on the notorious *The Beatles Live! At The Star-Club in Hamburg, Germany 1962* recordings, underscoring their key role in the band's development rather than assigning them — given their crude origins and, worse yet, even cruder sound quality — to the dustbin of rock history. In her perceptive study of Paul McCartney's vocal control on "Hippy Hippy Shake," for example, she notes the song's raw, raunchy undercurrents and their echoes of the singer's evolving work on "I Saw Her Standing There," the track that eventually kicks off their first album. In this way, O'Toole shrewdly couches *The Beatles Live! At The Star-Club in Hamburg, Germany 1962* as an opportunity for fans to eavesdrop on the primitive, unvarnished sound of the pre-Beatlemania bandmates in postwar, vice-ridden Hamburg, their most famous proving ground.

O'Toole's discussion of early albums like *With the Beatles* brings the group's unbridled energy and musicianship into full flower with such tunes as "Hold Me Tight" and "All I've Got to Do." In her extensive reading of George Harrison's songwriting debut with "Don't Bother Me," she draws a line from his first composition through his more nuanced work to come. In similar fashion, she reflects on an early, pre-Ringo Starr vocal performance of "Honey Don't" for the BBC with John Lennon as lead singer demonstrating his playful frenzy and unabashed love of rock and roll.

Likewise, O'Toole astutely reads the non-standout tracks on *A Hard Day's Night* as densely packed instances of artistic growth. She recognizes songs like "I'll Be Back," the album's wistful closer, as signifying shifts in the ways in which Lennon and McCartney "address complex themes of love and loss, idealism and cynicism, innocence and maturity." She takes on tracks like "When I Get Home" and "I'll Cry Instead" — songs that the bandmates themselves could scarcely stomach in the sober backcast of history — and sagely reminds us about their origins, skillful creation, and lasting impact. To this end, O'Toole reads "Things We Said Today" as a brilliant depiction of "future nostalgia." As with "I'll Be Back," songs like "Things We Said

Today" reveal just how strong the band's corpus is beyond their slew of hit-making numbers.

With *Beatles for Sale*, easily one of the group's most disrespected long-players, O'Toole reinterprets songs like "Baby's in Black" and "What You're Doing" as conduits for understanding the band's later work. For her part, O'Toole can't help poking fun at the album's despondent status among the Beatles' albums — a corpus that, by any measure, is riddled with masterpieces: "As you begin deliberations, ladies and gentlemen of the jury, I ask you to put aside all prejudices as you pull out your *Beatles for Sale* copy," she writes. With "What You're Doing," for instance, she describes producer George Martin's piano accents as being coherent with a possible shift in romantic mood in the songwriters' approach to their craft. O'Toole's work regarding *Beatles for Sale* is highlighted by her spirited defense of the oft-maligned "Mr. Moonlight." "Can anyone make a better case for Lennon being one of the great rock vocalists by hearing his opening line?" she asks. "When he shouts 'Mr. Moonlight,' one can hear his cords shredding a la 'Twist and Shout.' This technique perfectly sets the mood for the heart-rending lines describing the narrator as praying and begging while on his knees."

O'Toole offers similar eye-opening analyses of tracks from *Help!* and *Rubber Soul*, reading songs such as the former's "Tell Me What You See" as signposts along the pathways of the band's musical and lyrical development. In addition to ascribing *Rubber Soul*'s "The Word" as a kind of musical and lyrical foreshadowing of the Summer of Love, she succeeds in re-situating "Run for Your Life," with its dour, hard-driving masculinist ethos, as a touchstone along Lennon's larger, lifetime progress towards redeeming the violence of gender politics in *Sgt. Pepper's Lonely Hearts Club Band*'s "Getting Better" and later concluding that process in such solo efforts as *Imagine*'s "Jealous Guy" and *Double Fantasy*'s "Woman." Through such moments, O'Toole observes, Lennon "understands his cruelty and vows to change."

Not surprisingly, O'Toole mines fewer and fewer "deep cuts" as she explores the bandmates' works from *Revolver* through the twilight of the group's career. As the band's accolades continued to pile up, the stakes of authorship rose ever higher, resulting in many fewer tracks that don't enjoy classic status. Along the way, O'Toole still finds plenty of key moments to examine, including the sophisticated musical arrangement at the heart of Harrison's "I Want to Tell You" on *Revolver*, as well as Lennon's multi-textured performance on *Sgt. Pepper*'s "Good Morning Good Morning." Her study of *The White Album* is highlighted by a piercing interpretation of Lennon's overt heroin motifs in "Everybody's Got Something to Hide Except Me and My Monkey," which O'Toole rightly extols for its raucous rock-and-roll energy. "Raunchy and loud?" O'Toole asks. "Mission accomplished."

Rounding out the Beatles' career, O'Toole pauses to admire the lyrical power inherent in such *White Album* tracks as "Savoy Truffle" and "Cry Baby Cry," while pausing to enjoy the ethereal beauty and aesthetic bliss of the bandmates' breathtaking vocal performances on *Abbey Road*'s "Because." In a similar vein, she reclaims songs like Lennon's "Dig a Pony" and McCartney's "I've Got a Feeling." Writing about the former, O'Toole questions attempts to dismiss the track "as a throwaway. Yet the lyrics contain complexity beneath the surface, and the rumbling guitars, gospel-tinged piano, skilled drumming, and tight harmonies elevate the song from *Let It Be* curiosity to a prime example of Lennon's sophisticated wordplay."

In so doing, O'Toole adeptly reminds us what great music criticism is all about: learning, in an ever deeper and more meaningful fashion, how to appreciate the popular artifacts that we consume with unchecked abandon. She also succeeds in earning the greatest tribute that any Beatles book can offer: O'Toole's volume will find you seeking out those deep cuts in your own music library and listening to the songs as you read along with the author's analyses. In such moments, the group's music comes alive yet again — and in new and unforgettable ways. To paraphrase McCartney's insightful lyrics from which this wonderful book draws its title, we always come back to the songs we were singing — and for very good reason. O'Toole's thoughtful book reminds us why we return, time and time again, to enjoy the company of the Beatles and their near-masterworks.

Kenneth Womack is the author of The Beatles Encyclopedia: Everything Fab Four *and* Long and Winding Roads: The Evolving Artistry of the Beatles. *Womack has also edited collections such as* Reading the Beatles: Cultural Studies, Literary Criticism and the Fab Four *and* The Cambridge Companion to the Beatles.

PART ONE
1962-1964

"Like Dreamers Do"
Decca Audition (January 1962)

In 1962, the Beatles did not pass the audition. January 1 of that year was supposed to be the Beatles' huge break, as manager Brian Epstein had secured an audition with Decca Records. Decca A&R rep Mike Smith had attended the group's December 13, 1961 Cavern Club show. Liking what he heard, he approached the Beatles and Epstein to record an audition tape for the label. The recording session was set for December 31, 1961. What followed was a virtual comedy of errors.

First, road manager and assistant Neil Aspinall agreed to drive the boys from Liverpool to Decca's West Hampstead Studios. However, the group encountered a snowstorm during the trip, resulting in Aspinall getting lost. When they finally arrived at 10 p.m. December 31, they had been on the road over ten hours. Epstein (who had arrived earlier via train) and Smith rescheduled the session for the following day, hoping the boys would be well rested.

When a freezing January 1 dawned, the Beatles' anxiety was palpable; they felt tremendous pressure over performing to the label's satisfaction. Meanwhile, Smith had thoroughly enjoyed New Year's Eve, thus he arrived late to the recording studio. To make matters worse, Smith insisted that the Beatles use Decca's amplifiers rather than their own, thus increasing the group's anxiety over using unfamiliar equipment. Relying on their Hamburg and Cavern Club setlists, George Harrison, John Lennon, Paul McCartney and then-drummer Pete Best recorded 15 tracks during their one-hour session. Featuring mostly covers and a handful of Lennon/McCartney originals, the audibly nervous Beatles rushed through their tracks.

As Mark Lewisohn points out in *Tune In*, what happened next remains murky. Previous accounts claimed Decca A&R Head Dick Rowe rejected the group, informing Epstein that "guitar groups are on the way out." Instead, Lewisohn found evidence suggesting Decca had made an offer, but Epstein turned Rowe down, believing he could find a better deal elsewhere. In any case, the Beatles would go on to sign with EMI and replace Best with Ringo Starr, thus finalizing the band's lineup.

Meanwhile, the Decca audition tape resurfaced through bootlegs, with select tracks later appearing on the *Anthology 1* collection. Did the Beatles' performance really merit Rowe's harsh assessment? Listening to the tracks today, is the band's talent and originality evident in their voices? The debate rages, but the Decca tapes are an important historical document of the Beatles' early sound. The next few "Deep Beatles" columns will examine songs from these sessions, inviting fresh evaluations of their most famous audition.

Kicking off the series is "Like Dreamers Do," one of Paul McCartney's earliest compositions. Written in 1957, McCartney and Lennon performed the song as far back as their Quarrymen days. As the Beatles grew in confidence, they decided to sneak it into setlists from their early 1960s Cavern Club shows. During this period, most bands never dared to perform original songs, preferring to please the crowd with familiar tunes. As McCartney told biographer Barry Miles, "For you to write it yourself was a bit plonky, and the songs obviously weren't that great, but I felt we really had to break through that barrier because if we never tried our own songs we'd just never have the confidence to continue writing." According to *Tune In*, Harrison believed "Like Dreamers Do" was heavily influenced by McCartney's father Jim's interest in George Gershwin tracks, such as "I'll Build A Stairway to Paradise."

In the recording studio, the Beatles played their usual positions. Paul McCartney on bass and lead vocal, John Lennon on rhythm guitar, George Harrison on lead guitar and Pete Best on drums. His voice at first noticeably quivering, McCartney sings that he first saw his beloved in his dreams, and predicts that they will eventually fall in love. He appears to gain confidence after delivering the first chorus, playfully stretching out the syllable "I" as well as rhythmically chanting the word "you," letting his voice gradually modulate downward before crooning the next verse.

McCartney's Liverpudlian accent charmingly creeps in at various points, such as pronouncing "saw" as "saw-r." At other times he imitates Elvis Presley's style, which is particularly noticeable in the lines "You, you came just one dream ago, and now I know that I will love you." He draws out the second syllable in "ago," turning the word into "ago-uh." The word "know" receives the same treatment, this time turning it into a two-syllable term ("know-uh"). McCartney's stage name early on in his music career was "Paul Ramon," and he sounds as if he was channeling that persona here.

What "Like Dreamers Do" portrays is a very young band searching for their distinctive sound. Paul McCartney and the others are in the "imitative" stage, emulating their idols and popular songs of the day. Yet unlike their peers, the Beatles began composing their own material, risking the disapproval of audiences craving familiar songs. Lennon and McCartney recognized that a catchy hook would attract listeners, and writing about universally relatable subject would ensure that teenagers would purchase the singles. They would refine the technique in a remarkably short period of time, but "Like Dreamers Do" is an admirable first attempt.

Interestingly, "Like Dreamers Do" would gain new life once Beatlemania took over. As the Beatles rehearsed for a television appearance in 1964, they met then-rising UK beat group the Applejacks. Riding high on their top ten hit "Tell Me When," the group also became notable for having a female bass guitarist. Impressed, Lennon and McCartney offered an original composition to them: "Like Dreamers Do." The group's spirited cover would peak at No. 20 on the UK pop charts.

One more interesting fact: What was the Applejacks' record label? Decca.

Originally published May 1, 2015 at http://somethingelsereviews.com/2015/05/01/beatles-like-dreamers-do-decca-audition/

"Hello Little Girl"
Decca Audition (1962)

Last week's Deep Beatles took a closer look at the Beatles' 1962 audition for Decca Records. Since manager Brian Epstein wanted to present Decca's A&R department with a vivid picture of the Beatles' live shows, he asked the band to perform covers of Buddy Holly, Chuck Berry, Barrett Strong, and many others. Unlike many bands of the time, though, the Beatles brought in original songs as well: "Like Dreamers Do," "Love of the Loved," and "Hello Little Girl."

After the audition, the group tossed aside these early John Lennon/Paul McCartney compositions in favor of more mature, sophisticated fare. Studying tracks like "Hello Little Girl," however, reveals their influences and amazingly rapid creative growth.

Although Lennon composed "Hello Little Girl" in 1957, the song did not surface on any recording until 1960 (they had performed the song as well as "Like Dreamers Do" as the Quarrymen in concerts since 1958). Lennon, McCartney, George Harrison, and then-bassist Stu Sutcliffe recorded a demo of the track reportedly at McCartney's boyhood home.

Only available on bootleg, the song suffers from murky sound quality, some sloppiness (it is a demo, after all), and half-finished lyrics. The tempo is slightly slower, perhaps because Pete Best apparently did not take part in this session. Still, the close harmonies reflect the Everly Brothers, while the chord progression resemble Holly's early work.

In one of his last interviews, Lennon cited another unlikely muse: Cole Porter and his 1936 classic "It's De-Lovely." "I remember some Thirties or Forties song which was [singing]

'You're delightful, you're delicious and da da da. Isn't it a pity that you are such a scatterbrain,'" Lennon joked with writer David Sheff. "That always fascinated me for some reason or another. It's also connected to my mother. It's all very Freudian. She used to sing that one. So I made 'Hello Little Girl' out of it."

Fast forward to January 1, 1962, when a clearly nervous Beatles entered Decca Studios to record an audition tape. Eager to show off their still-developing songwriting skills, they performed the now-more-polished "Hello Little Girl." They never performed it again except for an audition for BBC radio on February 12, 1962. However, the track gained new life when it was offered to another Merseybeat group, the Fourmost, in July 1963. Not coincidentally, George Martin was producing the band at the time. Just two weeks before, Gerry and the Pacemakers had recorded a demo of the song, but ultimately elected to release another single, "I Like It."

The Fourmost's version reached No. 9 on the UK charts; according to McCartney, the song suited the group's lighthearted image. "Unfortunately the words aren't too wonderful. They're a bit average, but the Fourmost were eager to have a hit and they were very good friends of ours," McCartney told biographer Barry Miles.

In a very short time, the legendary Lennon/McCartney songwriting team proved they could write memorable hits like "Love Me Do" and "Please Please Me." While "Hello Little Girl" does not rank in quality with those songs, it represents an important stage in the Beatles' career. They quickly learned that they had to leave the tougher image behind, perform polished sets, and write songs that, quite frankly, would sell.

Clearly Lennon had listened closely to the hits of the day, and mimicked them in "Hello Little Girl." The tight harmonies recall early Everly Brothers hits such as "Bye Bye Love" or "Wake Up Little Susie," while the beat and chord changes echo now-classics like "Rave On!," and "Oh Boy!" Holly established himself as the master of the pop record, blending catchy hooks with intelligent lyrics; Lennon recognized that and tried to emulate Holly's gift.

In addition, listen closely to the rhythm and vocals for another reason: they anticipate the Merseybeat sound, the term denoting bands deriving from Liverpool. Gerry and the Pacemakers and the Searchers were two notable acts of the genre, and it's evident why "Hello Little Girl" was initially offered to the former group. The relentlessly upbeat, energetic sound, the close harmonies, and (somewhat) memorable chorus capture the sound perfectly.

The rest is history: The Beatles did not pass the Decca audition, but months later signed with Parlophone Records, a division of EMI. The three originals performed at the Decca session largely vanished from view until 1995's *Anthology* series. At Martin's urging, the band fired Best and hired drummer Ringo Starr. Soon the Lennon/McCartney team would demonstrate how they had grown as songwriters, and how they, like Holly, could blend catchy melodies with sophisticated chords and intelligent lyrics to create enduring hits.

Indeed, "Hello Little Girl" is one of the earliest signals of the change from the raucous "Silver Beatles" to the mature "Beatles."

Originally published March 15, 2013 at http://somethingelsereviews.com/2013/03/15/deep-beatles-hello-little-girl-1962/

"Three Cool Cats"
Decca Audition (January 1962)

Growing up in Liverpool, George Harrison, John Lennon and Paul McCartney had unique access to American R&B singles. Being a major port city, Liverpool imported American instruments and records. As such, the Mersey Beat sound would be heavily influenced by rock and R&B from the States. In fact, groups like the Beatles and the Rolling Stones would reintroduce American audiences to their own artists through covers. (Think Arthur Alexander and Larry Williams.) Harrison, Lennon and McCartney were particular fans of the songwriting team Jerry Leiber and Mike Stoller, the duo who penned numerous hits for the Coasters and other classics such as "Kansas City."

By 1959, the future Beatles became obsessed with another single: "Three Cool Cats," the B-side to the Coasters' "Charlie Brown." It became a staple of their early stage shows, thus they naturally selected the song for inclusion in their Decca audition. As it turned out, "Three Cool Cats" was one of the true highlights of the Decca tapes.

According to Mark Lewisohn's *Tune In*, the period found Harrison, Lennon, and McCartney constantly practicing the three-part harmonies essential to the song's success. Then known as the Quarrymen, they would perform the track at the Casbah along with then-drummer Pete Best. After enthusiastic audience response, they kept "Three Cool Cats" in their setlists through Hamburg and their eventual return to Liverpool, most famously at the Cavern Club. Fans cheered Harrison's lead vocals as well as Lennon and McCartney's backing harmonies, particularly when Lennon would utter the line "Hey man, save one chick for me" in funny voices.

The Beatles' cover of the Coasters' "Three Cool Cats" became an obvious choice for the Decca audition. After all, the track always performed well in the clubs, and it showcased their onstage charisma.

The Beatles' lineup for this track included Harrison on vocals and lead guitar; McCartney on backing vocals and bass; Lennon on backing vocals and rhythm guitar; and Best on drums. Harrison performs a decent guitar solo, but his voice is the star. It suggests that he sang the track with a wink, appreciating the sly lyrics. He enunciates the words, stressing how these "cats" are actually penniless. Still, they try to pick up "three cool chicks" who are amusingly "splitting up a bag of potato chips."

Next comes the dialogue, with John Lennon and Paul McCartney assuming the roles of the other two "cats." McCartney and Lennon cry out which "chick" they each want, both using bizarre voices. The three Beatles harmonize on the title phrase as well as the "three cool chicks" lines, demonstrating that their endless rehearsals had resulted in tighter vocals. (This technique would reappear in such original Beatles tracks as "Yes It Is," "I'm a Loser," and "Baby's in Black," among many others.)

Lennon and McCartney may have also been inspired by the song's "twist ending," a method they would employ in the Beatles' "Drive My Car." The three main characters suffered from the delusion that they were cool; in actuality, George Harrison reveals, "three cool chicks made three fools out of three cool cats."

Unlike other Decca tracks, "Three Cool Cats" features a more confident performance and a glimpse into the Beatles' early stage shows. They had learned to "mach schau" during their Hamburg days, and their spirited rendition of the Coasters B-side proved they had internalized this lesson. By 1962, the Beatles had learned how to engage audiences with humor and musicianship.

While the Beatles would eventually drop the song from their concert setlists, "Three Cool Cats" remains an early favorite among fans and one of the few standouts from the infamous Decca audition. Judging from the *Get Back/Let It Be* sessions, the Beatles never lost affection for the track; at one point they broke into a spontaneous slower version of "Three Cool Cats," as if reminding themselves of their previous camaraderie.

Originally published May 15, 2015 at http://somethingelsereviews.com/2015/05/15/beatles-three-cool-cats-deep-beatles/

"Loved Of The Loved"
Decca Audition (January 1962)

Primarily a McCartney composition, "Love of the Loved" features a slight Latin rhythm and a vocal performance that demonstrates the singer had worked on refining his range and phrasing. The Beatles never officially released the song, although it was later covered by a fellow Liverpudlian.

According to Mark Lewisohn's *Tune In*, McCartney first penned the track in 1959 while walking home, either from a date or John Lennon's house. His then-girlfriend Dot Rhone later claimed he had written the lyrics with her in mind, but Paul McCartney never publicly commented on this assertion.

Lewisohn points out that the bridge resembles the Teddy Bears' "To Know Him Is to Love Him" — a distinct possibility, since the Beatles performed the song in their sets. It became a staple of the Beatles' (then the Quarrymen's) concerts, with McCartney utilizing the crooning manner he employed on "Til There Was You" and "Besame Mucho." While playing Cavern Club shows, McCartney would sing "with his face turned up and angled, big eyes fixed on the far end of the tunnel, above the heads of the crowds," Lewisohn writes.

By the time manager Brian Epstein secured the audition with Decca Records, the Beatles had amassed a live repertoire composed of covers and originals, the latter an unusual trait for groups of the time. Thus Epstein urged the boys to perform "Like Dreamers Do," "Hello Little Girl," and "Love of the Loved" to demonstrate Lennon and McCartney's versatility and songwriting ability.

When the Beatles cut the Decca audition tape on January 1, 1962, their nervousness was evident on various tracks, and "Love of the Loved" is no exception. Paul McCartney's voice slightly quivers and he repeatedly overemphasizes the "k" in the word "look." Pete Best's drumming is unremarkable and lacks power, although John Lennon and George Harrison play decent rhythm and lead guitar, respectively.

Since "Love of the Loved" was an early composition, McCartney was still learning the songwriting craft and had yet to write sophisticated lyrics. Where the familiar McCartney shines through is at the very end, when he sings the title phrase and emits a falsetto "ooh," a technique that would become a trademark of future Beatles recordings.

Once the Beatles secured their contract with EMI, they shelved "Love of the Loved" for other originals. By 1963, Brian Epstein wanted to build a roster of performers, and on September 6 signed his lone female artist: singer Cilla Black.

Epstein persuaded Paul McCartney to dust off "Love of the Loved" and present it to Black. Thus George Martin produced her first single, "Love of the Loved," and it was released on September 27, 2963. Unfortunately, the song did not perform well, only reaching No. 30 on the UK charts.

Cilla Black's rendition differs greatly from the original in that the drumming remains very much in the foreground, with horns blaring throughout the recording — perhaps to complement Black's big, brassy voice. Her vocals do reveal the slight catchiness of the chorus and bridge, and demonstrate that Paul McCartney was rapidly developing an ear for memorable hooks.

"Love of the Loved" may not have earned the Beatles the Decca contract, nor did it score a hit for Black, but it nevertheless retains historical significance in the Beatles' development as songwriters and performers.

Originally published May 29, 2015 at http://somethingelsereviews.com/2015/05/29/the-beatles-love-of-the-loved-deep-beatles/

"Crying, Waiting, Hoping"
Decca Audition (January 1962)

As the Beatles finished their rocking rendition of "Get Back" at the conclusion of their 1969 Apple rooftop concert, John Lennon joked "I would like to say thank you on behalf of the group and ourselves and I hope we've passed the audition." While unbelievable today, there was one time when the Beatles did not pass the audition: January 1, 1962.

That day, the Beatles recorded their demo for London's Decca Records. A very nervous Lennon, Paul McCartney, George Harrison, and then-drummer Pete Best tore through selections from their live shows (mainly eclectic covers) as well as a few Lennon/McCartney originals ("Like Dreamers Do," "Hello Little Girl," and "Love of the Loved"). Head of A&R Dick Rowe famously rejected the group, stating that "guitar groups are on the way out." Luckily, manager Brian Epstein ignored the advice and later secured a deal with EMI.

The oft-bootlegged Decca session, however, showcases the Beatles at their earliest, as they were transforming from a rough Hamburg-trained rock act to a professional group. This month, Deep Beatles takes another look at these audition tapes, beginning with their cover of Buddy Holly's "Crying, Waiting, Hoping."

In 1961, Epstein was busily shopping around his new clients to various London labels with no luck. Their fortunes seemed to change on December 13, 1961, when Decca A&R rep Mike Smith attended one of the Beatles' Cavern Club shows. Smith then approached the band to record an audition tape, and they set a date: December 31, 1961. Road manager and assistant Neil Aspinall agreed to drive the group to the West Hampstead Studios; unfortunately a snowstorm, along with Aspinall getting lost, made the trip last over 10 hours.

They all arrived at 10 p.m. (Epstein had already arrived, as he had traveled by train), so the recording session was rescheduled for the following day.

The next day found the nerve-wracked Beatles at Decca studios, on time. Smith arrived late, having partied late the night before; to further make the situation difficult, he insisted that the group use Decca's amplifiers instead of their own. In just about an hour, the Beatles (at this point still called "The Silver Beatles") recorded 15 songs, all selected by Epstein. With Decca producer and ex-Shadows drummer Tony Meehan behind the control board, the group tore through numerous songs they had performed in their club shows, including "Crying, Waiting, Hoping."

Their appreciation of the Holly track should come as no surprise — the rocker was an early influence on the group's playing style, and his distinctive chord changes and lyrics created a model for the budding songwriters. Numerous Merseybeat groups covered the track, and the Beatles were no different. Harrison assumes the lead vocal here, slightly mimicking Holly's vocal tics, and faithfully reproduces original guitarist Donald Amone's solo. The song's merits are clear: the call-and-response motif, the uptempo rhythm, and simple but memorable chorus would draw positive responses from crowds. Remarkably poised, Harrison croons the first lines: "Crying, waiting, hoping, you'll come back; I just can't seem to get you off my mind." During the bridge, the group demonstrates their tight harmonies, particularly on the "do do do" backing vocals.

One question remains: How was Best as a drummer? Debate still rages whether Best deserved the negative criticism from future producer Martin. On "Crying, Waiting, Hoping," Best had to execute a somewhat complex drum pattern, and does so adequately. However, he lacked Ringo Starr's pounding, bass-heavy technique, which became a crucial factor in early hits like "I Want to Hold Your Hand." That unique style injected youthful energy into the track, accelerating the excitement already present in their teenage fans. Best was not a terrible drummer, but Starr possessed a flair needed to distinguish the Beatles from other so-called "beat groups" of the time.

The rest is history: Decca rejected the Beatles, instead choosing competing band Brian Poole and the Tremeloes. While that act scored a hit with their cover of the Contours' "Do You Love Me" in 1963, they never matched the Beatles' creativity or popularity. Meanwhile, Epstein finally persuaded EMI to give them a chance, Martin liked what he heard, and Starr soon joined the band. Interestingly the Beatles revisited the song in 1963, when they performed the song for BBC radio.

While the Decca sessions may not present the Beatles at their best, they hint at the originality and enthusiasm that would soon propel their career.

Originally published March 1, 2013 at http://somethingelsereviews.com/2013/03/01/deep-beatles-crying-waiting-hoping-1962/

The Beatles Live! At The Star-Club in Hamburg, Germany 1962 (1977)

"The Star Club Tapes": this very phrase inspires spirited debate among Beatles fans. Are they garbage, or do they serve as an important historical document? Should they be officially released, or has Apple been correct in prohibiting a Beatles-sanctioned Star Club album?

Love it or hate it, *The Beatles Live! At The Star-Club In Hamburg, Germany 1962* provides a murky-sounding snapshot of a crucial crossroads in Beatles history. Ringo Starr had recently joined the group, and they had just scored their first UK hit, "Love Me Do." They were unknown in America and just gaining popularity in Britain, and their set list still reflected their earlier Hamburg shows — heavily favoring covers over original songs. In a few months, Beatlemania would detonate, ending their small club shows for good.

For the next few columns, "Deep Beatles" will explore highlights from the Star Club recordings, examining how their sound was shaped by these early performances. In a slight departure, this edition will focus not on one song, but the history of the entire album. An understanding of the *Live! At the Star-Club's* long and winding journey provides crucial context for appreciation of these primitive-sounding recordings. As our *Something Else!* editor Nick DeRiso said: "It doesn't get any deeper than this."

The story begins on December 17, 1962, when the Beatles returned — this time, reluctantly — to Hamburg for the fifth and final time. According to Mark Lewisohn's *The Beatles Live!*, they had previously committed to the gig, which also included Liverpool acts Johnny and the Hurricanes, the Strangers, King-Size Taylor and the Dominoes, Tony Sheridan Roy Young, and Carol Elvin.

Their club residency lasted from December 18-31, and during this time at least three sets were recorded, thanks to King-Size Taylor and the Dominoes leader Ted Taylor. He had recently purchased a reel-to-reel recorder, and Star Club manager Adrian Barber borrowed it to record the various musicians' sets. Placing a microphone on a table in front of the stage, Barber operated the equipment, recording at a tape speed of 3¾-inches per second. After recording at least three sets, Barber then presented the tapes to Taylor. Questions of ownership have dogged the tapes ever since.

Taylor claimed that one of the Beatles allowed him to record the show in exchange for buying rounds of beer for the band. When the Beatles soared in popularity, Taylor offered to sell manager Brian Epstein the Star Club tapes, but was apparently unsuccessful. However, the tapes would resurface in 1972, when the Beatles' early booking agent Allan Williams somehow gained possession of the recordings.

According to Williams, Taylor had left the tapes with a recording engineer, but the recordings were eventually abandoned. In 1972, Williams said he, Taylor, and the engineer retrieved the tapes to find a buyer. A year later, they met Starr and George Harrison at Apple headquarters, offering to sell them the Star Club tapes for £5,000. When the duo declined, Williams sold the tapes to Paul Murphy, then head of BUK Records. Murphy established a new company, Lingasong, to press the recordings; he then sold distribution rights to Double H Licensing. Both parties spent over $100,000 to remix and remaster the poor sound quality in preparation for release.

Four years passed before *The Beatles Live! At The Star-Club In Hamburg, Germany 1962* was set for release. The footage was edited to a 26-track double album, but work soon halted when an Apple lawyer contacted Murphy in January 1977. According to *The 910's* article "The Beatles vs. Lingasong: The Star Club Litigation," Apple did not want the Star Club album to conflict with an official release: *The Beatles at the Hollywood Bowl*, a live collection due out that May. After Murphy initially agreed to slightly delay the release, he then sent apples to reporters, inviting them to a press conference at Apple headquarters to announce the Star Club release. The event was actually not held at that location; a Lingasong representative directed people from Apple to the actual venue.

Furious over being explicitly linked to the project, Apple decided to begin proceedings to block *Live! At the Star-Club's* release. After attempting to reach Murphy to settle the matter out of court, Apple and the Beatles filed an injunction on April 1, 1977.

The intricacies of the filing are too complex to describe here, but in sum, the plaintiffs (Apple and the Beatles) argued that releasing the double album would cause them irreparable commercial and creative harm. They also claimed Murphy's actions violated the Dramatic and Musical Performers' Protection Act of 1958, and interfered with their trade or business.

The judge largely rejected Apple's assertions, and Murphy resumed preparations for the *Star-Club's* German release just a week later. The UK received copies in May, while the U.S. saw a June 1977 release by Lingasong in association with Atlantic Records. Interestingly, the American version differed in that four songs — "I Saw Her Standing There," "Twist And Shout," "Reminiscing," and "Ask Me Why" — were replaced by four others from the same tapes: "I'm Gonna Sit Right Down And Cry (Over You)," "Where Have You Been All My Life," "Till There Was You," and "Sheila."

Why did the Beatles want the Star Club performances suppressed? As Lewisohn writes in *Tune In*, these performances reflect the rawer, less-polished days, when they played songs at "breakneck speed — Prellies pace," a reference to their days popping speed to keep up with their grueling performance schedule. In a letter to the court, John Lennon said "the sleeve note, apart from being inaccurate, seems to have been written with a court case in mind ... THIS IS A FUCKING FAKE!"

George Harrison used equally harsh words during his 1998 testimony in yet another Apple/Beatles suit attempting to block Sony's re-release of the tapes: "One drunken person recording another bunch of drunks does not constitute a business deal," he said. He added it was one of the "crumbiest" recordings ever made of the Beatles, dismissing it as "a lot of teen-agers ... getting drunk and playing rock 'n' roll."

This time, Apple and the band successfully argued that they were under contract to EMI at the time of the performance, thus only they should own the tapes. Since the 1998 Copyright Act had recently been passed, the judge granted full ownership to Apple.

After that ruling, Apple has held on to the recordings and apparently has no plans to release them, other than a few brief clips in the *Anthology* documentary. However, all those years in litigation allowed numerous bootleggers to issue their own versions, thus Star Club albums can be had fairly easily. Technology has allowed labels such as Purple Chick and, most recently, Ox Tango, to remove some of the tape hiss and background noise that plagued the Lingasong and other earlier versions.

Today, fans still debate the merit of the Star Club tapes. While the sound quality is rough, it provides a crucial glimpse into the Beatles' development. In a very short time, they would play to massive audiences, and would rely much less on the early rock and R&B covers that dominated their earlier set lists. Lennon and Harrison would later assert that their best days as a live band were in their Liverpool and Hamburg days, and these recordings document that time period, flaws and all.

Originally published April 25, 2014 at http://somethingelsereviews.com/2014/04/25/deep-beatles-the-beatles-live-at-the-star-club-in-hamburg-germany-1962-1977/

"Ask Me Why"
The Beatles Live! At the Star-Club in Hamburg, Germany 1962 (1977)

As the Beatles fulfilled their previous commitment to playing Hamburg's Star Club, they were probably thinking about returning to England to begin work on their debut album. Few audiences had heard John Lennon and Paul McCartney's original compositions, as the band still leaned heavily on cover versions of familiar rockers.

By December 1962, Lennon and McCartney embarked on their unprecedented run as songwriters, already penning impressive songs like "I Saw Her Standing There," the previously released "Love Me Do," and "P.S. I Love You." Their major breakthrough single "Please Please Me" was less than a month away from release, and would propel them to stardom.

While that song does not appear on the Star Club album, the 45's flipside does: "Ask Me Why," a blend of Motown and doo wop that features Lennon, McCartney and Harrison's impeccable harmonies. They seemingly executed these vocals perfectly — not a surprise, since they had recorded the track just a month earlier.

Lennon and McCartney wrote "Ask Me Why" in spring 1962, reportedly after hearing the 1961 track "What's So Good about Goodbye" by Smokey Robinson and the Miracles. According to the Beatles Bible, Lennon adapted the guitar motif introducing "What's So Good about Goodbye" for the riff weaving throughout "Ask Me Why." As McCartney told Barry Miles for the biography *Many Years from Now,* Lennon brought the idea to McCartney, and the duo sat down and composed it together.

While the Beatles recorded six takes of the song in November 1962, they had actually attempted it previously during their first session at Abbey Road on June 6, 1962. Unfortunately no tapes of this session exist, as EMI reportedly erased all the master tapes from that day.

They did perform the song for BBC during that time, however, demonstrating that this earlier attempt must have differed little from the November sessions. By the time the Beatles took the Star Club stage, they had obviously rehearsed "Ask Me Why" frequently, which explains their smooth performance.

Featuring heavier drums than on the studio version, "Ask Me Why" sounds more polished than the other Star Club performances. Harrison, Lennon, and McCartney execute flawless harmonies, with Lennon turning in a typically impassioned vocal.

Unlike their June 1962 and subsequent BBC appearances, the Star Club rendition finds Lennon in a more aggressive mood. Here, he sounds raspier, alternating between shouting and crooning. This technique adds more drama to such lines as "you're the only love that I've ever had." The lyrics convey the pleasure and sometimes anguish of new love, with the narrator admitting to often crying in happiness. Yet, he seems to fear that this love could vanish overnight, with Lennon's voice dropping in volume and range as he sings that he cannot believe that this new romance could result in more "misery." Harrison and McCartney occasionally join in on words and phrases, as if to highlight the uncertainty to the narrator's experiences.

Despite his rawer sound, Lennon also convincingly delivers the song's more tender lines, such as in the lines concerning that he may cry not because of grief, but that she represents his first true love. Harrison and McCartney join in on the title phrase as well as key lines such as "I love you" and the word "misery," effectively propelling the song's story. Starr's drums are a great presence, echoing Lennon's more unrestrained singing style.

While the instrumentation is solid, the lead vocal and harmonies are the stars here. The earlier BBC version of "Ask Me Why" is lovely, as is the subsequent *Please Please Me* album rendition. But the more unrestrained sound at the Star Club coaxes out the deeper, complex emotions expressed in the track's heartfelt lyrics.

Originally published May 23, 2014 at http://somethingelsereviews.com/ 2014/05/23/deep-beatles-ask-me-why-star-club-1962/

"The Hippy Hippy Shake"
The Beatles Live! At the Star-Club in Hamburg, Germany 1962 (1977)

From the Quarrymen to the Silver Beatles to the early Beatles days, the group relied heavily on covers in their set lists. Their choices reflected the music they grew up on: American R&B and rock, along with some unusual choices ("Till There Was You," "Besame Mucho," and "The Sheik of Araby," to name a few).

A favorite rocker among Liverpudlian groups was "The Hippy Hippy Shake," a minor American hit in 1959 that later caught on with British teens. While its originator Chan Romero remains a somewhat obscure figure in early rock, the song has risen in popularity over time.

The Beatles performed it frequently, obviously intending to energize audiences and allowing Paul McCartney to utilize his screaming Little Richard vocals. While the band recorded five versions of "The Hippy Hippy Shake" for the BBC, their 1962 Star Club rendition sounds rawer and more reflective of the record's spirit.

The song came from the mind of Romero, a Latino singer/guitarist who penned the track at only 16 years old. A Montana native, the teenager and his first band were playing gigs in their home state when local DJs and audiences noted how Romero resembled Ritchie Valens in sound and appearance.

After Valens' tragic death, Montana DJ Don Redfield sent a tape to Bob Keane, Valens' former manager. Excited at the prospect of signing another Valens, Keane flew Romero to Los Angeles, where he recorded his first records (as a side note, Valens' mother invited Romero to stay with her while he was in Los Angeles; he has remained close to the Valens family ever since).

His debut single, "The Hippy Hippy Shake," was released in July 1959, attracting only modest interest in America. The song fared much better in England and Australia; he even toured the latter with Jerry Lee Lewis in 1960.

Meanwhile, as a teenaged McCartney was listening to as much rock and R&B as possible, he came across an import copy of "The Hippy Hippy Shake" and took an instant liking to the gritty rocker. Along with other Liverpudlian bands, the Beatles worked the song into their live repertoire. Interestingly, they never recorded a studio version, instead bringing it out for BBC sessions. In 1963, Merseybeat peers the Swinging Blue Jeans would score a major UK hit with the track.

While the BBC version sounds clearer, the Star Club take retains more of the raw rock sound of the original. Played at a slightly faster tempo, "The Hippy Hippy Shake" features McCartney at his best, shouting, growling, and howling the lyrics. Like Romero, he screams "whoo!" at various points, as if provoking the audience as well as the band to maintain the energy. In a short time those "whoos" would become a Beatles trademark, albeit in a slightly different manner. Here, McCartney does not hold the note, instead barking the "whoo" as punctuation.

Ringo Starr's drumming style is on full display, his patented hard-pounding technique already present. George Harrison executes a fun solo, while presumably John Lennon plays pulsating rhythm guitar to accent the jubilant — if slightly naughty — bridge instructing listeners to "Shake it to the left / Shake it to the right." This down-and-dirty sound is just about urging the crowd to their feet to dance and get a little wild: two major elements of rhythm and blues. Those qualities were carried over to early rock and roll, and the Beatles prove themselves adept students in both musical styles.

Their then-current single "Love Me Do" symbolized their smoother, pop-oriented sound, but their rambunctious take on "The Hippy Hippy Shake" at the Star Club represents the group in their earliest and more dangerous form. Even toward the end of their career, the Beatles enjoyed revisiting the track, as they performed a more restrained version during the *Get Back* sessions.

Originally published May 9, 2014 at http://somethingelsereviews.com/2014/05/09/deep-beatles-the-hippy-hippy-shake-star-club-1962/

"I Saw Her Standing There"
The Beatles Live! At The Star-Club in Hamburg, Germany 1962 (1977)

The final entry in our four-week exploration of *Live! At the Star-Club* involves a favorite song in very different clothing. On the surface, "I Saw Her Standing There" epitomizes the energy, excitement, and relative innocence of the Beatlemania era. After all, the Beatles were simply singing about holding hands and falling in love — certainly nothing scandalous.

Yet underneath these romantic words was something more sexual, symbolized by the opening lines: "Well she was just seventeen — you know what I mean." The playful handclap-driven beat may have somewhat tempered these lyrics in the *Please Please Me* studio version, but their 1962 Star Club rendition more accurately captures the intended raunchiness of the original.

Written by John Lennon and Paul McCartney in September 1962, "I Saw Her Standing There" first took shape in McCartney's Liverpool home. McCartney composed the first line alone; he and Lennon wrote the rest of the lyrics in a Liverpool Institute exercise book. Sitting with their guitars, the duo painstakingly worked on every line. Most famously, Lennon disliked McCartney's original opening words: "Well she was just seventeen; she'd never been a beauty queen." In *Anthology*, McCartney dubbed this a "cringe line" and explained that he and Lennon devised the deliberately ambiguous phrase "you know what I mean."

Interestingly, McCartney later admitted that he lifted the bass line from Chuck Berry's "I'm Talking About You" for the song.

The Beatles' affection for the track is obvious, since they frequently covered it in their live sets — including their Star Club appearances — and BBC radio shows.

The group continued tinkering with the track, changing the tempo and revising the lyrics. In late 1962, the Beatles rehearsed "I Saw Her Standing There" at the Cavern Club, and the differences are remarkable: Lennon contributed harmonica while George Harrison played guitar; Ringo Starr's tempo is slightly slower; and the "my heart went boom" line was still a work in progress.

In this subsequently bootlegged version, Lennon and McCartney instead sang "Well, we danced all night" and broke into laughter upon crooning this line; perhaps expressing their discomfort with the revision.

By the time they performed this song during their December 1962 Star Club set, they had greatly progressed on the composition. The arrangement closely mirrors the final *Please Please Me* album version, but contains some slight differences. A particularly welcome addition, curiously absent from the studio rendition, is the "Peter Gunn" guitar riff after the first verse.

The original "well, we danced all night" lyric has vanished; clearly Lennon and McCartney had recently added the "well, my heart went boom" lines. McCartney's screaming vocals are almost identical to the final version, with slight modulation on the line "and I could see." Starr furiously bashes on the drums, driving the Beatles much harder than in the Decca recordings featuring Pete Best.

Finally, Harrison's thrashing guitar solo — augmented by Lennon's pounding rhythm guitar — lends a much harder edge to "I Saw Her Standing There." The tempo seems faster, although it actually differs little from the *Please Please Me* version. Wisely, the group had eliminated the harmonica section.

The rest is history: On February 11, 1963, the Beatles entered Abbey Road for their legendary all-day recording session. That morning, producer George Martin recorded nine takes of the track (three of which were complete). After deeming take one to be best, the Beatles overdubbed handclaps that afternoon. In a fateful move, Martin later added McCartney's "One, two, three, FOUR!" count-in from take nine.

Listening to the various takes, it is evident that the group valiantly battled with increasingly flagging energy; McCartney's count-in rallied the Beatles.

"I Saw Her Standing There" went on to become not only a huge hit, but a landmark cut in the history of rock. McCartney continues performing the song in concerts, to ecstatic audience reaction.

While the *Please Please Me* version remains a favorite, the Star Club rendition possesses a rawness not present on the more familiar album cut. Since no recordings from their earlier Hamburg days apparently exist, the Star Club performances help fans visualize what the pre-Beatlemania group sounded like.

The album remains controversial for its poor sound quality, but the spirited, arguably just-as-good-as-the-original rendition of "I Saw Her Standing There" is worth the price of admission alone.

Originally published June 20, 2014 at http://somethingelsereviews.com/2014/06/20/deep-beatles-i-saw-her-standing-there-star-club-1962/

"Kansas City/Hey-Hey-Hey-Hey!"
Cavern Club Performance (1962)

What is a well-known Beatles track like "Kansas City/Hey-Hey-Hey-Hey!" doing in a column called "Deep Beatles"? After all, their cover has appeared on official releases three times: *Beatles for Sale*, *Live at the BBC*, and *Anthology 1*.

Well, a rare performance has surfaced online, one dating from a period where only a few precious artifacts still exist. This complete live version of "Kansas City/Hey-Hey-Hey-Hey!" dates from 1962, and finally completes fragments previously heard in the *Anthology* documentary. Listening to the track, one can experience the excitement and rawness of the performance, imagining what lunchtime crowds heard in those pre-fame lunchtime Cavern Club appearances.

The track's origins date back to 1952, when the legendary songwriters Jerry Leiber and Mike Stoller composed the song. They gave the track to Little Willie Littlefield, a Texan boogie woogie pianist/singer who released it under the title "K.C. Lovin.'" However, it wasn't until 1959 that the renamed "Kansas City" found a mass audience, when R&B singer Wilbert Harrison's cover reached No. 1.

As was customary at the time, a slew of other versions quickly followed, including Little Richard's unique take on the track. He released his screaming version the same year as Wilbert Harrison, scoring a minor hit. Richard then later incorporated it into his live shows, fusing it with another obscure song: "Hey-Hey-Hey-Hey!" — the original B-side to the 1958 smash "Good Golly Miss Molly."

Meanwhile, the Beatles were slowly honing their skills, eventually arriving in Hamburg in 1960. For two years, they performed at various Hamburg clubs, learning how to connect with audiences and function as a tight unit. By 1962, Richard had staged a European comeback tour, having previously taken time off to concentrate on spiritual music. Beatles manager Brian Epstein caught wind of these successful appearances, and arranged for the group to open for Little Richard on select dates.

The Beatles first opened for the singer at New Brighton's Tower Ballroom in October; in November, the Beatles returned to Hamburg to perform with the R&B legend at the famed Star-Club. In the past, the group saw Little Richard perform "Kansas City/Hey-Hey-Hey-Hey!" and decided to incorporate it in their own act. Acting as a mentor, Richard instructed the Beatles in how to perform his tracks, and famously taught Paul McCartney his "ooh" trademark yell.

Before Richard's tutoring sessions, the Beatles played the mini-medley for their Cavern Club appearances. Performing for lunchtime crowds at the Liverpool hangout, the Beatles excited audiences with their professional — yet still rock and roll — renditions of covers and a few originals. On August 22, 1962, Granada Television filmed the group at the Cavern, where they captured the band rocking the club with "Some Other Guy." Intended to air on the program Know the North, the clip initially failed to air due to substandard sound.

Technician Gordon Butler returned to the Cavern on September 5 to create a better quality recording. Using three microphones, Butler recorded the Beatles for an hour — though only "Some Other Guy" and "Kansas City/Hey-Hey-Hey-Hey!" survived. Butler made five acetate discs of the two songs; according to the *Beatles Bible* website, one acetate was sold at Christie's auction house in August 1993.

Up to now, only fragments of the "Kansas City" performances were available, although other concert versions exist on bootlegs and the *Live at the BBC* collection. Thus, it is exciting to hear this previously unreleased complete rendition.

McCartney's voice stands front and center, using a slightly different style on the "yeah yeah" sections on this recording. Unfortunately, Harrison and Lennon's voices cannot be heard as clearly (perhaps due to insufficient microphone placement), so the call and response portion of "Hey-Hey-Hey-Hey!" is a bit muted. Harrison's guitar solo has a muddied sound quality, as well. The excitement remains, and the cheers at the end demonstrate the small the Cavern was. In a short time, the Beatles would play packed stadiums and incessantly screaming audiences, so it is a treat to experience them as they sounded pre-stardom.

The Beatles would largely drop the medley from their setlists in 1963, although they rerecorded the track for select BBC appearances and the *Beatles for Sale* album. However, "Kansas City/Hey-Hey-Hey-Hey!" has endured due to its symbolic nature. It represents the group's early raw power, and demonstrates how they drew from early rock and R&B to forge their unique and still unequalled sound.

Originally published July 26, 2013 at http://somethingelsereviews.com/2013/07/26/deep-beatles-kansas-cityhey-hey-hey-hey-1962-cavern-club/

"I'll Get You"
Past Masters (1963)

"That was Paul and me trying to write a song ... and it didn't work out," John Lennon said in a 1980 interview. Despite Lennon's opinion, 1963's "I'll Get You" exemplifies the Beatles' growing ability to absorb pop and rhythm and blues, then transform them into their unique sound. Featuring close harmonies, a strong Ringo Starr backbeat and intriguing lyrics, "I'll Get You" should be known as more than just the B-side to the "She Loves You" single.

Originally written as the followup to the hit "From Me to You," the song has a confusing history. Experts such as Bill Harry claim that Lennon was the primary songwriter, although Paul McCartney recalled it being a true collaboration in *Many Years from Now*. In 1994, McCartney admitted he borrowed the unusual chord change during the line "it's not easy, to pretend" from a Joan Baez song entitled "All My Trials."

Later, he told biographer Barry Miles that Lewis Carroll also greatly influenced Lennon's lyrics, particularly through the frequent use of words like "imagine" and "picture." "This idea of asking your listener to imagine, 'Come with me if you will …,' 'Enter please into my …,' 'Picture yourself in a boat …,' It drew you in. It was a good little trick, that," McCartney said.

Believing that the beat echoed "From Me to You," the group figured "Get You in the End" (the working title) would be a worthy followup. But that changed in late June 1963, when Lennon and McCartney penned "She Loves You" while on tour. After the band decided that would be the stronger single, "I'll Get You" was soon relegated to the B-side. Thus on July 1, the Beatles spent the first half of the day recording "She Loves You" at Abbey Road, leaving "Get You in the End" for the evening session. Little information exists on how many takes it took to perfect the track, although they were certainly under pressure to finish it quickly due to their strict touring schedule as well as the exigency of issuing a new single. Presumably Lennon's harmonica and the hand claps must have been overdubbed later in the session.

Mixing commenced on July 3; since the track was only issued as a single, Martin and Emerick made a single mono mix, although later "fake stereo" mixes were created. Of course, a stereo version finally appeared in 2009 as part of the remastered Beatles catalog. The final mono mix, now retitled "I'll Get You," was released as the B-side to the "She Loves You" 45 in Britain on August 23, 1963, and the A-side naturally received more attention and became a massive hit.

Despite being the B-side to such a classic song, "I'll Get You" receives little airplay today. Why this is remains a mystery, as the track represents how the Beatles could listen to other genres, then incorporate select elements into truly original works. The group made no secret of admiring Motown, and Starr's strong backbeat suggests that he spent time listening to the Funk Brothers' envied sound. Lennon's harmonica, first on prominent display in "Love Me Do," makes a welcome return.

Many Merseybeat groups listened to American blues, and the Beatles were no exception. Lennon's harmonica lends a slightly harder edge to an otherwise upbeat, pop-oriented song. Then there are those close Lennon/McCartney harmonies, which echo the Everly Brothers' patented vocals here. Add in McCartney's admission of borrowing a chord from folk singer Baez, and what results is a conglomeration of styles that creates a new, fresh sound in rock and pop music.

The lyrics demand the listener's attention by consistently using the second person. While they address the love interest, inviting her to dream about their budding love, the chorus sounds somewhat odd: "So I'm telling you, my friend, that I'll get you, I'll get you in the end," the words suggesting a little aggression. Calling his beloved "my friend" is unusual as well, even though the two harmonize on otherwise romantic lines conquering how they think of their beloved constantly.

The bridge showcases Lennon and McCartney's ability to work in perfect synchronization, harmonizing as closely as Don and Phil Everly. They croon that the woman will soon change her mind and surrender to their charms. Then comes another curious line where they say that she might as well "resign" herself to their wishes. "Resign" implies giving in, not altogether willingly; does this reinforce the aggressive tone of the "I'll get you" chorus? Underneath the rapid rhythm, the catchy "oh yeahs," and the hand-clapping beginning and ending lie some atypical lyrics, particularly for a love song. This exemplifies the Beatles' ability to turn song conventions upside down and add some sophistication to the pop charts.

"I'll Get You" appears on the *Past Masters* CD, but it received even more attention in 1995 during the *Anthology* mania. The first in the CD trilogy, *Anthology 1*, contains a rare live version of the track which equals — and perhaps improves upon — the original. Recorded at the London Palladium on October 13, 1963, the song gains from the crowd's energy (particularly during the hand-clapping parts) and the superior vocals. Luckily the audience's screams do not overwhelm the Beatles, giving listeners a sense of how few artists could touch them as a live band at the time.

While not as well known as other tracks, "I'll Get You" stands as a superior example of the Beatles' early material, and contrary to Lennon's opinion, really did "work out."

Originally published October 5, 2012 at http://somethingelsereviews.com/2012/10/05/deep-beatles-ill-get-you-1963

"Misery"
Please Please Me (1963)

Last week marked the 50th anniversary of a cultural revolution: the release of the Beatles' *Please Please Me.* Their first effort, recorded over 12 hours on a single day, stands as one of the most impressive debuts in rock history.

Even more astonishing for a 1963 band, they included their own compositions besides covers; of course, the title track, "Love Me Do," "I Saw Her Standing There," and "Twist and Shout" are just a few examples of the Beatles' early hits. Nevertheless *Please Please Me* contains some hidden gems as well, including the John Lennon/Paul McCartney-penned song "Misery."

It represents their burgeoning talent for taking traditional subjects and turning them inside out, lending their own unique take on a love song.

"Misery" originates from the Beatles' January 1963 tour with singer Helen Shapiro; in fact, they wrote the track with her in mind. "John and I were a songwriting team, and what songwriting teams did in those days was wrote for everyone," McCartney said in 1988. "'Misery' was for Helen Shapiro, and she turned it down. It may not have been that successful for her because it's rather a downbeat song … It was quite pessimistic."

According to the *Beatles Bible*, they began writing the track before the band's performance at the King's Hall, Stoke-on-Trent on January 26; later they completed the lyrics at McCartney's family home in Liverpool.

In 1980, Lennon claimed that it was "kind of a John song more than a Paul song, but it was written together." Interestingly, McCartney told biographer Barry Miles that it represented their first attempt at a ballad and contained a spoken introduction. McCartney stated he and Lennon were "hacks" that were just completing a job for someone.

After Shapiro rejected "Misery," the duo offered the track to singer/actor Kenny Lynch, who was on the same tour. Lynch wound up scoring a minor hit with the single and, more importantly, ranks as the first artist to ever record a Lennon/McCartney original (Lynch would later appear as one of the "escapees" on the *Band on the Run* album cover for Wings).

The Beatles entered the recording studio on February 11, 1963, during which they would record an astonishing 10 songs. They performed 11 takes of "Misery"; as evidenced by the accompanying demos here, the takes varied little from one another. Breakdowns occurred because of flubbed lyrics, George Harrison's difficult guitar part, and their increasingly rough voices. Producer George Martin recorded the track with the tape running at a faster speed — this allowed room for a later piano overdub, recorded at the slower speed.

On February 20, Martin laid down said piano part, and the day also marked the first time Geoff Emerick served as second tape operator. The Beatles were not present for this session. Further editing took place February 25, when Martin and engineer Norman Smith edited and remixed "Misery" as well as numerous other *Please Please Me* tracks.

To promote the album, the Beatles performed "Misery" frequently for the BBC. Curiously, the 1994 release *Live at the BBC* includes none of these performances, although they exist on a variety of bootlegs. Through much of 1963 they played the track live for BBC shows including "Saturday Club," "On the Scene," "Side by Side," "Easy Beat," and their own special, "Pop Go the Beatles." The live BBC version below particularly showcases Ringo Starr's pounding drums, Harrison's guitar work (listen for the flair he lends to the song's conclusion), and those tight Lennon/McCartney harmonies.

"Misery" is a noteworthy track in that it foreshadows their later experiments with expanding the limits of rock music and composition. When the piano and guitar start the song, they seemingly predict that this will be a tender ballad; as Lennon and McCartney croon the opening lines, they underscore the melancholy mood: "the world is treating me bad — misery." Suddenly the bass kicks in, and Starr's strong drumming drastically increases the tempo.

Thus, the tune becomes an oxymoron, with the upbeat instrumentation contrasting with the "lost love" theme. While the narrator is clearly mourning for his beloved, he manages to undercut his sadness with a touch of anger. He will fondly look back on their time together, but he predicts she will soon regret her decision. By the end, however, the story is one of loneliness. He wants someone to send her back to him, for without her love he will dwell in "misery." Lennon and McCartney harmonize on the word "misery," emphasizing the track's overall theme.

But listen closely: the rapid tempo, chiming guitar, and cheerful vocal style all suggest that the Beatles are performing these rather depressing lyrics with a sly wink.

Are they parodying conventional ballads, or perhaps tweaking the rip-your-heart-out dramatics of Johnny Ray and other 1950s vocalists? It may have been the songwriting duo's "first stab at a ballad," as McCartney later said, but they seem to have absorbed the common characteristics of a teen love song, then turned those cliches inside out.

While the Beatles did not perform "Misery" on subsequent tours, it remains an early standout that previews the group's groundbreaking creativity. Quite simply, a pop song doesn't get much better than this.

Originally published March 29, 2013 at http://somethingelsereviews.com/ 2013/03/29/deep-beatles-misery-1963-1/

"There's a Place"
Please Please Me (1963)

Many fascinating stories have emerged from the landmark 1963 recording of the *Please Please Me* album. The all-day marathon session signaled the beginning of The Beatles' rock and pop reign and produced an impressive array of singles: "Love Me Do," "I Saw Her Standing There," "Twist and Shout," and the title track, just to name a few. Yet other album tracks and B-sides remain overlooked, perhaps due to the fact that *Please Please Me* contains an embarrassment of riches. One such track that deserves a second listen is "There's A Place," an upbeat song that not only features impressive harmonies by John Lennon, George Harrison, and Paul McCartney; its sophistication differentiated the group from other pop bands of the time.

Primarily written by Lennon, "There's A Place" represents his attempt to write a Motown song. "'There's A Place' was my attempt at a sort of Motown, black thing," he explained in 1980. "It says the usual Lennon things: 'In my mind there's no sorrow…' It's all in your mind." In *Many Years from Now*, McCartney recalled working with Lennon on the track, with the two meeting at McCartney's home on Forthlin Road in Liverpool. He told author Barry Miles that they loosely based the song on the lyrics from *West Side Story's* "Somewhere," but changed the theme to intellectual rather than purely romantic. In this case, the place existed solely in the mind. "This was the difference with what we were writing: we were getting a bit more cerebral," he explained.

Lennon and McCartney brought their composition to the now-legendary February 11, 1963 session at Abbey Road Studios. They recorded "There's A Place" along with "I Saw Her Standing There," both taking place during just a few hours. In ten takes, George Martin and The Beatles completed the backing track and vocals; McCartney remembered singing the high harmony, Lennon the lower harmony and melody. "This was a nice thing because we didn't actually have to decide where the melody was till later when they boringly had to write it down for sheet music," he told Miles. After a break, Lennon commenced overdubbing the harmonica part onto take 10. After three attempts, the last take — take 13 — became the final version. Interestingly, Harrison originally played the lead line on guitar; Martin and the group then replaced it with the harmonica solo.

Despite its strengths — complex harmonies, catchy melody, and uptempo sound — "There's A Place" ended up relegated to the B-side of the 1964 US "Twist and Shout" single. The rest is history, of course; "Twist and Shout" became a huge hit, while "There's A Place" faded into relative obscurity. To this day, casual fans may not be aware of the track, and radio stations rarely play it, making it one of the "lost" Beatles songs from their vast catalog.

"There's A Place" stands out for many reasons, the first being the lyrics. Unlike typical love songs of the period, the tune concerns introspection and reflection. Lennon and McCartney sing that they have a special place, a retreat from sadness. On first listen, one expects this "place" to be with a lover, to bask in the romantic glow. But the song confounds the listener's expectations: instead of a physical place, it's the person's mind. Here being alone is not a negative situation, but rather an opportunity to think and re-energize. The narrator reflects on his beloved, but on her words and actions rather than beauty. Meditating alone is nothing to pity, as it is not about loneliness. In case anyone has missed that point, the bridge emphasizes the narrator's happiness, that sadness does not exist in his mental space. In other words, do not feel sorry for this character — just leave him alone with his thoughts, and he will never feel lonely. Lennon would return to this general theme repeatedly, celebrating the value of contemplation and seemingly doing nothing in later tracks like "I'm Only Sleeping," "Tomorrow Never Knows," and "Watching the Wheels," among many others.

Another fascinating aspect of "There's A Place" lies in its gorgeous harmonies. Listen carefully for how Lennon and McCartney let their voices flutter on ending words like "place" and "go," and the intricate harmonies during the bridge. Their close singing remains some of the underrated pleasures of this song and the Beatles' music in general. Both the lyrics and these vocals stood out from typical pop of the time, adding a level of sophistication heretofore unheard of in rock and roll. As a sidenote, "There's A Place" slightly predates the similarly themed "In My Room" by the Beach Boys.

The Beatles rarely performed the song live except for a BBC appearance in 1963. New technology has presented expanded opportunities to appreciate Beatles music, from remastered CDs to MP3s via iTunes. Hopefully these releases (along with the recent vinyl remasters of the catalog) will breathe new life into this unfairly overlooked track. If nothing else, "There's A Place" further signals the change The Beatles brought to popular music, fusing rock and pop with complicated harmonies and deeper lyrics. Grab a pair of headphones and fully indulge in all the subtleties of this still poignant song.

Originally published November 16, 2012 at http://somethingelsereviews.com/2012/11/16/deep-beatles-theres-a-place-1963/

"Hold Me Tight"
With the Beatles (1963)

Some Beatles tracks forged new sonic territory, and others just rocked hard. "Hold Me Tight," a track off 1963's *With the Beatles*, harkens back to their beginnings in Hamburg and Liverpool, driving audiences mad with their hard-driving guitars and unflagging energy. While never released as a single, "Hold Me Tight" remains one of *With the Beatles'* hidden gems and a perennially underrated song in their catalog.

Originally intended for inclusion on *Please Please Me*, "Hold Me Tight" was born out of songwriting sessions at Paul McCartney's Forthlin Road, Liverpool home circa 1961. McCartney later told biographer Barry Miles that when the Beatles began their careers, they had to write singles rather than simply album tracks. The time frame had to fit the two and a half minute time frame in order to be played on the radio. Thus he labeled "Hold Me Tight" as "a failed attempt at a single which then became an acceptable album filler." In Mark Lewisohn's *Complete Beatles Recording Sessions*, McCartney added that he and John Lennon were emulating the Shirelles, perhaps meaning harmonically or their "call and answer" format.

In any case, the group began including the song in their live set lists in 1961, then brought it to Abbey Road for the marathon February 11, 1963 recording session.

During the *Please Please Me* sessions, the Beatles recorded 13 takes of the track. Unfortunately, the tape containing these versions was subsequently destroyed, thus no bootlegs exist from that day. When the group converged to work on their followup, *With the Beatles*, they resurrected "Hold Me Tight," completing nine takes on September 12,

1963. Luckily footage exists of takes 20-29; producer George Martin edited versions 26 and 29 together to create the final album edition, completing work on September 30.

Sadly, the Beatles thought very little of "Hold Me Tight." In typical "own worst critic" fashion, Lennon later dismissed the track as a "pretty poor song" and was "never really interested in it." McCartney was slightly kinder to the song in 1988: "I can't remember much about that one. Certain songs were just 'work' songs — you haven't got much of a memory of them. That's one of them. You just knew you had a song that would work, a good melody.'Hold Me Tight' never really had that much of an effect on me."

Upon close listening, "Hold Me Tight" does have a rushed quality, with some flubbing of the lyrics and McCartney's less than perfect vocal. However, these imperfections only enhance the energy and the "live" feeling of the recording, emulating what a Cavern performance may have sounded like.

As the Beatles reworked the song, it's apparent that they experimented with a different introduction in take 20. Wisely they chose what exists on the *With the Beatles* album version: the handclap-heavy beat with Lennon's driving rhythm guitar. Clearly the long sessions took a toll on McCartney's voice; as evident in the accompanying videos, his vocals grew strained, cracking and wavering from the effort. He as well as Lennon and George Harrison would occasionally forget the lyrics (leading a frustrated McCartney to yell "bloody hell!" after once again missing the words).

However, Lennon's chugging rhythm guitar — accented by George Harrison's lead — Ringo Starr's thunderous drumming, and the call-and-answer vocals significantly add to the song's power. The handclap-dominant percussion adds a crucial element to the track, as it lends a "live" aspect to the track, as if hearing the Beatles perform it at a small club.

Lyrically, "Hold Me Tight" does not break any new ground. However, its suggestive lines perfectly blend with the song's nervous energy, injecting it with sexual as well as youthful vitality. After Harrison, McCartney, and Lennon harmonies on the title phrase, McCartney adds that he hopes to continually love his girlfriend. The trio increases the sense of urgency by harmonizing on the words "tonight, tonight," with McCartney concluding his plea with a statement of monogamy, that he will make love to only her. "Making love to only you."

Starr somewhat tempers the drums during the bridge, with handclaps and guitar rising to the foreground. He professes that no one can understand how much it means to him to spend time alone with his girlfriend, keeping her in his embrace. McCartney sings alone, his slightly quavering voice communicating anxiety, excitement, and anticipation. The trio finally reenters the scene by loudly emphasizing the line "It feels so right."

With its harder-rocking feel, sexually tinged lyrics, and overall exuberance, "Hold Me Tight" embodies everything the early Beatles stood for: youth, energy, pulsating excitement, and newness. It offers a glimpse into the group's rougher roots, sporting leather head to toe while performing for rowdy audiences. In addition, the song highlights how the Beatles excelled as a straight-ahead rock and R&B band guaranteed to entrance the crowds.

Lennon and McCartney may not have thought much of "Hold Me Tight," but its raw power endures and encapsulates the changes the Beatles brought to teenagers and early '60s pop culture.

Originally published April 11, 2014 at http://somethingelsereviews.com/2014/04/11/deep-beatles-hold-me-tight-from-with-the-beatles-1963/

"Don't Bother Me"
With the Beatles (1963)

As a composer, George Harrison developed his craft at an astoundingly rapid pace. Compare his first effort, 1963's "Don't Bother Me," with his sophisticated contributions to Abbey Road: "Here Comes the Sun" and "Something." In just five years, Harrison established himself as a first-class songwriter every bit as talented as his gifted bandmates John Lennon and Paul McCartney. Yet Harrison later disdained his debut moment, dubbing it as not a "particularly good song" and failing to include it on subsequent setlists.

Is "Don't Bother Me" worth such a dismissal? A closer examination reveals its importance in the Harrison catalog.

Sickness inspired the song; while on a 1963 tour in Bournemouth, England, Harrison fell under the weather. Convalescing at the Bournemouth hotel, Harrison challenged himself to write a track for the next Beatles album. Written as a reaction to his illness as well as his vanishing privacy (due to Beatlemania), "Don't Bother Me" stands as Harrison's first attempt at writing a song for his own voice.

As McCartney explained in *Anthology*, he and Lennon first wrote songs for Harrison and Ringo Starr to showcase their voices. "A lot of the girls were mad on him, so we always wanted to give him at least one track," McCartney said. "Then George started to catch on: 'Why should you write my songs?' And he started writing his own."

After recording very basic demos in his hotel room, Harrison brought the song to Abbey Road Studios for the *With the Beatles* sessions on September 11, 1963 After a very long day of laying down tracks for "I Wanna Be Your Man," "Little Child," "All I've Got to Do," and "Not A Second Time," the Beatles began work on the track. They recorded seven takes — three of which were overdubs — but elected to scrap them and try again the next day.

Several more tracks were recorded, as well as messages for Australian radio stations, before they finally attempted "Don't Bother Me" once more. They recorded ten more takes: four of the basic track and six overdubs. Basic track take 13 was deemed best, and overdubs from take 15 featuring a secondary Harrison lead vocal, McCartney on woodblock, Lennon on tambourine, and Starr on Arabian bongos were used. Producer George Martin and engineer Norman Smith finished mono mixes of "Don't Bother Me" on September 30, 1963, and *With the Beatles* finally hit store shelves less than two months later.

"Don't Bother Me" contains two important elements that would reappear in several Beatles songs: the tempo and the complex subject matter. Since their Hamburg days, the Beatles were fascinated with incorporating rhythms not typical of rock music. They particularly enjoyed Latin percussion, as evident on "Besame Mucho" and "P.S. I Love You," as well as later songs such as "And I Love Her" and "I Feel Fine."

While this track may not represent the Beatles' first attempt at integrating world music with rock, it stands as Harrison's earliest venture into international sounds that would permeate much of his subsequent Beatles compositions as well as solo work. Here, Latin rhythms are established through McCartney and Starr's catchy percussion; these ingredients, along with Harrison's piercing lead guitar, distinguish "Don't Bother Me" from other *With the Beatles* tracks.

Another key characteristic that "Don't Bother Me" foreshadows is Harrison's biting lyrics. His overt pessimism on the track marks a departure from early Beatles material. Although Harrison penned tender love songs, he returned to his world-weary, darkly humorous wordplay in songs such as "Only A Nothern Song," "Taxman," and "Piggies" along with solo tracks like "This Song," "Sue Me, Sue You Blues," and "Devil's Radio."

Here, Harrison directs his venom not only at an ex-lover, but at overzealous fans and the press. He admonishes them to leave him alone, that he has no time for their crazy behavior. A hint of romance enters the picture when he croons the bridge, admitting that he still desires his girlfriend's company. If she doesn't return his affections, his live will be forever changed. He demonstrates some vocal versatility on these lines, hitting higher notes than on previous cuts.

After his early effort, Harrison would rapidly mature as a songwriter; therefore "Don't Bother Me" symbolizes an important stage in his artistic development. In 1980, Harrison reflected on his first song: "I don't think it's a particularly good song. ... It mightn't even be a song at all, but at least it showed me that all I needed to do was keep on writing, and then maybe eventually I would write something good."

"Don't Bother Me" is the first step toward reaching his ultimate goal. Its brief inclusion in *A Hard Day's Night* also ensures its longevity.

Originally published July 4, 2014 at http://somethingelsereviews.com/2014/07/04/deep-beatles-dont-bother-me-from-with-the-beatles-1963/

"All I've Got To Do"
With the Beatles (1963)

As any Beatles student knows, the four made no secret of their love for R&B. Before they conquered the world, they cut their teeth on tracks by Little Richard, Arthur Alexander, Smokey Robinson and the Miracles, Larry Williams, and numerous Motown acts. Throughout their careers, The Beatles (as a group and as solo artists) interpreted soul and blues in a unique fashion, adding that pounding Ringo Starr backbeat and John Lennon's slightly raspy vocals to lend them an edge. "All I've Got to Do," a standout track from their second album *With The Beatles* (1963), blends rock and soul in a particularly sophisticated yet catchy way.

In 1980 Lennon, the song's primary composer, labeled "All I've Got to Do" as "me trying to do Smokey Robinson again." While Lennon lacks Robinson's patented falsetto, he does turn in a memorable vocal on this song. In fact, his emotion-packed singing ranks as one of his finest performances, both in his Beatles and solo years. When he professes his devotion, that he will always stand by his lover, his voice rises in pitch and volume. Lennon repeats these lines toward the track's end, effectively dramatizing the lovestruck man who will do anything for his beloved. "All I've Got to Do" also showcases the Beatles' still-impressive harmonies, which they gradually honed until they reached near-perfection on *Abbey Road*. Paul McCartney and George Harrison's combined voices punctuate and echo Lennon's lead vocal, emphasizing his commitment. They stress the title phrase as well as the "call on me" line, essentially convincing Lennon's lover of his devotion.

Another standout in this track is Starr, whose slightly off-kilter drumming distinguishes this song from others circa 1963-1964. Few songs featured such start-stop rhythms instead of a typical 4/4 pattern. Starr's trademark power-drumming accents the R&B roots of "All I've Got to Do," also accompanying McCartney's bass. When Starr's beat briefly hesitates, it stresses Lennon's passion while singing how he will seduce her with loving words whenever he wants to kiss her. Having Lennon's voice laid so bare must have been difficult for the rocker, as he famously disliked his own singing and often employed studio tricks to distort his vocals. However, such effects would have dulled the impact of the lyrics' emotion.

The ending of "All I Got to Do" intrigues as well. Instead of fading out over the Beatles singing the lyrics, the song ends with Lennon humming the melody with McCartney and Harrison crooning "oohs" behind him. After the intense feelings expressed in the final verses, the song downshifts to conclude on a quieter note. Has the narrator successfully convinced his lover of his devotion, thus transitioning into a laid-back, gently romantic tone? As is typical of many Beatles songs, the four leave it to listeners to determine for themselves.

Even early in their careers, the Beatles proved themselves masters of manipulating words and sounds to create a mood or evoke a feeling within the listener. In 1963, the Beatles were gradually experimenting with taking elements of already existing music, tearing them apart, and reconstructing them using their unique talents as glue. This action resulted in forever altering the rock landscape by expanding the very definitions of "rock" and "pop," demonstrating that there may not be such a thing as "pure" soul or "pure" rock. Instead, these genres borrow from other fields to create new kinds of music. "All I've Got to Do" represents their early stage in this process, and album by album they further established themselves as "mad scientists" expanding the rock and pop worlds. While not as adventurous as later cuts like "Tomorrow Never Knows" or "A Day in the Life," "All I've Got to Do" perfectly illustrates the Beatles' pastiche technique.

Originally published July 26, 2012 at http://somethingelsereviews.com/2012/07/26/deep-beatles-all-ive-got-to-do-1963/

"Honey Don't"
Live at the BBC (1963)

For the next few columns, "Deep Beatles" shines a spotlight on their BBC performances. Before incessant screaming and the rigors of touring took their toll, the Beatles had become one of the most polished live bands on the road. From 1962-1965, the group performed on 52 BBC programs, beginning with a March 1, 1962 appearance on "Teenager's Turn-Here We Go," and ending with the special "The Beatles Invite You to Take a Ticket to Ride" (recorded on May 26, 1965).

On these shows the Beatles performed covers even more than their own compositions, and can be heard joking around with the DJs. For decades, this material was available only on bootlegs such as the *Beatles at the Beeb* and poor quality recordings like *Youngblood*. Fans finally got their wish in 1994 when Apple released the collection *Live at the BBC*, which featured remastered selections from their many BBC performances. One of the choice cuts from this compilation is "Honey Don't," a Carl Perkins cover that, unlike *Beatles for Sale*, has John Lennon on lead vocals.

"Honey Don't" goes back to some of the Beatles' 1962 shows; then, Lennon always sang lead on the cut. But when the group entered Abbey Road Studios on October 26, 1964, Ringo Starr had been chosen as the new vocalist. As Starr explained in the *Anthology* documentary, the song appealed to him because of his deep love for country music.

"It was one of those songs that every band in Liverpool played. I used to love country music and country rock. I'd had my own show with Rory Storm, when I would do five or six numbers... that's why we did it on *Beatles For Sale*. It was comfortable. And I was finally getting one track on a record: my little featured spot."

Starr's performance demonstrated his charm and ability to capture the wit of the words. A year before, however, Lennon continued singing lead. They recorded a live version of "Honey Don't" for BBC radio's "Pop Go the Beatles" special, and Lennon's gritty voice gave the song a sexier edge. His shouts seem to energize the band, with George Harrison executing a solo very similar to that of Perkins. Paul McCartney plays rapid bass lines while Starr uses his uniquely heavy rock drum style. But on this version, Lennon's rank as one of the best rock singers in music is solidified.

Two wonderful vocal moments occur during Lennon's take on "Honey Don't." First, when he revisits the chorus beginning "Well I love you baby on a Saturday night," listen to how he lets just a bit of hoarseness enter his voice as he slightly ups the volume. It lends the line a more seductive edge, and one can picture the young Lennon standing onstage, legs akimbo, clad in all leather, making girls faint at the Star Club or Cavern Club. Toward the song's conclusion, he begins ad libbing, adding a "bop do bop" line after repeating the title.

Here, he demonstrates playfulness and energy, and clearly communicates how much he loves classic rock and roll. Lennon's charisma shines through, and he illustrates how slight voice modulation can completely change the meaning of a track.

Starr's later version of "Honey Don't" has its merits, most notably how Starr manages to retain the song's original country roots. But Lennon transforms it into the embodiment of rock: sexy and a bit dangerous.

Throughout his life, Lennon famously hated his own singing voice. "Honey Don't" instead proves how he ranks among the top rock vocalists.

Originally published April 12, 2013 at http://somethingelsereviews.com/2013/04/12/deep-beatles-honey-dont-live-at-the-bbc-1963/

"Some Other Guy"
Live at the BBC (1963)

Years ago, low-quality footage surfaced of the Beatles performing "Some Other Guy" at the Cavern Club on October 22, 1962. Filmed by Manchester-based Grenada Television, the brief clip captures the Beatles playing before a packed lunchtime crowd at the Cavern.

Originally intended for a program entitled "Know the North," its grainy quality made it unsuitable for broadcast — until the Beatles hit it big in 1963, naturally. After it finally aired on November 6, 1963's edition of "Grenada's Scene" at 6:30, the footage only appeared on bootlegs or frustratingly briefly in documentaries. However, a complete performance of "Some Other Guy" surfaced on 1994's *Live at the BBC* compilation, one that presents listeners with a picture of how their Hamburg and early Liverpool shows must have sounded.

The group stumbled onto the Richie Barrett R&B single through Brian Epstein. As George Harrison explained in *Anthology*, the Beatles would scour the racks at Epstein's NEMS record store, hunting for songs to play in their shows. The store's extensive selection included songs that were not hits in Britain or the U.S., offering the band a unique opportunity to discover more obscure tracks.

While "Some Other Guy" may not have been a huge success, its pedigree was impressive: it was co-written by Barrett, Jerry Leiber, and Mike Stoller. Barrett's original version leaned more toward R&B than rock, with an electric piano prominently featured.

Due to its rough sound and fast tempo, British bands in addition to the Beatles began featuring the song in their sets. London act Johnny Kidd and the Pirates recorded their own version in 1963, although it was not released until 1990. Therefore another Liverpool band, the

Big Three, scored a minor hit with their take on the rocker.

When the Beatles hit the Cavern Club stage, they were clad in their matching sweater vest and ties, signaling their more professional image. Another new addition: Ringo Starr, who had joined the group only days before. In the clip below, a fan can be heard screaming "We want Pete!" at the very end — of course, referring to former drummer Pete Best.

While the Beatles never recorded "Some Other Guy" for any album, they performed the song for the BBC three times. The first time was for the "Saturday Club" program on January 22, 1963; the second version was recorded at the BBC Paris Studio; and the final recording is the one included on *Live at the BBC*.

On June 19, 1963, the group performed the song in front of a live audience at London's Playhouse Theatre; six days later the BBC broadcast the concert as part of their "Easy Beat" show.

The "Easy Beat" performance's sound quality certainly does not rival their studio recordings; however, it still brims with energy and raw rock and roll. Paul McCartney and John Lennon sing in tandem, blending so well that they become a single voice. Lennon's enthusiasm particularly shines, shouting "owww!" at various points. Starr easily handles the complicated, slightly offbeat drum pattern, while Harrison plays a guitar solo recalling the energy of the oft-bootlegged Hamburg shows.

Listening to this performance, one can imagine being packed into the Cavern Club like sardines, condensation dripping from the walls, watching the local boys just on the brink of stardom.

"Some Other Guy" represents the Beatles' never-ending love of obscure American R&B, and demonstrates how they could transform the original recording into their own unique sound.

Originally published April 26, 2013 at http://somethingelsereviews.com/2013/04/26/deep-beatles-some-other-guy-bbc-1963/

"Nothin' Shakin' (But the Leaves on the Trees)"
Live at the BBC (1963)

Concluding our three-week look at select BBC performances, "Deep Beatles" focuses on a memorable George Harrison performance: "Nothin' Shakin' (But the Leaves on the Trees)," a rocker the Beatles had performed since their Hamburg days. Harrison excels on this track, demonstrating his singing prowess and ability to confidently lead the group.

"Nothin' Shakin'" traces its origins to 1958, when Cirino Colacrai, Diane Lampert and John Gluck, Jr., and Eddie Fontaine cowrote the track. Fontaine, a rockabilly vocalist, was previously known for performing at DJ Alan Freed's first live rock show. In addition, he had appeared in the classic film *The Girl Can't Help It* in 1956. "Nothin' Shakin'" eventually became his signature song, and the Beatles' 1963 version revived the tune.

Interestingly, Fontaine focused on acting from the 1960s until his death, making guest appearances on shows such as *Happy Days*, *The Rockford Files*, and *Quincy*. His frequent run-ins with the law, however, eventually overshadowed his once promising career.

Flash forward to December 1962, when the Beatles incorporated "Nothin' Shakin'" into their set lists in Hamburg. The bootleg *Live! At the Star-Club* features a brief version of the track, and the effects of the Preludin (or speed) they were constantly ingesting shows through their lightning-fast rendition.

Unlike Fontaine's rockabilly version, the Beatles' take is straight-ahead rock, with a fierce lead vocal by Harrison.

A year later, the Beatles decided to revive the song for a BBC appearance. On July 10, 1963, they played the song for the sixth edition of "Pop Go the Beatles." Recorded at the Aeolian Hall, London, the song finally aired during the July 23, 1963.

Interestingly, the BBC version stresses the track's country roots more than the Hamburg rendition — and even Fontaine's original. Harrison's guitar solo reveals how much he revered Carl Perkins' picking style, as it recalls his solos on "Matchbox" and other classics. Paul McCartney's bass accents the rhythm, and Starr displays his usual flair and ability to hit those drums hard, in perfect time. Lennon plays rhythm guitar on the track, letting his other bandmates shine on this rocker.

Harrison is often underestimated as a rock vocalist — unlike many singers, his voice contained wit as well as musicality. While "Nothin' Shakin'" mainly addresses teenage lust, Harrison manages to evoke the humor present in the words. Just listen to his delivery of the lines concerning her being a "doggone tease" and how he would go to shows where "the cats are stomping on their heels and toes." The words may be silly, but Harrison convincingly dramatizes the narrator's immaturity, his bright tones on lines concerning how he is learning about love sounding particularly youthful.

The Beatles' BBC performances remain the best way to hear how the band excelled at live shows. As the tornado that was Beatlemania hit, their voices and instruments were drowned out by hysterical fans. Thoroughly burned out and believing their live performance skills were deteriorating, they retired permanently from the road in 1966.

Other than bootlegs and the official *Live at the BBC* compilation, few early live recordings exist. Tracks like "Nothin' Shakin'" demonstrate how closely the Beatles listened to early rock and roll, mastered those songs, and eventually would carve their own musical niche.

Originally published May 10, 2013 at http://somethingelsereviews.com/2013/05/10/deep-beatles-nothin-shakin-but-the-leaves-on-the-trees-bbc-version-1963/

"I'll Be Back"
A Hard Day's Night (1964)

This year marks the 50th anniversary of the Beatles' *A Hard Day's Night*; to celebrate, a newly restored version is playing in select theaters and will be released on DVD and Blu-ray. The soundtrack album, released in the UK on July 10, 1964, featured a double-sided treat for fans: side one included songs that were in *A Hard Day's Night*, while side two offered tracks written during filming but ultimately dropped from the movie.

At the surface a superb pop/rock album, *A Hard Day's Night* also signals an early turning point in the Beatles' career. It marks the first time they issued a disc featuring all original material, and it shows signs of their evolving musical experimentation. The title track crashed onto the nation's consciousness with that resounding opening chord, while "And I Love Her" further explored Latin rhythms in creating a classic ballad.

The songs included in *A Hard Day's Night* have become ingrained in fans' memories, due to their astounding quality and enduring accompanying images. Who could forget the Fab Four romping on the field to "Can't Buy Me Love," or John Lennon jokingly singing to a pouting Ringo Starr during "If I Fell"? The songs left out of the film, however, deserve just as much attention for their innovative qualities. For the next few columns, "Deep Beatles" will explore these lesser-known *Hard Day's Night* tracks; while "Any Time at All" has already been discussed, several other songs remain unjustly buried. This "Deep Beatles" salute kicks off with the moody "I'll Be Back," a classic example of how the Beatles were growing as songwriters and musicians.

Proving that ideas come from interesting places, "I'll Be Back" has roots tracing back to Del Shannon. In 1980, Lennon explained that the song was his reworking of the chords from Del Shannon's hit "Runaway." In Barry Miles' *Many Years from Now*, Paul McCartney recalled that "I'll Be Back" was mainly Lennon's idea, although he contributed a few lines. As usual, Lennon later criticized the track: "A nice tune, though the middle is a bit tatty," he said in a 1972 interview with *Hit Parader*.

Recording commenced on June 1, 1964, and took 16 takes before the group and producer George Martin were satisfied. As evident on *Anthology 1*, Lennon originally conceived of "I'll Be Back" as a waltz. He and the band quickly abandoned the idea after Lennon complained that the lyrics were too difficult to sing at that tempo. By take three, the Beatles decided on a more manageable 4/4 rhythm. This version, however, featured electric guitars rather than the acoustic guitars that dominated the album cut. Ultimately, the first nine takes recorded the rhythm track, and the last seven laid down double-tracked and harmony vocals as well as an acoustic guitar overdub.

Musically, "I'll Be Back" illustrates the Beatles' rapidly developing sophistication and willingness to abandon traditional pop song formulas. Essentially the song contains no chorus; instead, three bridges anchor the track. Second, the chords alternate between A major and A minor, lending a melancholy tone that reflects the emotional words (for a thorough analysis of the chord structure, read Alan Pollack's entry in his excellent "Notes On" series).

Lennon's grittier vocals reveal the narrator's inner conflict and despair over a faltering relationship. His acoustic guitar drives the song's rhythm, although George Harrison contributes lead acoustic as well. McCartney and Harrison supply harmony vocals, with McCartney also playing bass. As usual, Starr contributes drums, displaying his ability to play subtle patterns as well as pounding, straightforward rock.

Lyrically, "I'll Be Back" contains some of Lennon's most introspective and mature lines up to that time. He vows that he will always return to his lover, even if they fight. He sings how how he left her once before but returned, all while executing perfect harmonies with McCartney and Harrison. The chord changes dramatize the fragility of the relationship, even though Lennon's voice increases in volume, power, and confidence when he sings that he still loves and wants her. Interestingly the narrator's girlfriend serves as the aggressor in the next lines, when Lennon argues that she could find "better things to do" than to hurt him.

His tone and perspective changes in the next few verses, focusing more on his own misdeeds. He sings that next time he will prove that he is "not trying to pretend," and that she would soon realize her mistake if he walked away from the relationship. Before the song ends, Lennon suggests that the road to romance is never smooth: "I wanna go, but I hate to leave you," he bemoans. Unlike the pure, idealistic romance expressed in "And I Love Her," or "I'm Happy Just to Dance with You," "I'll Be Back" reveals the underside of love, perhaps closer to the ambivalence omnipresent in "If I Fell."

Lennon would further explore complicated themes on the Beatles' next album, *Beatles for Sale*, and even more on *Help!* "I'll Be Back" can be seen as a precursor to such tracks as "I'm A Loser," "You've Got to Hide Your Love Away," and "Help!," as they all address complex themes of love and loss, idealism and cynicism, innocence and maturity. An inexplicably underrated *Hard Day's Night* track, "I'll Be Back" foreshadows later Lennon-penned masterpieces — and signals the beginning of the end of the early "Fab Four" era.

Originally published July 18, 2014 at http://somethingelsereviews.com/2014/07/18/deep-beatles-ill-be-back-from-a-hard-days-night-1964/

"When I Get Home"
A Hard Day's Night (1964)

Deep Beatles' look at *Hard Day's Night* songs that did not appear in the film continues with one of the lesser-known tracks in the band's catalog: "When I Get Home." A sampling of comments posted in the song's *Beatles Bible* entry represents some fans' attitude toward the track. Just a few examples: "well below average lyrics," "the worst recording on any Beatles song ... and the performance ranks somewhere at the bottom too," and "one of the few Beatles songs I always forget exists. Then I listen to it and remember why."

Does the song deserve such scorn? While it may not rank among their all-time best tracks, "When I Get Home" contains energy and a hard-charging beat that could have easily been included in concert setlists. A live version may have improved its sound, and its driving rhythm would have fit in nicely with other uptempo tracks from that period.

Frustratingly little information exists on this particular *Hard Day's Night* track. Written by John Lennon, they recorded "When I Get Home" on June 2, 1965, with George Martin producing and Norman Smith serving as engineer. They tackled the song on the final day of the *Hard Day's Night* sessions, with the usual lineup: Lennon on lead and backing vocals as well as rhythm guitar; Paul McCartney on backing vocals and bass; George Harrison on backing vocals and lead guitar; and Ringo Starr on drums.

Lennon later explained that "When I Get Home" was his attempt at emulating current R&B: "That's me again — another Wilson Pickett, Motown sound — a four-in-the-bar cowbell song," he said in 1980. They recorded the tune in 11 takes, laying down the instrumental track and overdubbing vocals. Martin and Smith created a mono mix on June 4, but it was never used; instead, their June 22 stereo and mono mixes were the final versions.

While not their most popular track — the Beatles never included it in set lists or performed it for the BBC — "When I Get Home" is worth a closer listen due to several factors:

The unusual beginning: In typical Beatles fashion, the song opens cold with the chorus rather than an instrumental introduction. They clearly enjoyed playing with intros and outros in their music, a trend they would continue throughout their careers The harmonies (along with Starr's pounding drums) crash into the scene, demanding the listener's attention.

Lennon's gritty rock vocal: While he famously disliked his own voice, Lennon showed great vocal versatility in his Beatles and solo material. He could modulate his singing to evoke the tender feelings of a ballad, or increase the volume and intensity to communicate anger or passion in uptempo songs. "When I Get Home" is an early example of his emerging skills — when he sings how he has no time for "trivialities," his insistent voice leaves no doubt of his intentions.

Starr's drumming: Lennon and Harrison's chugging guitars help establish the rhythm, but Starr's distinctively powerful style propels the track into harder rock territory. His fills and rolls add urgency to the song, underscoring the narrator's impatience in lyrics describing his rush to see his lover.

The vague lyrics: Note how the perspective changes once the narrator has arrived home. He plans to embrace her "till the cows come home." Suddenly the perspective changes, with Lennon admitting that he really should not spend so much time with his girlfriend, that he has too much to do. Why would he shift tone and subject? His impatience is now directed at his love for preventing him from other business. Why the change? Does this explain the aggressive sound of the entire record? Fans must interpret the meaning for themselves, as Lennon, Harrison, and McCartney simply repeat the chorus at the conclusion, returning to the lyrics' original perspective.

Does "When I Get Home" deserve such mixed-to-negative reviews? True, "I'm gonna love her till the cows come home" does not stand alongside the best lines the Lennon/McCartney duo ever wrote. However, it contains a rawness reminiscent of the Beatles' earliest Hamburg and Cavern days, suggesting that it could have been a shake-the-rafters concert highlight.

Unfortunately, the group chose to never perform the song live, so we'll never know how it might have sounded. It can still be enjoyed on the *Hard Day's Night* soundtrack (or *Something New* for American release fans), and be appreciated as a buried gem in the Beatles canon.

Originally published August 15, 2014 at http://somethingelsereviews.com/ 2014/08/15/deep-beatles-when-i-get-home-from-a-hard-days-night-1964/

"I'll Cry Instead"
A Hard Day's Night (1964)

Next in the "Deep Beatles" series on *A Hard Day's Night* album tracks that did not appear in the film is one song that almost graced a famous sequence.

Everyone remembers an iconic scene in *A Hard Day's Night*: The moment when the Beatles break free from a television rehearsal to frolic in a field — actually Thornbury Playing Fields in Isleworth, south London. When Lennon presented director Richard Lester with a new composition for the segment, Lester opted for another song: "Can't Buy Me Love." Thus "I'll Cry Instead," a country-inflected tune, appears only on the soundtrack album. It was restored in a new opening collage segment for the movie's 1986 rerelease.

While the "Can't Buy Me Love" segment ranks among the most memorable scenes in movie history, "I'll Cry Instead" is also a strong example of a sophisticated Lennon/McCartney composition.

In 1980, John Lennon told interviewer David Sheff that he originally wrote the song for use in the *Hard Day's Night* film, but that director Dick Lester passed on the song. "I like the middle eight to that song, though — that's about all I can say about it," Lennon concluded. In typical Lennon fashion he proved his own worst critic, underestimating the track's complex subject matter and notable instrumentation.

The group convened at Abbey Road Studios on June 1, 1964 to record "I'll Cry Instead" in addition to "Matchbox" and "Slow Down." The Beatles assumed the usual roles: Lennon on vocals, acoustic rhythm guitar, and tambourine; Paul McCartney on bass; George Harrison on lead guitar; and Ringo Starr on drums.

Interestingly, the group recorded the track in two parts, dubbed "Section A" and "Section B"; the former took six takes, the latter two. Producer George Martin and engineer Norman Smith then edited the two best versions together on June 4.

As was typical for the UK and American Beatles releases of the era, "I'll Cry Instead" differs slightly in even the mono versus stereo versions. To summarize the complicated tale: the mono mix contains an extra verse where Lennon repeats the first verse at the end. This lengthened version was spliced together originally to accompany the romping scene in *A Hard Day's Night,* but as previously mentioned Lester ultimately elected to use "Can't Buy Me Love." The stereo mix omits the repeated verse, shortening the song by 20 seconds.

Not surprisingly, these two versions appear differently on the UK and American editions of the *Hard Day's Night* soundtrack. The UK albums include both the mono and stereo versions, which exclude the extra verse; in the U.S., the mono and stereo mixes contain the additional verse. While the longer version also appears on the Capitol single and the mono version of *Something New,* the shorter edit only is included on the U.S. stereo mix of *Something New.* The original, full-length "I'll Cry Instead" is currently available through *The Capitol Albums, Volume 1*.

Aside from its confusing history, "I'll Cry Instead" is significant for its country leanings, its clever wordplay, and the themes of heartbreak, insecurity, and anger that Lennon would revisit several times as a Beatle and a solo artist. It took great courage to begin a pop song with a line declaring his anger instead of an upbeat sentiment, and it signals the track's overriding theme.

The song also contains what ranks among the greatest Beatles lyrics: "I've got a chip on my shoulder that's bigger than my feet." Here Lennon perfectly captures the narrator's pain and anger from failed romance. Hints of later tracks such as "I'm Loser," "Help!" and "You've Got to Hide Your Love Away" linger in subsequent lyrics, where Lennon expresses feelings of isolation and depression. He avoids people because he fears crying in public, thus creating a scene. One wonders if "I'll Cry Instead" may have partially inspired Smokey Robinson to pen similarly themed songs like "Tears of A Clown" or "Tracks of My Tears." Both feature narrators wrecked by lost love and feeling isolated even in a crowd.

Gradually, however, "I'll Cry Instead" undergoes a transformation. Lennon's words reflect a man struggling to regain his pride and uses anger as a crutch. He vows to return in the near future, adding that the girls should avoid him because he plans on breaking each of their hearts. Clearly these are vengeful acts that he hopes his ex-love will somehow witness. His declaration to exact his revenge also argues that her destruction of the relationship is to blame for destroying other women's hearts.

Lennon would revisit this theme in the controversial "Run for Your Life," considered the most misogynistic track in the Beatles catalog. In any case, "I'll Cry Instead" differs from the overwhelming sadness of 1963's "Misery" or other *Hard Day's Night* tunes like "You Can't Do That" or "Tell Me Why"; in those tracks, the narrator mourns his relationship's demise but does not seek retribution.

Musically, McCartney's bass stands out during the "lovin' man can do" line, adding aggression and a blues tinge to the track. The chugging bass amplifies the narrator's defiance and vengeful desires. Harrison's guitar picking reveals Carl Perkins' lasting influence, with the sound closely resembling recordings such as "Honey Don't" and "Matchbox," both of which the Beatles covered. Not surprisingly, the great country guitarist Chet Atkins later released his own instrumental version of "I"ll Cry Instead" on his 1966 album *Chet Atkins Picks on the Beatles*.

The jangly guitar sound as well as the downbeat lyrics indicate how the Beatles were evolving artistically, foreshadowing the acoustic sound of *Beatles for Sale* and *Rubber Soul*, in particular. Lennon would continually explore dark subjects on subsequent Beatles albums as well as his own work, and "I'll Cry Instead" represents an early example of this thematic shift. "I'll Cry Instead" may have ultimately been omitted from the movie *A Hard Day's Night*, but its country-rock sound and darker subject matter rank the song as an important Beatles track.

Originally published August 2, 2014 at http://somethingelsereviews.com/2014/08/02/deep-beatles-ill-cry-instead-a-hard-days-night-1964/

"You Can't Do That"
A Hard Day's Night (1964)

In retrospect, "You Can't Do That" could have been titled "Shoulda Been." It should have been in the *Hard Day's Night* film; it should have been a lead single. Instead, due to various circumstances, "You Can't Do That" is a non-movie track that remains one of the Beatles' "shoulda been" hits. Featuring lyrics concerning anger and insecurity, "You Can't Do That" is a prime example of the Beatles' ability to record accessible yet sophisticated pop. It remains a deep track that should have been considered in the same league as "A Hard Day's Night" or "Can't Buy Me Love."

According to past interviews, Lennon wrote "You Can't Do That" partially to break away from his usual rhythm guitar parts. In 1964, he told *Melody Maker* that "I'd find it a drag to play rhythm all the time, so I always work myself out something interesting to play." With "You Can't Do That," Lennon explained, "there really isn't a lead guitarist and a rhythm guitarist on that, because I feel the rhythm guitarist role sounds too thin for records. Anyway, it drove me potty to play chunk-chunk rhythm all the time." He acknowledged that George Harrison contributed stellar lead guitar, but that sometimes Lennon liked to take the reins.

Sixteen years later, Lennon claimed the track was his attempt at emulating Wilson Pickett: "You know, a cowbell going four-in-the-bar, and the chord going 'chatoong!" he said. After penning the track, Lennon and the band assembled on February 25, 1964 at EMI/Abbey Road Studios to record it, along with "And I Love Her" and "I Should Have Known Better." Only "You Can't Do That" was completed during this session, with the Beatles laying down nine takes of the song (only four takes were complete). As the *Beatles Bible* notes, the song marks the first time Harrison used his soon-to-be-trademark Rickenbacker 12-string guitar. As previously mentioned, "You Can't Do That" also features Lennon's lead guitar debut on a Beatles single.

While it does not appear in the released version of *A Hard Day's Night*, "You Can't Do That" was originally intended for inclusion during the final concert sequence. In addition, the track was slated to be the sixth UK single until Paul McCartney composed "Can't Buy Me Love." Thus, Lennon's song was not only left on the cutting room floor, it was also relegated to the B-side of the "Can't Buy Me Love" single in the U.S. and UK, showing up only as an extra tune on the *A Hard Day's Night* soundtrack. Interestingly, after the "Can't Buy Me Love/You Can't Do That" single was released on March 20, producer George Martin overdubbed a piano part onto take nine on May 22, according to Mark Lewisohn's *Complete Beatles Recording Sessions*. This version, now take ten, was never used.

Despite these setbacks, "You Can't Do That" received acclaim via the Beatles' 1964 concerts and BBC radio appearances. According to the *Beatles Bible*, the omitted *Hard Day's Night* footage was aired on the *Ed Sullivan Show* on May 24, 1964 to promote the film. In 1995, take six of the song appeared on the *Anthology 1* collection, a version notable for including Lennon's original guide vocal.

"You Can't Do That" begins and ends with Harrison's distinctive guitar picking, the sound slightly predating the Byrds' folk-rock sound, as well as reflecting the group's interest in spanning musical genres. The heavy rhythm, punctuated by Starr's drums and McCartney's accompanying cowbell, reveals the group's well-known R&B roots.

Lennon then enters the scene with a raspy rock vocal, perfect for communicating the narrator's message. He warns that he will most likely cause pain through this words, snarling that if he catches his girlfriend talking to a certain man again he will "leave you flat." He plays the tough guy, sounding possessive as he confronts her. This marks the second time he has caught her with another man, and reminds her that this seeming betrayal is a "sin." He repeats the title phrase, clarifying his feelings concerning her even speaking to another man.

Obvious thematic comparisons can be made to other Lennon compositions such as "Run for Your Life," "No Reply," "Not A Second Time," or the resentment expressed in "I'll Cry Instead." On "You Can't Do That," however, Lennon admits his insecurity, suggesting that the problem may lie with him. Other men are jealous that he won his girlfriend's love, and that he fears being humiliated in front of friends. If they caught her with another man, he surmises, that they would laugh at his cuckolded status.

So, while he commands the girlfriend to listen to him if she wants to be his lover, he admits that he has little control over his emotions, which would lead to the relationship's demise. Lennon would later atone for his overly possessive feelings and mistrust in songs like "Jealous Guy" and "Woman."

Another essential ingredient of "You Can't Do That" is Harrison and McCartney's backing vocals. The call-and-response motif, particularly when Lennon sings the line about how he will leave her, lets the other two function as a Greek chorus — underscoring important aspects of the tune. Listen to their harmonies on the words "green" and "seen," as well as the phrase "laugh in my face." Their voices are found high in the mix, serving as exclamation points, dramatizing the rage and anguish of the narrator. Harrison and McCartney repeat the title words during Lennon's guitar solo, the repetition adding to the overall aggressive tone of the lyrics and sound.

While the catchy beat and jangly rhythm guitar may energize the song, the lyrics reveal its darker nature. The Beatles consistently proved they could tackle difficult subjects but not sacrifice accessibility. They would continually test the boundaries of pop with each subsequent album, but "You Can't Do That" stands as an early illustration of this experimentation. It may not have appeared in the film or been released as the A-side of a single, but "You Can't Do That" contains one of Lennon's finest vocal performances and should be ranked among the Beatles' best early rockers.

Originally published August 29, 2014 at http://somethingelsereviews.com/ 2014/08/29/deep-beatles-you-cant-do-that-from-a-hard-days-night-1964

"Any Time at All"
A Hard Day's Night (1964)

BOOM! Ringo Starr's forceful drumbeat provides an abrupt, attention-grabbing introduction for "Any Time at All," a *Hard Day's Night* track that was never released as a single, but stands as an extraordinary example of the Beatles' gift for creating sophisticated yet catchy songs.

"Any Time at All" originates from June 2, 1964, when principal writer John Lennon brought the rough draft into Abbey Road Studios. That afternoon, The Beatles first recorded seven takes of the rhythm track, then Lennon's lead vocal. After breaking to record two more songs, they returned to the song in the evening. They recorded four more takes, overdubbing piano, guitar, and vocals. According to the *Beatles Bible* website, the track was mixed for mono on June 4; this mix was discarded, and new stereo and mono mixes were completed on June 22.

As is typical of many Lennon/McCartney compositions, Lennon and Paul McCartney did not sit side by side, writing the music and lyrics. Instead, Lennon wrote the song on his own. In his 1980 *Playboy* interview, Lennon explained that the tune was "an effort at writing 'It Won't Be Long' — same ilk: C to A minor, C to A minor with me shouting." By this time, Beatlemania was in full swing, which meant that their manager Brian Epstein, and their label wanted to fully exploit their (erroneously) presumed fleeting fame. Therefore, in between shooting *A Hard Day's Night* scenes, the foursome would quickly pen songs and record in the studio late into the evening. This tight time limitation led to "Any Time at All" being released in a relatively unfinished state. When Lennon presented the song to the group, he lacked lyrics for the middle eight. McCartney suggested a series of piano chords, with the intention of writing additional lyrics over them. As the deadline loomed, however, the band and producer George Martin abandoned this plan and left in just the piano-infused middle eight.

Despite leaving it "unfinished," the Beatles otherwise carefully crafted this hidden treasure. After that pound of the drums, Lennon and McCartney alternate between the refrain's lyrics, repeating the title phrase and adding the lines telling the lover that whenever she calls, he will be there. Lennon's slightly raspy voice lends the song a sharper rock edge, while McCartney's higher but clear tones keeps it from becoming too suggestive.

The rest of the lyrics aren't particularly novel — they describe a man telling his lover that he sympathizes with her pain, that he will bolster her spirits if she needs him. He clearly will do anything to make her smile. George Harrison's lead guitar, layered over acoustic guitars, clearly influenced the Byrds, who would meld the Beatles' electric guitars with soft folk strumming just a year later. McCartney's piano and Harrison's guitar lines interweave with each other in the bridge, returning to Lennon's almost screaming vocal on the refrain. Bringing the song full circle, the conclusion is signaled by Starr's strong drumbeat followed by the guitar reverb gradually fading out.

Like "It Won't Be Long," "Any Time at All" combines the Beatles' patented backbeat, searing voices, memorable refrain, and distinctive beginnings and conclusions. Why didn't Parlophone/EMI release the track as a single? After all, it has all the ingredients of a solid hit. The answer remains a mystery, but "Any Time at All" is an underrated track from the Mop Top era.

Originally published July 11, 2012 at http://somethingelsereviews.com/2012/07/11/deep-beatles-anytime-at-all-1964/

"Things We Said Today"
A Hard Day's Night (1964)

Concluding "Deep Beatles'" look at *Hard Day's Night* tracks that did not appear in the film is a gem: "Things We Said Today," a Paul McCartney-penned song that he still performs live. In 1980, John Lennon cited it as one of his all-time favorite McCartney compositions. Its acoustic guitar-driven sound foreshadows the folk-rock sound of *Rubber Soul,* an album they would release just a year later.

As McCartney told biographer Barry Miles, he wrote "Things We Said Today" on a yacht in May 1964. Cruising the Virgin Islands with then-girlfriend Jane Asher, as well as Ringo Starr and his wife Maureen, McCartney penned the wistful track in a cabin below deck. Fighting off seasickness, McCartney jotted down the words while trying to ignore the smell of oil and the roar of the yacht's engine.

His lyrics tell the story of an uncertain relationship, of choosing to remember the good times while facing a vague future. It can be argued that McCartney was referencing his rocky romance with Asher, as their careers and wildly differing lifestyles ultimately drove them apart. They did not officially end their relationship until 1968; interestingly, McCartney wrote this song four years before that event.

In any case, McCartney described the song to Miles as "a future nostalgia: we'll remember the things we said today, sometime in the future, so the song projects itself into the future and then is nostalgic about the moment we're living in now."

The Beatles cut the track at Abbey Road Studios on June 2, 1964; amazingly, it took only three takes to perfect "Things We Said

Today." Take one was a false start; take two was complete; and the final version involved overdubbing McCartney's second vocal part, Lennon's piano, and Starr's tambourine, according to the *Beatles Bible*. They meant to omit the piano from the final mix, but it was still picked up by other microphones during the recording, as the instruments were not recorded on separate tracks. Therefore the piano can still be heard in the released version. (Listen closely to the bridge for the faint piano section.)

Another interesting aspect of the song is that McCartney harmonizes with only himself; he double-tracked his vocals, mostly singing in unison but occasionally harmonizing. Lennon and George Harrison never sing a note, but they still performed vital roles: Lennon plays that striking rhythm guitar, while Harrison adds lead guitar.

While "Things We Said Today" was not a hit on its own, it did receive welcome exposure. It was released as the B-side to the "Hard Day's Night" single on June 2, 1964, and it subsequently appeared on the film soundtrack album in the UK. American fans could not buy it until the *Something New* collection was released on July 20.

The tune benefitted even more from live treatments, as the band performed it twice for BBC radio and briefly included in their August and September 1964 tours of the U.S. and Canada; Harrison provided the harmony vocals on stage.

Lennon's strident rhythm guitar begins "Things We Said Today," another example of the Beatles' ability to draw the listener in from the first note. By rarely straying from a minor key, the song maintains its moody tone. Starr's drums punctuate each guitar riff as McCartney begins his vocals, singing that even after he must leave her, she will continue to think of him. Already the listener senses impermanence in the relationship: the couple is visualizing their future breakup. McCartney harmonizes on the next two lines, emphasizing this uncertainty. When he'll feel lonely, he will revel in the memory of tender words they told one another. His lover then assures him that she will love him forever, but he admits that these feelings may not be everlasting.

Lennon and Harrison furiously strum their guitars and Starr slightly increases the tempo at the crucial bridge. McCartney expresses how lucky he is to be in love, even though he is unsure of the future. They may be deceiving themselves that their romance will be permanent, but for now, their love is enough. McCartney sings these emotional lines, his voice double-tracked in perfect synchronicity.

In other words, he encourages both of them to live in the moment, to revel in these words of love and not think of their relationship's possible transience. Yet he concludes this section by singing "we'll go on and on." He suggests that their words may outlast their romance, that language possesses an infinite quality that love may not.

Perhaps McCartney's lyrics rendered "Things We Said Today" too complex for the generally upbeat tone of the film. He clearly retains great affection for the tune, as he included it in his 1989-1990 world tour (the attached live version is available on the *Tripping the Live Fantastic* album) and his 1991 *MTV Unplugged* appearance. In addition, McCartney occasionally performs it during soundchecks.

A Hard Day's Night stands as not only a landmark film, but as a soundtrack packed with hidden gems as well as enormous hits. The songs appearing in the movie remain memorable, partially due to indelible images such as the Beatles romping in a field or jamming on a train. However, the album-only songs should not be overlooked, and should receive radio airplay and acclaim as much as "Can't Buy Me Love" or the title track.

Delve into deep *Hard Day's Night* tunes, and hear hints of the band's impending musical evolution — when they moved from the Beatlemania years to Beatles 2.0, starting with *Rubber Soul*. These under-appreciated songs are experimental in their own way, and portend how the Beatles would soon transform rock and roll.

Originally published September 12, 2014 at http://somethingelsereviews.com/ 2014/09/12/deep-beatles-things-we-said-today-from-a-hard-days-night-1964/

"I Call Your Name"
Past Masters (1964)

This week's edition of Deep Beatles could be retitled "A Tale of Multiple Mixes."

Originally intended for the *Hard Day's Night* soundtrack, the Beatles' "I Call Your Name" stands out for its cowbell-led percussion, unusual musical structure, and distinctive guitar solo. While omitted from the album due to its slight similarity to "You Can't Do That" (chiefly its cowbell), "I Call Your Name" resurfaced on the Beatles' 1964 UK EP *Long Tall Sally* and the U.S. Capitol release *The Beatles' Second Album*. Today, it can be found on the *Past Masters* compilation.

John Lennon had been hanging on to "I Call Your Name" since the Beatles' pre-Hamburg days, according to a 1980 *Playboy* interview. "That was my song. When there was no Beatles and no group, I just had it around," he said. "It was my effort as a kind of blues originally, and then I wrote the middle-eight just to stick it in the album when it came out years later. The first part had been written before Hamburg even. It was one of my 'first' attempts at a song." In a 1994 interview, Paul McCartney recalled helping Lennon revise the track before the recording.

Lennon first gave "I Call Your Name" to Billy J. Kramer, a singer Brian Epstein had recently signed to his roster of artists. Kramer and his backing band the Dakotas recorded the song along with another early Lennon/McCartney composition, "Bad to Me," in 1963; Parlophone then released the single, but chose "I Call Your Name" as the B-side. A year later, John Lennon apparently decided enough time had passed for the Beatles to record their own version. In *The Complete Beatles Recording Sessions*, Mark Lewisohn said Lennon could be heard discussing Kramer's version in the control room. "Do you think it's a bit much doing Billy J's intro and solo? 'Cos it's our song anyroad, innit?" he said before the group attempted take one.

The Beatles assembled at Abbey Road Studios on March 1, 1964 to record "I Call Your Name," along with "I'm Happy Just to Dance with You" and "Long Tall Sally." The lineup included John Lennon on vocals and rhythm guitar; Paul McCartney on bass; George Harrison on lead guitar; and Ringo Starr on drums and, even more importantly, cowbell. Under George Martin's direction, the Beatles recorded seven attempts, completing only three takes. Take seven was deemed best, with another Lennon lead vocal and Starr's cowbell added to the final version. Harrison's solo was added in from take five.

"I Call Your Name" may not have been a hit, but it marks a significant change in the Beatles' repertoire. Although John Lennon may have written the track early in his career, it demonstrates how the group wanted to incorporate musical forms outside of straightforward rock. As Alan Pollack states in his "Notes On" series: "The style of this one is not easily pigeon-holed; somewhat bluesy in flavor, but not at all in form; more like pop, or even jazz, than the predominantly harder rock songs which chronologically surround it." What makes the song even more distinctive is its instrumental section, an early attempt at an emerging genre out of Jamaica: ska.

A precursor to reggae and rocksteady, ska features a fast tempo, a strong off beat, and elements of rock, jazz, calypso, and American R&B. The Beatles were most likely exposed to ska through Blue Beat, a British record label that struck a deal with Jamaican record producers to distribute that country's music in the UK. The foundation of the label coincided with a mass migration of Jamaican artists to Britain, hoping to earn their fortunes outside of their home country. The label featured early ska pioneers Wilfred "Jackie" Edwards, Laurel Aitken, Owen Gray (his hit "Please Let Me Go" combines Fats Domino's New Orleans sound with a calypso feel), trombonist Rico Rodriguez, Kentrist Fagan (aka Girl Satchmo), and Millie Small, who recorded ska's best-known early hit: 1964's "My Boy Lollipop."

Ska earned a cult following among "mods" in the 1960s, and its Blue Beat-powered heyday spanned the years 1960-67. Presumably John Lennon did not hear the genre until the early 1960s, thus he most likely added the instrumental break around 1964. Compare "My Boy Lollipop" to Ringo Starr's brief change in drumming style and George Harrison's offbeat guitar solo.

Another interesting aspect of the Beatles' "I Call Your Name" is its complex story of multiple mixes: the U.S. mono and stereo versions, and the U.K. mono and stereo mixes. Each varies when Starr's cowbell enters the song, and the U.S. stereo version (found on the stereo mix of *The Beatles' Second Album*) also adds reverb. The first mono mix occurred March 3, 1964, a rushed effort to have the songs ready for the upcoming *Hard Day's Night* soundtrack. George Martin and engineer Norman Smith prepare the track for inclusion in the film. Ultimately "I Call Your Name" was dropped from the movie, thus this initial mix was scrapped. This would not conclude the mixing journey, of course; so many were created that a timeline is needed to keep track of the releases.

The Beatles' Second Album **mono version:** On March 4, Martin returned to Abbey Road to create the mono mix that would appear on this project, released only in the U.S. The cowbell enters the song almost immediately, although it drops out briefly right before Harrison's solo. Why? A previous take of the instrumental section was edited into take seven, as mentioned earlier. Also, listen to how the mono mix introduces the cowbell immediately as the song begins:

The Beatles' Second Album **stereo version:** Martin and Smith created this first stereo mix on March 10, 1964. First, the cowbell enters the song right as John Lennon sings the word "call." Note how George Harrison's introductory guitar solo slightly differs from the previous mono mixes. The cowbell also drops out right before Lennon sings the last "I call your name" before the guitar solo, yet another variation on how Martin and Smith edited in the instrumental break from a previous take. Even more importantly, the entire mix features an echo effect. Does the reverb enhance the quality of the song or detract from the original mono mix? You be the judge:

Long Tall Sally **U.K. EP mono version:** This mono mix was created on June 4, 1964, and is almost identical to the U.S. mono version. The cowbell appears at the very beginning of the track, and the edit of the instrumental section occurs right before Lennon sings the final "I call your name" before the instrumental; the cowbell returns after

Lennon croons "don't you know I can't take it."

UK stereo mix: Martin, Smith, and Geoff Emerick reunited on June 22, 1964 to complete several mixes, including created and editing together two stereo versions of "I Call Your Name." This hastily completed version featured Lennon's voice single-tracked at the very beginning of the song, and the cowbell placement once again varies slightly at the start and conclusion of the instrumental section. This mix first appeared on the 1976 compilation *Rock 'N' Roll Music*, and is now available on the *Past Masters* collection. Listen to the U.K. stereo mix as found on *Past Masters*. After Lennon sings the title phrase, the cowbell begins right before sings "but you're not there."

No matter which version you prefer, most can agree that "I Call Your Name" illustrates the Beatles' rapid artistic development. The tempo changes twice; unusual chord changes appear in the two bridges; and the instrumental section stands as an early indicator of the Beatles' interest in incorporating world music into rock and roll. "Ob-La-Di, Ob-La-Da" owes its existence to this prior experimentation with ska. Clearly, Ringo Starr still holds great affection for the unique track — as he, Tom Petty, and Jeff Lynne rendered a charmingly energetic version for the 1990 TV special *Lennon: A John Lennon Tribute*.

Originally published June 26, 2015 at http://somethingelsereviews.com/ 2015/06/26/the-beatles-i-call-your-name-deep-beatles/

"Eight Days a Week"
Beatles for Sale (1964)

Note: This was the first "Deep Beatles" column I wrote for Something Else Reviews, thus material that repeats anecdotes from this book's introduction has been deleted.

While not necessarily a "deep track," I'll kick off this column with "Eight Days A Week," the song that hooked me 27 years ago. A song fading out at the end was common, but here the guitars gradually fade in at the beginning, which instantly demands the listener's ear. As evidenced on the *Anthology* collection, the Beatles experimented with earlier versions of the song, including adding an "ooo" vocal in lieu of the fade in. But the group wisely chose the experimental introduction. As for the typically humorous title (reminiscent of "A Hard Day's Night"), McCartney has offered two explanations for the unusual wording. In 1984 he claimed it stemmed from a Ringo Starr malapropism; in another interview he recalled it being a statement from his then-chauffeur.

Interestingly, John Lennon thought "Eight Days A Week" was one of their weaker tunes; in 1972, Lennon stated that "we struggled to record it and struggled to make it into a song. It was his (Paul's) initial effort, but I think we both worked on it. I'm not sure. But it was lousy anyway." Regardless of Lennon's subsequent opinion, "Eight Days A Week" stands as a stellar illustration of their pop sensibilities, a textbook example of writing a memorable song with lyrics and chord changes that linger with the listener long after the record ends.

Originally published June 26, 2012 http://somethingelsereviews.com/2012/06/26/deep-beatles-eight-days-a-week-1964/

"Baby's in Black"
Beatles for Sale (1964)

When the Beatles released *Beatles for Sale* in the UK on December 4, 1964, fans were startled by the group's haggard appearance on the album's somber album cover. Indeed, that year they had been swallowed up in the Beatlemania hurricane, playing innumerable concerts, taping television appearances, recording music, and, of course, shooting their film debut *A Hard Day's Night*.

Because of their hectic schedule, the group had little time to develop an album consisting entirely of originals. Thus, their just-in-time-for-the-holidays release *Beatles for Sale* included eight compositions and six covers, most dating from their Hamburg and Cavern Club days. One of the originals, "Baby's in Black," stands as one of the darkest yet most harmonic tracks in the Lennon-McCartney pantheon.

John Lennon and Paul McCartney penned the song together in a hotel room while on tour. In *Anthology*, McCartney explained that they wanted to experiment with waltz time. In addition, they wanted to explore darker themes and further expand the limits of pop music. "I think also John and I wanted to do something bluesy, a bit darker, more grown-up, rather than just straight pop. It was more 'baby's in black' as in mourning. Our favourite color was black, as well," McCartney said.

While the lyrics tell the story of a man wooing a woman who is still mourning the loss of her past love, speculation abounds that the words refer to a real-life figure. While in Hamburg, the Beatles befriended a circle of German intellectuals and artists, one of which was artist and photographer Astrid Kirchherr. She fell in love with the group's then-bassist, Stu Sutcliffe, who soon left the band to remain with her in Hamburg. Their love story would be cut tragically short when aspiring painter Sutcliffe died of a brain hemorrhage in April 1962.

Regardless of the song's actual subject, "Baby's in Black" results from a full collaboration between Lennon and McCartney. The former stated in his 1980 *Playboy* interview that they were "together, in the same room" while penning the words and music. McCartney would add to this statement years later in *Many Years from Now*, telling Barry Miles that he and Lennon cowrote the song:

> Sometimes the harmony that I was writing in sympathy to John's melody would take over and become a stronger melody. ... When people wrote out the music score they would ask, 'Which one is the melody?' because it was so co-written that you could actually take either. We rather liked this one. It was not so much a work job, there was a bit more cred about this one. It's got a good middle.

Recording commenced on August 11, 1964, also the first day of the *Beatles for Sale* sessions. According to Mark Lewisohn's *Complete Beatles Recording Sessions*, they recorded 14 takes, only five of which were complete. The major difficulty occurred with the opening guitar note — George Harrison experimented with several variations, bending it with his tremolo arm to emphasize and extend the sound (none of these attempts were used). Lennon and McCartney sang into the same microphone to perfectly synchronize their harmonies.

Interestingly, Lewisohn notes that the session signified a change in the Beatles' working relationship with producer George Martin: During takes, Martin can be heard asking how the boys wanted the beginning to sound, an indication that Martin was no longer fully dictating the sessions. Clearly, the group had demonstrated their confidence in songwriting and musicianship in just a short time.

After the marathon recording session, the Beatles, Martin, and engineer Norman Smith regrouped at Abbey Road Studios on August 14 to record several other tracks and complete rough mono mixes of "Baby's in Black." The mixes were finally completed on October 26, also the last day of the *Beatles for Sale* sessions.

A waltz with a country twang, "Baby's in Black" succeeds due to Lennon and McCartney's Everly Brothers-style vocals and Harrison's piercing guitar. Ringo Starr's pulsating drums, particularly toward the end as other instruments drop out of the track, propel the song's unusual tempo.

"Baby's in Black" works well thematically with other *Beatles for Sale* tracks such as the pessimistic "I'm A Loser" or the angry "No Reply." "What can I do?" the narrator reiterates throughout the song. His love interest will not let go of her former boyfriend; constantly draping herself in black, she mourns either their failed romance or his death. The lead character's frustration increases as the track progresses. "I think of her, but she thinks only of him," Lennon and McCartney's voices seamlessly blend as they sing their lament: they think of her, but she thinks only of her lost love. Curiously, they label her sadness "only a whim," although her attire and emotion suggest otherwise.

"Baby's in Black" reaches a crescendo in the bridge, when the two singers' pitch and volume rise. They carefully enunciate an important line, asking how long it will take for the woman to stop living in the past. Cleverly, the lyrics alternate between the colors black and blue, an indication that the narrator has been emotionally wounded as well as his love interest. Harrison's country leanings shine through in his solo, with idols Carl Perkins and Chet Atkins looming large in every note.

While never released as a single, "Baby's in Black" played a big part in the Beatles' concerts, making its final appearance at their farewell Candlestick Park show on August 29, 1966. Thematically, it seemed a curious choice for the setlist, as its dour mood contrasted with the more upbeat numbers.

Hearing their Hollywood Bowl and Shea Stadium renditions of "Baby's in Black" can be a jarring experience. As Lennon and McCartney crooned very serious and introspective words, teenage girls screamed throughout the entire song, seemingly oblivious to the song's bleak meaning. (This was most likely due to not being able to hear the group.) As their tours continued, however, they did begin adding more thematically complex songs like "Yesterday" to their repertoire.

Along with other *Beatles for Sale* tracks, "Baby's in Black" signaled the Beatles' rapidly growing interest in musical experimentation. The song's tempo and grim subject matter further expanded the boundaries of typical beat group fare, preparing audiences for even more complex works such as the aforementioned "Yesterday" and "Eleanor Rigby." It also provides a lesson in both interpretative singing as well as skilled harmonization, courtesy of Lennon and McCartney's patented vocal blend.

Originally published April 3, 2015 at http://somethingelsereviews.com/2015/04/03/the-beatles-babys-in-black-beatles-for-sale-deep-beatles/

"What You're Doing"
Beatles for Sale (1964)

Like "Baby's in Black," "What You're Doing" exemplifies the somber mood pervading some tracks on 1964's *Beatles for Sale*. Describing a turbulent relationship, "What You're Doing" is primarily a Paul McCartney composition featuring jangly guitar, an unusual drum beat, intricate chord changes, and creative lyrics. Astoundingly, McCartney would later dismiss it as "filler," but the track merits more than that label. Instead, it further anticipates the 1960s folk rock movement and introspective songwriting that would characterize much of the Beatles' later work.

Thought to be inspired by his shaky romance with actress Jane Asher, McCartney penned the words and music on a whim. He told Barry Miles that the song may have derived from just talking, with one of them asking "Hey, what'cha doing?" McCartney claimed that he first wrote the verses, hoping they would inspire a memorable chorus. Apparently he believed he had not achieved his goal, telling Miles that he felt it was a better recording than a song. In other words, the recording quality enhanced what he believed to be an average track.

The *Beatles Bible* notes how "What You're Doing" departed from then-traditional Beatles songs and set the tone for future recordings. The four-bar solo drum pattern introduces the song and returns in the fadeout; the distortion of the lead and rhythm guitars create a fuzzy sound; and the piano and bass break right before the song's conclusion signal the Beatles' willingness to experiment with song structure.

Recording began at Abbey Road on September 29, 1964; during

this session they completed seven versions of the rhythm track. The next day they attempted the track five more times; according to the *Beatles Bible*, at this point the instrumental section was an octave higher. In the video below, note how Lennon and McCartney initially tried harmonizing on virtually all the lyrics rather than double tracking McCartney's voice. Listen for a brief pause before the instrumental fadeout. The clip begins with take five, an incomplete attempt that breaks down quickly but features amusing studio chatter.

They did not return to the track until October 26, the final day of the *Beatles for Sale* sessions. After recording seven more takes, they finally decided on their final attempt, take 19, as the final version. With that, the Beatles completed not only the song but the entire album.

"What You're Doing" immediately seizes the listener's attention with Ringo Starr's thumping drums, the bass drum underscoring the plodding beat. The four-bar section ushers in McCartney's bass, John Lennon's acoustic rhythm guitar, and George Harrison's lead guitar. The resounding notes clearly anticipate the Byrds' brand of folk rock as well as the sound dominating their 1965 release *Rubber Soul*. McCartney's double-tracked voice then enters the picture, with key words such as "look" and "I'm" emphasized through Lennon and Harrison's backing vocals (shouted more than sung).

While the song addresses a serious subject — loss of love — McCartney's creative rhymes introduce an element of playfulness. He near-rhymes "doin'" with "blue an,'" repeating the technique in the second verse, rhyming "runnin,'" and "fun in." Harrison and Lennon harmonize in the background as McCartney delivers the title phrase, dramatizing the frustration the narrator feels.

The bridge — which usually, is repeated twice — employs some unusual chord changes and dissonance that musicologist Alan Pollack cites as "jazzy." He points out that the final section of the bridge, particularly the way McCartney's voice modulates on the word "me," adds an element of conflict to the track.

"The sustaining of the A-Major chord for two measures coupled with the descending melodic melisma on the word 'me' is an essentially relaxing or winding-down kind of gesture," Pollack writes. "In sharp contrast to this, the rhythm backing takes the opportunity to use the last beat of the last measure as an energetic springboard into the next verse, and the overlap of the two gestures makes an uncanny effect; kind of like you're being pulled in two directions at once." In other words, the bridge adds an element of tension that is resolved as McCartney's voice descends on "me." Thus, the emotional climax is tempered, the song returning to the dominant storyline.

As the song concludes, George Martin's piano creates a shaky, uncertain mood. Can this romance be repaired? As the narrator repeats the lines questioning just what the love interest is doing to the narrator, the listener is left to reach one's own conclusions.

While not as well known as other Beatles tracks, "What You're Doing" should be considered an important creative step for the group. In its structure and lyrics, the song illustrates how the Beatles were experimenting thematically and musically. Unlike "Love Me Do," "What You're Doing" concerns the complexities of love, the narrator gazing inward to determine just why his romance is so unstable. The intricate and unexpected chord changes move beyond typical pop songs of the time, incorporating jazz elements. Structurally, the song defies traditional rock/pop single construction by repeating the bridge twice.

Finally, the instrumentation foreshadows how the Beatles would test the limits of rock, using distinctive guitar sounds that would become quite pervasive in mid-to-late '60s music. Starr also demonstrates his ability to adopt different drumming styles, and McCartney shows a propensity for stretching his voice to fit the mood of a song. For these reasons, "What You're Doing" is worth a deeper listen and represents a significant phase of their artistic development.

Originally published April 17, 2015 at http://somethingelsereviews.com/ 2015/04/17/the-beatles-what-youre-doing-deep-beatles/

"Mr. Moonlight"
Beatles for Sale (1964)

Ladies and gentlemen of the jury, I stand before you to defend the reputation of the Beatles' 1964 cover of "Mr. Moonlight." Since its first appearance on *Beatles for Sale*, fans and critics have derided the track as corny, cheesy, and overdone, unworthy of the band's otherwise stellar recordings.

Music theorist Alan Pollack summarizes common criticisms: "It must be something about the self-consciously campy vocal, lugubrious Hammond organ, and generally queasy blend of doohwhop [sic] and Latin musical styles." But is "Mr. Moonlight" guilty of these crimes? Should it be labeled as one of the worst Beatles songs of all time? Its backstory and a closer look at the Beatles' performance may influence your musical deliberations.

First, I present the facts of the case:

In 1962, bluesman William "Willie" Lee Perryman's group Dr. Feelgood and the Interns (pictured below) issued a single appropriately titled "Dr. Feelgood." The b-side, written by Interns guitarist Roy Lee Johnson, was a bluesy ballad entitled "Mr. Moonlight." Neither song charted, but the Beatles discovered the obscure track, similarly to how they found unfairly neglected American R&B artists Arthur Alexander and Larry Williams.

By the time the band embarked on their stint in Hamburg, they decided to incorporate little-known covers into their stage act to separate them from competing groups. When playing gigs like the Star Club in 1962, they would play few originals and more offbeat covers like "Besame Mucho," "Lend Me Your Comb," and, of course, "Mr. Moonlight."

In just two years, the Beatles found themselves at the center of the Beatlemania hurricane. While securing material for their fourth studio album *Beatles for Sale*, they resurrected some of the songs from their early set lists, one of them being "Mr. Moonlight." Fans may be surprised to learn that producer George Martin voiced no objection to this choice, as it became a popular number for "beat groups" of the time. The Hollies recorded their version of the tune in 1964, and acts such as the Lovin' Spoonful and Aretha Franklin drew inspiration from Dr. Feelgood and the Interns. Since "Mr. Moonlight" had received enthusiastic responses at early live shows, the Beatles apparently felt the song would fare well on an album.

Recording took place during two days: August 14, when they recorded four takes; and October 18, when they recorded four more. John Lennon sang lead and played acoustic rhythm guitar; Paul McCartney sang harmony vocals and played bass and the organ; George Harrison performed lead guitar and played African drums; and Ringo Starr rounded out the four on percussion. In his book *Here, There and Everywhere*, EMI recording engineer Geoff Emerick recalled Lennon recording his vocal part: "His searing vocal introduction sent shivers down my spine, even though it took him several tries to nail it," he wrote.

Instead of Harrison playing a slide guitar on the last two takes, McCartney performed a dramatic Hammond organ solo. Emerick claimed that previously Harrison experienced trouble executing the guitar solo: "Not the notes he was playing, but the odd, sped-up tremolo sound he was using, in faithful imitation of the Dr. Feelgood version that had been a minor hit a couple of years previously." While Lennon and Emerick approved of the unconventional sound, Martin "insisted that it was simply too weird. After some discussion, it was decided to overdub a cheesy organ solo instead. Even though I loathed the sound, I was most impressed to see Paul playing it — up until that point, I'd had no idea that he could even play keyboards." When editing commenced on October 27, Martin and engineer Norman Smith created the final version by merging takes four and eight, then mixing for mono and stereo.

Since *Beatles for Sale's* release, the prosecution — or critics, in this case — have heaped scorn upon the cut. *AllMusic's* Stephen

Thomas Erlewine dubbed it "arguably the worst thing the group ever recorded." *Pitchfork's* Tom Ewing seemed at a loss to describe the song, as he figured somehow "the ugliness of its organ solo [was] surely deliberate."

Ladies and gentlemen, I can understand how the straight-out-of-a-roller rink sound of the Hammond organ tainted the track. But should "Mr. Moonlight" be found guilty of cheesiness because of one flaw? No, and I ask that the following be entered into evidence:

Exhibit A: Lennon's vocal performance. Can anyone make a better case for Lennon being one of the great rock vocalists by hearing his opening line? When he shouts "Mr. Moonlight," one can hear his cords shredding a la "Twist and Shout." This technique perfectly sets the mood for the heart-rending lines describing the narrator as praying and begging while on his knees. Interestingly, Lennon clearly based his singing closely on the original recording. Listen to the phrasing in the Dr. Feelgood version here.

Exhibit B: The group's harmonies. *Beatles for Sale* tracks like "No Reply" and "Baby's in Black" illustrate how much Lennon and McCartney had developed their close harmonies. As this track fades out, one can hear the duo experimenting with chord changes and different harmonies on the title phrase alone.

Exhibit C: The Beatles' original live version. Judging from an admittedly murky recording from their 1962 Star Club appearance, the group's original intent was to hone the song's rougher edges. While Dr. Feelgood and the Interns emphasized the bluesy, R&B feel of the track, the Beatles highlighted its pure rock elements. In the live recording, Harrison plays the guitar solo, which maintains the song's consistency. When Martin substituted the Hammond organ on the studio version, it totally destroyed "Mr. Moonlight's" moody atmosphere. In retrospect, the group should have stood their ground and stuck with Harrison's melodic guitar solo.

As you begin deliberations, ladies and gentlemen of the jury, I ask you to put aside all prejudices as you pull out your *Beatles for Sale* copy. Focus on Lennon's shiver-inducing vocals, the patented Beatles harmonies, and Harrison and Starr's gentle percussion. Think of McCartney's Hammond organ solo as a rare misstep that should not reflect badly upon "Mr. Moonlight's" general sound.

Find the track not guilty of being one of the Beatles' worst songs, "'cause we love you, Mr. Moonlight."

Originally published September 21, 2012 at http://somethingelsereviews.com/ 2012/09/21/deep-beatles-mr-moonlight-1964/

PART TWO
1965-1970

"Tell Me What You See"
Help! (1965)

One of the least-known tracks off the Beatles' *Help!* soundtrack, "Tell Me What You See" has even been dismissed by its chief songwriter: Paul McCartney He dismissed the track as forgettable, telling Barry Miles that the song served as an album cut or B-side, but not much else. Is the song worthy of such a lukewarm review? While relatively obscure to casual fans, its variety of instrumentation and unusual structure further demonstrate the Beatles' growing experimentation and determination to expand the pop/rock landscape.

In Miles' *Many Years from Now*, Paul McCartney vaguely recalled that he composed the majority of the track, but that John Lennon may have assisted. Lennon claimed in his 1980 *Playboy* interview that McCartney alone wrote "Tell Me What You See." They presented the song to director Richard Lester for inclusion in the *Help!* film, but Lester passed on the tune. It did eventually find a home on the soundtrack album and, in the U.S., on *Beatles VI*.

The Beatles recorded the song at Abbey Road on February 18, 1965. Under the direction of producer George Martin and engineer Norman Smith, the band laid down three tracks during the marathon session: "Tell Me What You See," "You've Got to Hide Your Love Away," and the unreleased "If You've Got Trouble" (it finally surfaced on the *Anthology 2* compilation).

Recorded in four takes, "Tell Me What You See" features McCartney on vocals, bass, and electric piano; Lennon on vocals, rhythm guitar, and tambourine; Ringo Starr on drums and claves; and George Harrison on güiro, a Latin-American percussion instrument consisting of a hollow gourd with horizontal notches cut into one side. The musician rubs a stick along the notches to produce a unique sound. Another key instrument is the Hohner Pianet electric piano, played after the refrain.

Paul McCartney may not have considered "Tell Me What You See" "memorable," but it marks important stages in the Beatles' artistic development. First, percussion takes a central role on the song, with three different instruments used. Ringo Starr also demonstrates his ability to play different tempos and styles during one track; twice he breaks out of the dominant tempo to perform a riff that varies from the previous rhythm. After Lennon and McCartney harmonize on the title phrase, McCartney plays the electric piano, followed by a slightly offbeat, lumbering fill slightly reminiscent of "What You're Doing" from *Beatles for Sale*. The claves and güiro remain high in the mix, propelling the rest of the song.

Second, "Tell Me What You See" foreshadows the acoustic sound of *Rubber Soul*, released in December 1965. Compare the song with "You Won't See Me" — the harmonies, prominent percussion, piano, and introspective lyrics resemble the preceding tune, illustrating how the Beatles were progressing toward a folkier sound as early as February 1965. The electric piano solo may have been inspired by previous singles such as the Zombies' 1964 hit "She's Not There," a track that prominently featured the instrument to lend a haunting air to the tune.

Finally, the melancholy yet playful lyrics demonstrate just how much Paul McCartney had grown as a lyricist. His contrasting use of the sound-alike words "apart" and "a part" shows a willingness to experiment with language, similar to songwriting partner John Lennon's methods.

His constant references to vision communicate the narrator's attempts to convince his lover that he will stand by her. She may close her eyes and he seemingly disappears, as she apparently expects. But when the protagonist commands her to open her eyes and tell him what she see, he prompts her to admit that he still stands before her. The sky may darken, but his love and loyalty will brighten her world (yet another reference to vision. In other words, his love will lift the metaphorical darkness and help her see the world through different, positive lenses). He would use a similar technique in *Rubber Soul's* "I'm Looking through You," in that case using vision to express deceit.

Unusual instrumentation, a preview of the Beatles' folkier sound, and increasingly sophisticated lyrics: all of these elements earn "Tell Me What You See" more attention. It marks a significant phase in their history, which renders the song anything but forgettable.

Originally published June 12, 2015 at http://somethingelsereviews.com/2015/06/12/beatles-tell-me-what-you-see-paul-mccartney/

"I Need You"
Help! (1965)

This week shines the spotlight on another underrated *Help!* track: "I Need You," an early George Harrison composition that still sounds haunting and airy. Its tender lyrics, along with the shrewd use of a volume pedal, add up to one of the Beatles' most distinctive, yet unheard, songs.

The melancholy lyrics are thought to address Harrison's burgeoning relationship with future wife Patti Boyd. More significantly, "I Need You" represents the second Harrison composition included on a Beatles album, the first being "Don't Bother Me" from *With the Beatles*. Recorded over two days, the song features an unusual lineup and interesting sonic effects.

According to the *Beatles Bible* and George Martin's book *Playback*, Harrison played Spanish guitar and Paul McCartney wielded his usual Hofner bass. However, Ringo Starr added very different percussion, namely by hitting the back of a Gibson Jumbo acoustic guitar. John Lennon supplemented the rhythm by striking the snare drum on beats two and four. Lennon and McCartney also contributed backing vocals, and Starr provided additional accompaniment on cowbell.

Recording began on February 15, 1965 — the initial day of the *Help!* sessions. First, the group laid down the rhythm track in five takes; next, Harrison performed his guide vocals on track two of the tape. After adding more guide vocals with McCartney on track three, Starr contributed his cowbell section on track four. When the Beatles reentered Abbey Road Studios the following day, they erased track four so Harrison could record his lead vocal. Lennon and McCartney added their backing harmonies, thereby erasing track two (Harrison's original guide vocal).

Starr replayed his cowbell section, while Harrison performed the song's crucial ingredient: the distorted guitar. Playing a twelve-string Rickenbacker, Harrison plucked the notes while Lennon knelt in front of him manipulating the guitar's volume control. Clearly they group liked the jangling sound, as they would reemploy it for the track "Yes It Is."

While "I Need You" did not receive airplay, it earned a featured spot in the film *Help!*: The group performs the song in the Salisbury Plain sequence; the scene is memorable not only for the great track, but for Starr's visible shivering in the cold while trying to smile and mime playing the drums.

Lyrically, "I Need You" functions as a straightforward love song. The narrator has fallen deeply in love, and begs his lover to return to him. Lennon and McCartney's backing harmonies emphasize the desperation expressed in these lines, creating a mood appropriate for their downbeat sentiments.

The bridge shifts keys, and here Harrison displays the emotion he would fully unleash in his later material. His voice gradually rises as he sings of his deep hurt, and how he cannot continue feeling such pain. This perfectly leads into even pleas; he asks his girlfriend to remember how much he loves her, and that he cannot live without her. Repeating the word "please" in several key lines underscores his acknowledgment that their relationship's future is out of his control, and he asserts that his very existence depends on their love. "I Need You" serves as a version of "Help!" but this time the narrator cries out to a specific person: his lover.

The distinctive guitar effect adds another dimension to the track, lending a modern sound. Like a plane flying overhead, the notes sail through the air, landing at will. Clearly the Byrds and the Beatles influenced each other, as the song contains folk-rock elements that would soar in popularity over the next couple of years. Upon close listening, McCartney's bass lines are more complicated beneath the surface, effectively propelling the rhythm. Speaking of rhythm, Starr's cowbell plays a surprisingly crucial role in "I Need You": along with the guitar, the cowbell emerges as one of the most distinctive elements of the tune.

Despite these fascinating elements, relatively few artists have recognized this unique song. One notable exception is Tom Petty, who lovingly covered it for 2002's *Concert for George* tribute.

As a whole, *Help!* foreshadows the radical sound changes the Beatles would rapidly undergo. *Rubber Soul* dived headfirst into folk rock waters, while *Revolver* further experimented with distortion and other effects. "I Need You" predicts these two elements, symbolizing Harrison's growth as a songwriter — and the band's desire to push rock's boundaries.

Originally published March 28, 2014 at http://somethingelsereviews.com/ 2014/03/28/deep-beatles-i-need-you-from-help-1965/

"The Night Before"
Help! (1965)

Was "The Night Before" the Beatles' response to the Shirelles' 1960 hit "Will You Love Me Tomorrow"? The 1965 *Help!* track could be seen that way, as it deals with a common topic: what happens the morning after intimacy?

Mostly written by Paul McCartney, "The Night Before" describes an insecure narrator questioning his lover's sincerity. It also features stellar harmonies and terrific guitar work from McCartney and George Harrison, and driving piano courtesy of John Lennon. Despite its significant presence in *Help!*, "The Night Before" remains one of the Beatles' most overlooked album tracks.

McCartney composed "The Night Before" in his apartment on Wimpole Street in London specifically for the film; Lennon later claimed not to remember much about the tune (although he deemed the track "good" in 1965), while McCartney stated in a 1994 interview that "I would say it is mainly mine. I don't think John had a lot to with that." Amazingly, the group recorded "The Night Before" in just two takes on February 17, with George Martin producing along with engineer Norman Smith.

From 2 to 7 p.m., the group recorded vocals and backing tracks, with two notable differences: McCartney and Harrison played the guitar solo together, an octave apart, while Lennon pounded on the Hohner Pianet electric piano. His rhythmic style underscores Ringo Starr's drums, lending the track its driving beat. After double tracking McCartney's lead vocals as well as Harrison and Lennon's backing voices, the group moved on to the next song: Harrison's "You Like Me Too Much."

Over February 18 and 23, Martin and Smith completed mono and stereo mixes while the Beatles returned to filming *Help!* During a subsequent press junket for the movie, the group recorded a live version for the BBC on May 26, 1965; this along with live renditions of "Ticket to Ride," "Everybody's Trying to Be My Baby," "I'm A Loser," "Honey Don't," "Dizzy Miss Lizzy," and "She's a Woman" were broadcast as part of the show *The Beatles Invite You to Take a Ticket to Ride* on June 7, 1965.

"The Night Before" begins with Starr's light-touch drumming, accented by Lennon's heavily rhythmic piano. McCartney utilizes a raspier singing style, emphasizing the anguish and uncertainty the narrator feels. "Were you telling lies? Was I so unwise?" he asks. Harrison and Lennon harmonize on the phrase "ah, the night before," suggesting the man's longing to return the previous evening's romance. Yet his beloved's feelings have seemingly cooled, leading to the lines most reminiscent of "Will You Love Me Tomorrow." He recalls the intense experience he and his lover shared the night before, then expressing profound sadness at her current indifference. McCartney communicates his pain through his wailing vocals, raising his voice in volume and key on the word "cry." Starr accents this section with maracas, working in tandem with McCartney's vocals.

McCartney and Harrison then execute their shared solo, the sound piercing through the piano and drums. This technique creates a jolting effect, demanding the listener to pay full attention to the interlude. With the listener primed, the song leads directly into the lyric concerning how "sincere" she was as they made love the previous evening.

The track ends with a brief reprise of the dual guitar solo, the final resolved chord suggesting hope at reconciliation. Will they "say goodbyes," as McCartney sings, or to paraphrase the lines, will love remain in their eyes? The question remains open to interpretation.

Like many songs on *Help!*, "The Night Before" represents solid pop songwriting, an example of tapping into listeners' experiences with insecurity and hesitation toward commitment.

The Shirelles questioned whether to give in to their lust, asking their would-be lover "will you still love me tomorrow?" In "The

Night Before," the narrator has already taken the next step, but now feels regret. The Beatles invert the trope by inserting a male perspective, thus proving that both sexes experience similar difficulties when surrendering to love.

For these reasons as well as superior musicianship, "The Night Before" should be appreciated as a classic, if underrated, Beatles tune.

Originally published March 14, 2014 at http://somethingelsereviews.com/ 2014/03/14/deep-beatles-the-night-before-from-help-1965

"The Word"
Rubber Soul (1965)

1965 proved to be a busy year for the Beatles. Beatlemania continued to take over the globe, the group maintained a whirlwind touring schedule, they shot the film *Help!*, and they recorded two albums. In the midst of the chaos, the four showed subtle but definite signs that they were maturing artistically.

Cracks in the moptop image first surfaced on 1964's *Beatles for Sale*, when darker tacks like "I'm A Loser" and "Baby's in Black" stood out among uptempo songs that included "Eight Days A Week" and "Every Little Thing."

Help! showed more signs of their progression, with Dylan-esque tracks like John Lennon's "You've Got to Hide Your Love Away" and Paul McCartney's classical hybrid "Yesterday." But 1965 marked the beginning of the Beatles' transformation with the release of *Rubber Soul*, a quiet, introspective work that laid the groundwork for *Revolver* and all subsequent albums. The album contains numerous game-changing songs like "Norwegian Wood" and "Nowhere Man," but "The Word" stands out for its prophetic lyrics and its subject: love in general, not just romantic love.

In later interviews, Lennon and McCartney claimed they wrote the lyrics while stoned. For the first time, they smoked pot while composing the song by drawing the lyrics in multicolored words on a sheet of paper. According to Barry Miles' McCartney biography *Many Years from Now*, McCartney explained that they typically did not smoke pot while composing, as they wanted to keep their minds clear. In 1980, Lennon said that while McCartney helped with the lyrics, "it's mainly mine. You read the words, it's all about gettin' smart. It's the marijuana period. It's love. It's a love and peace thing. The word is 'love,' right?"

Indeed, "The Word" gives listeners a preview of what was to come just over a year later. Instead of singing that money can't buy love or declaring unending devotion, the Beatles address love in a much broader sense. Here, love means freedom, and Harrison, Lennon, and McCartney suggest that they have achieved a kind of transcendence by simply uttering the word. What is the word? "Love," they croon, arguing that love is a "new" topic that everyone is talking about. But this is another type of love — one that is abstract, tied to nature, and bigger than all of us.

The next verse finds Lennon proselytizing, acting as a preacher. He announces that he now understands the word, and wants to guide people toward this "light." In this role, he wants to share his discovery with listeners and bask in his newfound joy. He has clearly researched the topic, explaining that he has heard the word in the air, and the "good and the bad" books he ha read. The word is the way to truth, Lennon sings, and with McCartney and Harrison emphasizes his message's importance: say and live by the important word. The trio chants "love" as the harmonium takes over.

As the song fades out, one can digest the Beatles' concluding argument: this word will play a major part in the near future. By submitting to *Love* with a capital "L," we too can find this transcendence that others have thus far not achieved. Like Harrison demands in "Think for Yourself," the group lets us decide whether to follow their lead.

As usual, the Beatles' recording sessions proved astoundingly fast and efficient, as the track was arranged and recorded in a single evening on November 10, 1965. The basics — guitar bass, and drums — were laid down first, then other instruments like maracas and the harmonium (played by producer George Martin), and finally the tight harmony vocals. Lennon's voice is double tracked on the song, creating four-part harmony. Mixing commenced a day later, but the stereo mix had to be redone on November 15.

Rubber Soul went on to become one of the Beatles' most critically acclaimed albums, and represents a huge step in their creative development. In the *Anthology* documentary, Harrison noted that he always considered *Rubber Soul* and *Revolver* "volume one and volume two," resembling bookends. At the very least, *Rubber Soul* illustrated their interest in politics and their increasing awareness as spokesmen for their age group.

"The Word" remained a deep album track until 2006, when the Cirque du Soleil show Love included a mashup with "Drive My Car" and "What You're Doing." Perhaps inspired by this unique showcase, McCartney resurrected the tune during his 2011 On the Run tour. During his Bologna show on November 26, 2011, he performed "The Word" in a medley with "All You Need Is Love," a fitting song pairing thematically and chronologically. "The Word" foreshadowed the Summer of Love anthem and signaled an impending change in direction for rock and pop culture.

Originally published August 23, 2012 at http://somethingelsereviews.com/2012/08/23/deep-beatles-the-word-1965/

"Wait"
Rubber Soul (1965)

The Beatles' 1965 album *Rubber Soul* is an embarrassment of riches. In addition to its stellar material, it signaled the final days of Beatlemania and a transition into more experimental sounds and sophisticated songwriting. "Norwegian Wood" most famously embodies these qualities, but other tracks receive fewer accolades, including the catchy yet musically complicated "Wait." Even more interesting, "Wait" slightly predates *Rubber Soul*, as the group originally recorded it for the *Help!* soundtrack. The song proves that the Beatles' so-called "throwaways" were often some of the most underrated cuts in their vast catalog.

In between filming and other activities, Paul McCartney composed "Wait" while on location in the Bahamas. In Barry Miles' *Many Years from Now*, McCartney vaguely recalled writing the track while in the company of Brandon de Wilde, a former child star best known for his Oscar-nominated role in the 1952 classic *Shane*. McCartney recalled to Barry Miles that the actor loved the Beatles' music, and would often chat with McCartney. McCartney claimed that he wrote "Wait" in front of the fascinated de Wilde, and that Lennon did not have much involvement in the song's composition.

Recording began at Abbey Road on June 17, 1965, under the usual guidance of George Martin. McCartney performed vocals and bass; John Lennon assumed the rhythm guitar and vocals; George Harrison took over on lead guitar; and Ringo Starr, of course, played drums. The group recorded four takes, with the last being deemed the best. This initial version lacked tambourine and maracas, and contained less guitar and fewer vocals. Mysteriously the Beatles and Martin then decided to shelve the song, leaving it off the *Help!* soundtrack.

Flash forward to the *Rubber Soul* sessions later that year: in a hurry to finish the album in time for Christmas sales, the Beatles found themselves short one song for their upcoming disc. Thus they resurrected "Wait" by adding percussion (Lennon played the tambourine while Starr contributed maracas) and guitar parts (courtesy Harrison and volume pedals). Finally, Lennon and McCartney recorded additional vocals for the chorus and bridge, and McCartney laid down another vocal for the song's conclusion. The duo also performed handclaps to further accent the percussion; all of these revisions made "Wait" better fit the overall tone of *Rubber Soul*. Once they finished overdubs on November 11, 1965, "Wait" became the fourteenth track on the album.

"Wait" begins abruptly, with Lennon and McCartney's double-tracked voices displaying their typical tight harmonies. Percussion plays a large role in this track, with the start-and-stop beat reinforced by Starr's steady drumming and the prominent tambourine and maracas. Due to the subject matter, much of "Wait" is in a minor key, expressing the narrator's longing and impatience to see his lover again. Tambourine and Harrison's guitar provide background for the opening lines, with Lennon and McCartney proclaiming they are coming home after a long time away. Building the tension, the maracas and drums immediately enter the picture, emphasizing the narrator's anxiety at being alone for so long. They stress the melancholy tone by dropping the key on the word "alone." The chorus, however, suggests an upbeat tone and possible reunion that will make them forget any previous sadness.

The bridge introduces another level of uncertainty, with McCartney's voice in the forefront. He explains that he has been as faithful as possible, and that if his beloved believes in him, he will trust her to wait for him. McCartney's voice rises on the phrase "wait for me," hinting at optimism. Unlike a typical love song of this type, the lyrics apparently forecast a less-than-perfect restarting of their love. The lead actor states that he's been as faithful as possible, hardly a definitive declaration of his fidelity. Yet the next lines question his lover's loyalty: has she been faithful? Should the two trust each other? If so, he concludes, she will willingly wait for him. Their relationship, as presented here, appears fragile.

As the song concludes, Lennon and McCartney repeat their opening lines, but slow down on the "I've been alone" phrase, with Harrison's slightly distorted guitar emitting lower notes. In other words, "Wait" does not end with an exciting major chord, providing the listener with a resolution and happy ending. Instead, the Beatles depart with an air of uncertainty, leaving open the question of whether the lovers experienced a happy reunion and continuation of their relationship. Harrison's volume pedal-enhanced guitar weaves throughout, the somewhat eerie sound underscoring the sense of ambivalence and ambiguity pervading "Wait."

"Wait" does not represent the first or last time the Beatles revisited the themes of uncertain love and nervous anticipation (see "When I Get Home," "A Hard Day's Night," "Don't Let Me Down," "If I Fell," and "The Night Before," among many others). However, its instrumentation, harmonies, and opaque lyrics distinguish "Wait" from similar songs, and make it one of the Beatles' most unfairly overlooked tracks.

Originally published Febaruary 28, 2014 at http://somethingelsereviews.com/2014/02/28/deep-beatles-wait-from-rubber-soul-1965/

"Run For Your Life"
Rubber Soul (1965)

It's the song everyone loves to hate, the one containing squirm-inducing lyrics that are at least politically incorrect, at most misogynistic. Even John Lennon eventually distanced himself from the tune, calling it a "throwaway song."

Since its 1965 debut on *Rubber Soul*, "Run for Your Life" has occupied an uneasy place in the Beatles oeuvre. But does it deserve to be permanently buried or tossed into the never-play pile of songs such as "Revolution 9"?

Deep Beatles is all about fearlessly exploring the depths of the Beatles catalog, so let's dig deeper to uncover "Run for Your Life's" hidden meanings and, yes, charms.

The song's roots originate with Elvis Presley; his 1955 single "Baby Let's Play House" (itself loosely based on the country track "I Want to Play House with You" by Eddy Arnold) caught Lennon's attention, particularly the lines "Now listen to me baby, try to understand. I'd rather see you dead, little girl, than to be with another man." In his 1970 interview with *Rolling Stone*, Lennon explained that "I used to like specific lines from songs ... so I wrote it around that but I didn't think it was that important." Barry Miles' *Many Years from Now* offers Paul McCartney's analysis: at the time, Lennon was running away from his life. "He was married; whereas none of my songs would have 'catch you with another man.'" Overall he classified it as a "bit of a macho song."

Although Lennon later dismissed "Run for Your Life," it became one of the first songs recorded for *Rubber Soul*. Entering the studio on October 12, 1965, the four worked on his composition with Lennon on acoustic guitar, McCartney playing bass, George Harrison on electric guitar, and Ringo Starr manning the snare drum and tambourine. After four attempts, the Beatles finally finished the backing track on the fifth try. Next they overdubbed more electric guitar parts from Harrison and Lennon, lead vocals, and backing vocals. According to the *Beatles Bible* website, the entire session lasted four and a half hours. George Martin and engineer Norman Smith commenced mixing mono versions of "Run for Your Life" on November 9, with stereo mixes finished the next day.

"Run for Your Life" received little airplay; in fact, Ottawa radio station CFRA banned the song in 1992, believing its "anti-woman" status too offensive for modern tastes. Strangely, the track did appear on a 1966 episode of the Beatles cartoon series.

Does "Run for Your Life" retain any merit? Harrison apparently thought so, as Lennon once stated that it was one of his favorites from *Rubber Soul*. From an instrumental perspective, it represents a solid pop song with a catchy, shuffling beat. The driving acoustic rhythm guitar is a constant presence throughout, as is Harrison's lead guitar. Critics such as Ian MacDonald believe the guitar playing does not represent Harrison's best work, even suggesting that Lennon actually performed the solo. "The guitar-work, some of which is badly out of tune, is similarly rough, the piercingly simplistic blues solo suggesting that the player was not Harrison but Lennon himself," MacDonald writes in his book *Revolution in the Head: The Beatles' Records and the Sixties*. While not an absolutely perfect example of guitar work, the melody still lingers.

What the track does contain is the Beatles' patented tight harmonies, most evident in lines describing that the girl should run and hide to avoid the narrator's wrath. Lennon also turns in an effective vocal, the slight roughness of his voice adding to the words' sinister connotations. Just listen to how this raspiness lends an ominous tone to already confrontational lines concerning how he cannot spend the rest of his life forcing his lover to obey his wishes.

Lest anyone misinterpret the narrator's message, Lennon reiterates his argument later. He concludes that he means every word he said, and that he would rather see her dead than with another man. The tambourine weaves in and out during the song, taking the place of a harder drumbeat. After returning to the opening verse and a final return to the chorus, Lennon seemingly ad-libs as the song fades. One is left with a sense of confusion — how can such harsh words be delivered through such an apparently bouncy tune?

Yes, "Run for Your Life" does include some alarmingly chauvinistic imagery. However, Lennon and the Beatles weren't exactly new to this theme. "You Can't Do That" contained lyrics admonishing a girl for talking to another man. If she repeats the action, the words warn, he will humiliate and leave her. As time went on, the Beatles apparently changed with the times, admitting their previous macho attitudes — for evidence, listen to "Getting Better's" themes of redemption. The narrator used to torment his lover, beating her and isolating her from friends and family. Now, he claims, he understands his cruelty and vows to change. In Lennon's solo career, Lennon addressed his possessive side in tracks like "Jealous Guy" and "Woman."

While the lyrics may cause today's audiences discomfort, "Run for Your Life" should still stand as a catchy pop/rock song that effectively utilizes the Beatles' distinctive harmonies. It may not exemplify the Beatles' absolute best work, but the track does not deserve complete scorn.

Originally published January 18, 2013 at http://somethingelsereviews.com/ 2013/01/18/deep-beatles-run-for-your-life-1965/

"Rain"
Past Masters (1966)

Recently I've received requests to examine "Rain," the groundbreaking B-side to "Paperback Writer." Indeed, "Rain" has transformed into one of the Beatles' best-loved B-sides, a masterpiece both musically and lyrically. In addition to being simply a wonderful song, it signaled the next phase in the band's evolution, one which would see massive changes in their sound and image.

By 1966, the Beatles were coming off their next feature film, *Help!*, which maintained their early "mop top" look while subtly introducing more introspective lyrics ("You've Got to Hide Your Love Away"), sexuality ("Ticket to Ride"), and the beginnings of George Harrison's experiments with Indian music. These motifs continued in their followup, *Rubber Soul*, which represented an even greater leap forward in maturity ("In My Life") and sophistication ("Norwegian Wood"). After *Rubber Soul's* release and critical acclaim, the Beatles found themselves back at Abbey Road recording what would become one of their finest works, *Revolver*.

As was typical at the time, EMI/Capitol pressured George Martin and the group to issue a single; thus the tracks "Paperback Writer" and "Rain" were removed from the album-in-progress and released on May 30, 1966 in the US, and on June 10, 1966 in the UK. By itself, "Rain" peaked at No. 23 on the US: charts; billed as a double single with "Paperback Writer" in Britain, the song reached No. 1. Perhaps the seemingly radical change in sound, along with a trippy music video, confused some fans expecting "I Want to Hold Your Hand," but 46 years later "Rain" is widely considered one of their finest songs.

The story behind "Rain" remains somewhat muddled due to

conflicting memories. According to the *Anthology*, John Lennon wrote the track after the group arrived in a rain-soaked Sydney, Australia while on tour. "We were having hysterics, laughing. It was so funny, coming to Australia and getting on a big van, all soaking wet; we thought it was going to be sunny. We only got wet for about fifteen minutes, but the kids got wet for hours," Lennon later said. "How could we be disappointed when they came out to see us and stood in all the rotten wind and rain to wave to us? They were great, really great. I've never seen rain as hard as that, except in Tahiti." This incident inspired Lennon to compose a tune about "people moaning about the weather all the time." In *Anthology*, McCartney recalled "Rain" as a joint effort: "I don't think 'Rain' was just John's. We sat down and wrote it together. It was John's vocal and John's feel on the song, but what gave it its character was collaboration."

The Beatles commenced recording the track on the same day as "Paperback Writer": April 14, 1966. After spending much of the day working on "Paperback Writer," they began work on "Rain" in the evening session. Recording five takes, the Beatles utilized the same sound effects they had previously used on the *Revolver* track "Tomorrow Never Knows." According to engineer Geoff Emerick, that track taught them that the texture and depth of certain instruments sounded really good when slowed down. With "Rain," the Beatles played the rhythm track really fast so that when the tape was played back at normal speed everything would be much slower, changing the texture: "If we'd recorded it at normal speed and then had to slow the tape down whenever we wanted to hear a playback it would have been much more work."

While recording the original fast tempo version, Ringo Starr added his now famous drum part, which he has claimed many times was his finest performance. Harrison performed his lead guitar portion, and Lennon played rhythm guitar, heavily distorted in the final version, and his lead vocals. McCartney may have laid down a bass line, but he recorded the final version in the next session.

April 16 saw many more overdubs and finishing touches to "Rain." In a marathon 11-hour session, McCartney performed his complex bass part, Starr added tambourine, and McCartney, Lennon, and Harrison completed backing vocals. Then came one of the song's most fascinating elements: the backwards speech toward the end. Again, opinions differ as to whether Lennon devised this technique. In a 1980 interview, Lennon said that he always listened to the group's work from that day's recording session after returning home from the studio. "Somehow I got it on backwards and I sat there, transfixed, with the earphones on, with a big hash joint. I ran in the next day and said, 'I know what to do with it, I know … Listen to this!' So I made them all play it backwards."

However, Martin told Mark Lewisohn in 1988 that he had been playing around with the day's tapes and decided to experiment with altering Lennon's voice. "So I lifted a bit of his main vocal off the four-track, put it onto another spool, turned it around and then slid it back and forth until it fitted. John was out at the time but when he came back he was amazed. Again, it was backwards forever after that."

Despite this conflicting information, it cannot be denied that one particular element added an unmistakably psychedelic, hallucinogenic quality to "Rain." Once recording was completed, Martin and Emerick made four mono mixes of the track, with the third version being selected for the single. To promote the song, the group filmed three videos (all directed by Michael Lindsay-Hogg) for US and UK television: one where the group wanders in a garden and greenhouse, and the other two (one in black and white, the other in color) featuring the Beatles lip-synching to the song in a studio.

Several elements make "Rain" an outstanding song in the Beatles catalog. First, Starr proves his skill as a drummer by performing some off-kilter patterns, utilizing his typical powerful style. Second, McCartney's bass throbs throughout the track; listen closely to just his part to experience the complicated, swirling lines. In addition, Lennon demonstrates how he could alter his voice to fit a "role," this time a narrator guiding the listener through an otherworldly atmosphere. As a precursor to "Tomorrow Never Knows," "She Said She Said," "I'm Only Sleeping," "Lucy in the Sky with Diamonds," and numerous other compositions, "Rain" concerns a hallucinatory dream world, Lennon draws out some syllables, lets raspiness creep in, and fluctuates in tone to emphasize the fantastic lyrics. "Can you hear me, that when it rains and shines; it's just a state of mind?"

Lennon repeatedly stresses the words "state of mind," questioning whether real life conditions such as weather exist or are just figures of the imagination. "Rain" may have originally concerned weather, but this line suggests something more cerebral.

Other lines address another familiar Lennon theme: people not wanting to move beyond their borders, those "nowhere men" who resist change in thought or culture. When the "rain" arrives, people run as if to avoid experiencing something different. They become "dead," preferring to dwell in predictability and monotony. In contrast, this narrator declares that he welcomes the change, that he appreciates both rain and sun . Lennon uses another favorite technique — directly addressing the listener — by constantly asking if we can hear him, and offering to show us the way. Think of "Rain" as an extension of *Rubber Soul's* "The Word" or "Think for Yourself," this time overtly encompassing psychedelia and, through its sound, the emerging drug culture.

"Rain" may not have been a huge hit — in fact, it's difficult to believe it originated as a B-side — but it holds a very important position in the Beatles catalog. It marks the official transition from the "Beatlemania" years to the mature, experimental, forward-thinking band who would revolutionize rock music. Rubber Soul provided hints of this transition by moving even further away from traditional pop music, but "Rain" and later Revolver officially signaled Beatles, Mach Two.

Originally published December 4, 2012 at http://somethingelsereviews.com/2012/12/04/deep-beatles-rain-1966/

"I Want To Tell You"
Revolver (1966)

As the Beatles' career progressed, George Harrison gradually developed into a first-class songwriter on a par with the formidable John Lennon/Paul McCartney partnership. One of Harrison's more unusual compositions, "I Want to Tell You," fits in perfectly with *Revolver's* experimental vibe. The pounding piano, pervasive dissonance, and a subtle reference to Harrison's increasing interest in Indian music and culture add up to a classic and offbeat track.

In 1980, Harrison described the lyrics as addressing "the avalanche of thoughts that are so hard to write down or say or transmit." Indeed, the verses paint a picture of someone constantly struggling with language. He laments that he has many thoughts to express, but lacks the words to communicate them. In addition, he fears offending the person he's having the conversation with, explaining that he may appear "unkind," but it's not intentional — his mind is clear and pure, but the body cannot move as quickly as the mind.

For me, the best lines in the song concern his frustration with his inability to communicate, yet he ultimately surrenders to his imperfection. He can wait for his thoughts to unravel — he has the time. That sentiment fits in well with other songs on the album, as Lennon also advocates a laid-back lifestyles without worries in tracks like "Tomorrow Never Knows" (telling us to relax and float downstream" and "surrender to the void") and "I'm Only Sleeping." ("taking my time").

While Harrison's lyrics are clever, the instrumentation further distinguishes "I Want to Tell You" from other rock songs of the time. The galloping piano accents the rhythm through dissonant harmonies, and Ringo Starr's drumming easily navigates through some offbeat tempos. According to Alan Pollack, author of the "Notes On" series, Starr re-energizes the track with his driving percussion. "If you feel the momentum beginning to sag toward the end of this section, dig how that sudden burst of rapid triplets at the very end of the bridge helps to re-jump-start your momentum for the verse that follows," writes Pollack. Other percussion can be heard, including tambourine and handclaps.

As usual, the Lennon/McCartney/Harrison vocal harmonies sound tight, often singing entire lines instead of emphasizing certain words. As with many Beatles songs, the group experiments with beginnings and endings. Similar to "Eight Days A Week," the track gradually fades in, this time over the distinctive guitar riff. Even more interesting, the ending fades out over the repeated phrase "I've got time," and McCartney adds an unusual touch. As the sound fades, McCartney breaks into, as Pollack states, "free Indian-flavored melisma." In other words, he sang the word "time" while oscillating among various notes. The move adds a touch of sophistication and world-music influence to the rock track.

Harrison often found it difficult to title his songs; according to Mark Lewisohn's seminal work *The Complete Beatles Recording Sessions*, the cut's working titles included "Granny Smith," "Laxton's Superb" (another type of apple, foreshadowing later years) and "I Don't Know." On June 2, 1966, the Beatles entered the studio to lay down virtually all the track's elements; they put the finishing touches on "I Want to Tell You" the following day. Mixing was completed on June 6.

"I Want to Tell You" was never released as a single, and lingered in relative album track obscurity until years later. While touring in Japan with Eric Clapton in 1992, Harrison resurrected the song — to the delight of audiences. That version, which features extended guitar solos, appeared on the *Live in Japan* album chronicling the brief tour. Appropriately, ELO founder and frequent Harrison collaborator Jeff Lynne performed the track at the *Concert for George* ten years later. It may have taken over four decades, but "I Want to Tell You" is finally receiving deserved recognition for its sophisticated arrangement and Harrison's creativity in manipulating language.

Originally published August 8, 2012 at http://somethingelsereviews.com/2012/08/08/deep-beatles-i-want-to-tell-you-1966/

"Doctor Robert"
Revolver (1966)

The Beatles recorded their share of mysterious tracks such as "I am the Walrus" or even the self-parody "Glass Onion." Critics still analyze possible meanings of "Strawberry Fields Forever" or weird experiments like "What's the New Mary Jane." But the *Revolver* track "Doctor Robert" still baffles critics and fans alike. Were the lyrics based on an actual person? Is it a pro-drug song, or an extended joke? Besides these much-debated questions, "Doctor Robert" contains some stellar guitar playing and trademark close harmonies, all adding up to a memorable song that stands out among the other innovative *Revolver* tracks.

Multiple theories about as to the identity of "Doctor Robert." One involves a notorious April 1965 party hosted by John Riley, a London dentist and LSD enthusiast. George Harrison, John Lennon, and their wives attended this soiree, and unknowingly ingested the drug after Riley secretly dosed their coffee cups. Harrison later recalled their first LSD trip as a scary experience, subsequently identifying the doctor only as the "wicked dentist." Others speculate the song refers to Bob Dylan, who famously introduced the Beatles to marijuana. Yet another candidate includes London art dealer Robert Fraser, who provided various pills to the elite. In a 1980 interview, Lennon claimed he was Doctor Robert: "It was about myself. I was the one that carried all the pills on tour. Well, in the early days. Later on the roadies did it. We just kept them in our pockets loose. In case of trouble."

Paul McCartney attempted to set the record straight; he stated the inspiration was Dr. Robert Freymann, a New York drug supplier to the stars. While he ran a clinic on Manhattan's East 78th Street, he was better known for giving vitamin B-12 shots containing amphetamines to his tony clientele. McCartney told biographer Barry Miles that he and Lennon had heard of the "Great White Father," as Freymann was called, while touring in America. Building on the idea of a drug-providing doctor, McCartney explained, he and Lennon composed what he considered a parody. "John and I thought that was a funny idea — the fantasy doctor who would fix you up by giving you drugs. It was a parody on that idea," he said. "It's just a piss-take. As far as I know, neither of us ever went to a doctor for those kinds of things. But there was a fashion for it and there still is. Change your blood and have a vitamin shot and you'll feel better."

No matter the meaning, "Doctor Robert" took shape on April 17, 1966, when the Beatles entered Abbey Road Studios. Lennon took over lead vocals and played rhythm guitar and harmonium; McCartney contributed backing vocals and bass; Harrison played lead guitar, maracas, and sang backing vocals; and Ringo Starr, naturally, played drums. They recorded the backing track in seven takes, with the lead vocals added two days later. The video above separates some of the individual tracks.

On April 19, the Beatles reentered the studio to record vocal tracks and oversee mono mixing. Interestingly, the original version of "Dr. Robert" featured an extended jam session, including a Harrison solo. A section of his performance can still be heard on the mono mix, just before the first "well well well" line. Listen for the guitar to quickly fade out before the vocals kick in. A slightly longer mix can be heard on the US compilation *Yesterday ... and Today*.

One can have a field day analyzing the lyrics, trying to determine the subject's identity. Could "take a drink from his special cup" refer to the dentist? What does the reference to the "National Health" mean (thus poking holes in the Freymann theory)? If Lennon really was describing himself in the song, he states he is a "new and better man" and "a man you must believe, helping anyone in need." Here Doctor Robert sounds like an evangelist of sorts, one who enlightens others with his magic medicine. Not only will he make you feel good, he will help you understand life's mysteries. These words certainly suggest that Doctor Robert far from condemns drugs; instead, it suggests drug-taking as a way to expand one's consciousness and seemingly operate on a higher creative plane.

While one may not agree with the song's apparent pro-drug stance, there's no denying the Beatles' exquisite harmonies and gritty guitar work. When the refrain arrives, it sounds classically influenced and contrasts with the straight-ahead rock comprising most of the track. This highbrow/lowbrow comparison demonstrates Lennon and McCartney's dry humor, that this drug supplier is somehow better and more elevated in stature than everyone else. Listen closely to Harrison, McCartney, and Lennon's vocal blends at various points, and you'll experience how each voice individually contributes to the song's distinctive harmonies. Harrison's guitar, which cuts sharply through the track, adds a rougher edge that obviously contrasts with the chamber-music feel of the refrain.

Lyrically complicated and harmonically sophisticated, "Doctor Robert" remains one of the more underrated tracks from the milestone *Revolver* album.

Originally published July 5, 2013 at http://somethingelsereviews.com/ 2013/07/05/deep-beatles-doctor-robert-1966/

"I'm Only Sleeping"
Revolver (1966)

Revolver marked an important milestone for the Beatles: it represents the group at their most experimental to date. Backwards guitars, eerie sound loops, surrealist lyrics: nothing was off-limits for their 1966 masterpiece. A perfect example of this early innovation is "I'm Only Sleeping," the primarily John Lennon-penned track that features sound effects, a stellar Lennon vocal, and an unusual Harrison guitar solo.

While many fans believe "I'm Only Sleeping" refers to drugs, the words also refer to Lennon's habit of sleeping late. In his infamous interview with journalist Maureen Cleave on March 4, 1966, he claimed that that he was "physically lazy . . . I don't mind writing or reading or watching or speaking, but sex is the only physical thing I can be bothered with any more." Cleave even mentioned that "he can sleep almost indefinitely, is probably the laziest person in England." According to other sources such as *Rolling Stone* and the *Beatles Bible*, the story may also derive from Lennon's annoyance at Paul McCartney waking him up for a songwriting session. Lennon scribbled the initial lyrics on the back of an envelope, although McCartney mentioned in a 1994 interview that he helped revise the words.

Recording began on April 27, 1966, the same day that George Martin and engineer Geoff Emerick completed mono mixes of "Taxman," "And Your Bird Can Sing," and "Tomorrow Never Knows." The session involved rehearsals, with the Beatles experimenting with different instruments and arrangements. A particularly intriguing early backing track included vibraphones (it is unclear who played them); another featured Lennon accompanying his lead vocals with acoustic guitar. These fascinating versions eventually surfaced on bootlegs and on the *Anthology 2* compilation.

After rehearsing "I'm Only Sleeping," the band laid down 11 takes of the song. Lennon played acoustic guitar, McCartney performed bass, and of course Starr played drums. The final version was deemed best, although it contained a significant quirk. The Beatles performed the song in E minor, but for unknown reasons the tape machine was running fast, so it sounded slower and a semitone lower on playback, according to the *Beatles Bible*.

Not satisfied with their initial efforts, the Beatles made a second attempt at the backing track two days later. After five takes (only one complete) featuring percussion, acoustic guitars, and Lennon and McCartney on vocals, they decided to abandon these efforts and return to take 11. Thus the group overdubbed more instruments and Lennon's lead vocal onto this version. Once again, the tape machine was running at a different speed, thus the final take of "I'm Only Sleeping" contains a faster tempo and higher tone.

Next came a crucial element to the track: the backwards guitar solo. The Beatles met at Abbey Road on May 5, with Harrison recording two solos. Here the story becomes murky: Lennon claimed he had accidentally threaded the master tape the wrong way, resulting in the song being played backwards. Loving the sound, Lennon supposedly informed George Martin and Harrison that he wanted to reproduce the effect in "I'm Only Sleeping." Other accounts have Martin and/or Harrison suggesting the backwards looping.

Despite these conflicting stories, all agree that Harrison had to carefully plan and execute the solos to create the desired dreamlike effect. The lead guitarist wrote an Indian-inspired part that sounded good played backwards; next, he had to reverse the notes, then learn how to play the previous "backwards" solo normally. Martin then had to conduct Harrison beat by beat, with the guitarist ultimately recording two separate solos — one with "fuzz" effects or distortion, and one without. Martin then laid the tracks on top of one another, reversed them, and the final version was born. According to Emerick, the entire process took nine hours.

May 6, 1966 marked the final day of work on the complicated song, with Harrison, Lennon, and McCartney overdubbing additional vocals. Martin and Emerick created two reduction mixes, combining the second mix with the backwards guitar solos. The next two weeks involved competing mono and stereo mixes. Ultimately five mixes were created: the ordinal mono and stereo mixes, the US stereo and mono mixes, and according to Robert Fontenot, a "mono rechanneled into stereo" mix; this reverb-heavy version appeared on the first pressing of *"Yesterday"…And Today*, but was replaced with another stereo mix in subsequent editions.

In addition to these complicated effects, "I'm Only Sleeping" is notable for what would become a recurrent theme for Lennon: dreaming. In his 1980 *Playboy* interview, Lennon described the track as "me dreaming my life away." In this song as well as later compositions such as "Strawberry Fields Forever," "Watching the Wheels," and, to some extent, "Imagine," he extols the virtues of daydreaming. Here Lennon answers his critics who call him lazy — he retorts that people who are "running everywhere at such a speed" are "crazy." In contrast, he is taking time to simply observe and enjoy diving into his dreams. For him, sleep is an escape from tedium, and it transports him to another world where he can "float up stream." Why he feels the need for such mental excursions — the prison of fame, the grind of daily writing and recording, endless touring — is left to the listener's imagination.

Today, "I'm Only Sleeping" still sounds like no other song in the Beatles' catalog. Its hallucinogenic quality, vivid yet surreal lyrics, creative guitar solo, and unusual recording effects (such as the thudding of Starr's drums) were ahead of their time, and provided a hint of further sonic experiments to come.

Listen for a particular "Easter Egg" at the two minute mark, when McCartney can be heard yawning.

Originally published July 10, 2015 at http://somethingelsereviews.com/2015/07/10/the-beatles-im-only-sleeping-revolver/

"Good Morning Good Morning"
Sgt. Pepper's Lonely Hearts Club Band (1967)

A cacophony of guitars, brass, furious drums, John Lennon's lead vocal, and even animal noises, "Good Morning Good Morning" may stand as one of Lennon's most eccentric compositions. Yet its tale of suburban banality, contrasted with some blistering lead guitar, ranks as one of the standout *Sgt. Pepper's Lonely Hearts Club Band* tracks. A deconstruction of the track reveals its underlying meaning and stunning components, most notably Ringo Starr's complicated drumming.

Inspiration can come from unlikely places, and "Good Morning Good Morning" exemplifies this notion. While sitting at the piano and brainstorming song ideas in 1967, Lennon often had the television flickering in the background. An advertisement for Corn Flakes cereal aired, featuring the following jingle:

> Good morning, good morning
> The best to you each morning.
> Sunshine breakfast, Kellogg's Corn Flakes
> Crisp and full of fun.

The song's opening words appealed to Lennon, and he quickly penned the lyrics in his Kenwood home. In a 1968 interview, he stated that the words partially referred to growing up in Liverpool. "But it was writing about my past so it does get the kids because it was me at school, my whole bit," he said. As usual, he later dismissed the lyrics as "a bit of gobbledygook, but nice words" in 1972. In his biography *Many Years from Now*, Paul McCartney claimed that the words reflected Lennon's disintegrating marriage, that the singer felt trapped by his humdrum suburban life.

His home demo contains most of the final verses, although the tempo resembles a ticking clock. Lennon brought the track to Abbey Road Studios on February 8, 1967, and work progressed quickly. In eight takes, the Beatles laid down the rhythm track complete with drums, tambourine, rhythm guitar, and Lennon's guide vocal. On February 16, the group resumed work on take eight of "Good Morning Good Morning," with McCartney adding his bass part while Lennon contributed his lead vocal. At this point, McCartney and George Harrison also contributed backing harmonies. *Anthology 3* includes this overdubbed version of take eight's backing track.

The Beatles, George Martin, and engineer Geoff Emerick did not return to the song for almost a month. By March 13, Lennon decided it needed a brass section for a punchier sound. They recruited members of Sounds Incorporated, a band that had previously toured with the Beatles. A largely instrumental group that also backed Gene Vincent and Little Richard in Europe, they briefly served as members of Brian Epstein's stable of artists. The six-hour session added trombones, saxophones and a French Horn to the mix. In Mark Lewisohn's *The Complete Beatles Recording Sessions*, second engineer Richard Lush remembered "flanging, limiting and compressing it, anything to make it sound unlike brass playing it was typical John Lennon — he just wanted it to sound weird."

Two weeks later, Lennon added a second lead vocal, harmonizing with himself at times, and Lennon and McCartney overdubbed additional backing vocals. Then McCartney contributed his blistering guitar solo (Lennon and Harrison played rhythm guitars on the track), and they assembled the animal-sound effects from the Abbey Road archives. Final touches included harmonica courtesy of Harrison, Starr, Mal Evans, and Neil Aspinall, as well as an organ part played by Lennon. The last overdubs, including the tacking on of sound effects, occurred on March 29 and 31.

Singing in a flat, almost sarcastic tone, Lennon narrates the day of an average man. He trudges to work, clearly hating his job, but finds no relief once he leaves for home. Aimlessly wandering the streets, he finds emptiness, that everyone is "half asleep," no action is occurring, and that the bareness resembles a "ruin." He therefore paints a bleak picture of suburbia. Believing that revisiting his youth might cure his ennui, he visits his old school, but nothing has changed. Finally the lead character tries to find life in flirting with local girls while married men go home for "tea and meet the wife" (also the title of a popular British soap opera). Ultimately, he has "nothing to say but it's OK," again stressing the boredom in this workaday world. By repeating the title phrase ad infinitum, the song suggests this never ending cycle of tedium.

In addition to Lennon's biting lyrics, the instrumentation establishes this sense of irony and frustration, a circus-like atmosphere minus excitement and joy. A key component to "Good Morning Good Morning" is Starr's skillful drumming, made more impressive by the constant time changes. Anyone who doubts Starr's musicianship need only listen to the isolated drum track.

Elsewhere, McCartney's bass and lead guitar enhance the percussion and underscore Lennon's sharp vocals. Lennon and Harrison's rhythm guitars play in tandem with Starr's drumming, the distortion giving them a grungier sound. Finally, note the isolated vocals — Lennon's snarling voice contrasts with the tight harmonies. Injecting some humor, the Beatles gradually transition from chanting "good morning" to the German phrase "guten morgan."

"Good Morning Good Morning" works due to the sum of its parts. Lennon's satirical words still sting, while Starr's hard-driving drumming accentuates their bite. Add rhythm guitars, bass, lead guitar, and brass, and what results is a seemingly straightforward, upbeat rock track that tells a bleak story of discontentment.

Originally published November 7, 2014 at http://somethingelsereviews.com/2014/11/07/good-morning-good-morning-deep-beatles/

"Baby You're a Rich Man"
Magical Mystery Tour (1967)

The B-side to "All You Need Is Love," "Baby You're a Rich Man" stands as one of the Beatles' most innovative, funky, and underrated tracks. Originally intended to only accompany a segment of *Yellow Submarine*, the song instead surfaced on the 1967 *Magical Mystery Tour* soundtrack (although it never appears in the film). Its place on the former film soundtrack was restored in 1999, when a remastered version was included on the *Yellow Submarine Songtrack* collection. In addition to being one of the group's more unusual tracks, "Baby You're a Rich Man" also holds the distinction of being one of the fastest songs the Beatle ever recorded.

When the Beatles entered Olympic Sound Studios on May 11, 1967, they intended to record "Baby You're a Rich Man" for the upcoming *Yellow Submarine* project. According to Kenneth Womack's *The Beatles Encyclopedia*, the track resembles "A Day in the Life" in that it combines two previously separate song fragments: John Lennon's verses with a Paul McCartney-composed chorus.

As Lennon told *Rolling Stone*, his words poked fun at the upper class. "The point was, stop moaning — you're a rich man, and we're all rich men, heh heh, baby!" he said. In a 1980 interview, Lennon further expanded on the song's creation: "That's a combination of two separate pieces, Paul's and mine, put together and forced into one song. One-half was all mine. (sings) 'How does it feel to be one of the beautiful people / Now that you know who you are ...' Then Paul comes in with, (sings) 'Baby you're a rich man,' which was a lick he had around."

While George Martin produced the session as usual, the engineers included Keith Grant and Eddie Kramer, both of whom would play large roles in the recording. Lennon sang lead vocal and played piano and the Clavioline, an early electronic keyboard with its own amplifier. It could produce one note at a time and imitate several instruments. McCartney contributed piano, bass, and backing vocals; George Harrison played lead guitar, tambourine and sang backing vocals; and Ringo Starr provided all percussion. Kramer even performed on the record, playing the Vibraphone.

Once the lineup was in place, the group first rehearsed before laying down 12 instrumental takes. The final attempt was deemed best, with McCartney then overdubbing a bass guitar part, Lennon adding his lead vocals, and McCartney and Harrison contributing their backing parts. Once Martin, Grant and Kramer created two reduction mixes, the second was chosen for Harrison to overdub his lead guitar and for Lennon to add the Clavioline introduction. More vocals, backwards piano, and Kramer's Vibraphone were finally added, and the mono mix was completed. In all, the session lasted from 9 p.m. to 3 a.m. the following morning. According to Mark Lewisohn's *The Complete Beatles Recording Sessions*, it was the first Beatles single to be recorded and mixed outside of Abbey Road Studios.

A mystery remains: did two Rolling Stones appear on "Baby You're a Rich Man"? When Lewisohn searched the archives for his landmark book, he found two tape boxes labeled "+ Mick Jagger?" While Mick Jagger indeed attended the sessions, it is difficult to hear his voice anywhere on the record (although it is possible that he appeared during the shouted chorus toward the end). In addition, did Brian Jones play the oboe? Womack maintains that Jones appears on the record. Such a cameo appearance is plausible, as he infamously played on the Beatles track "You Know My Name (Look Up the Number)" just a week later.

Tape operator George Chkiantz told Lewisohn that Grant and Kramer were astounded by Lennon's voice. "They'd long been wondering what it would be like to record and they couldn't believe anyone could sing that well," said Chkiantz. Indeed, Lennon does experiment with his voice, alternating between his usual range and falsetto. The lyrics can be seen as an inner argument, a dialog between the singer's working class roots (falsetto) and later superstar status (natural range).

In the first verse the falsetto voices represent the "working class hero," functioning as a Greek chorus. After asking the famous question "How does it feel to be one of the beautiful people?" they follow with the thought that you understand your elite status. But Lennon's response suggests otherwise: do you really want to be one of the beautiful people? The chorus returns with followup questions concerning whether they had actually been to this perfect world, and what they saw in this special space. In other words, they inquire whether the "beautiful people" really do lead more fabulous lives than so-called ordinary folks. Lennon's voice takes on a flat quality when he answers the questions, sounding unimpressed, suggesting that reality does not live up to imaginings of the chorus. The responses are, in fact, rather boring.

The McCartney-written refrain, largely consisting of one note, repeats the title phrase and explains that the main character keeps his money in a "big brown bag / Inside a zoo." This line recalls the miserly character Lennon would revisit in "Mean Mr. Mustard" (albeit that title character is far from rich). Harrison, Lennon, and McCartney decry the rich man's greed. In the second verse, the Greek chorus again questions "Beatle John's" newfound life and happiness. He is now "tuned to a natural E" and seems content. But since he has found the new key, Lennon seems unsure as to what he will play. Wealth and fame bring complications, and the narrator must decide how these elements will reshape his life. He has reached the "toppermost of the poppermost," a cheer that he would recite to his bandmates in their early years. Now that he has achieved that goal, where does he go from here?

Another reading of "Baby You're a Rich Man" has been that the lyrics represent Lennon's disillusionment with manager Brian Epstein. As Womack points out, an oft-repeated anecdote claims Lennon chants homophobic and anti-semitic slurs during the song's fadeout. So much shouting occurs — along with McCartney's ad-libs — that it is virtually impossible to discern the words. Womack also states that the "beautiful people" phrase refers to the hippie generation, using then-contemporary slang.

While these are intriguing theories, the inner dialog and struggle with identity are consistent themes in Lennon's compositions. "I'm a Loser," "Nowhere Man," "Help!" and "You've Got to Hide Your Love Away" are just a few examples. As he later admitted, Lennon struggled with fame and self-esteem issues during the filming of *Help!*, dubbing it his "fat Elvis period." Thus, it is no stretch to read "Baby You're a Rich Man" as the struggle between the "working class hero" and "Beatle John as well as his search for solutions to his increasingly turbulent life.

In addition to the confessional lyrics, "Baby You're A Rich Man" succeeds because of McCartney's pulsating bass, which is highlighted by Grant's skillful engineering. Listening to the 2009 remastered version fully brings out the impressive and surprisingly soulful bass lines, and Grant should be commended for bringing out the booming sound. The reggae tinged "chuck chuck" of the guitar further accents the tempo, with Starr's drums sounding particularly powerful on the track. The Clavioline provides continuity, as it furthers the Beatles' ongoing experiments with world music. The notes lend a Middle Eastern quality, also underscoring the era's psychedelic trends.

Overall "Baby You're a Rich Man" hardly resembles any previous Beatles recording, demonstrating how the group's experimental and avant-garde tendencies reigned during this period. They would move away from such sonic innovations on the *White Album*, thus the *Magical Mystery Tour* LP and "Baby You're a Rich Man" serve as the last gasps of this artistic and inventive phase.

Originally published March 20, 2015 at http://somethingelsereviews.com/2015/03/20/the-beatles-baby-youre-a-rich-man-deep-beatles/

"Everybody's Got Something to Hide Except Me and My Monkey"
The Beatles (1968)

Would the Beatles' self-titled 1968 album (otherwise known as the *White Album*) have been stronger as a single-disc work? Was it as fragmented and disjointed as critics then claimed? As Paul McCartney exclaimed in the *Anthology* documentary, "I mean, it's great, it sold, it's the bloody Beatles *White Album*! So shut up!"

Initially, music critics like the *New York Times'* Nik Cohn dismissed it as "boring beyond belief," calling half the songs as "profound mediocrities." Today, *Rolling Stone* and *AllMusic* have reassessed the *White Album's* seemingly erratic feel, arguing that context is key to appreciating the work. "The band touches on anything and everything it can," writes *AllMusic's* Stephen Thomas Erlewine. "This makes for a frustratingly scattershot record or a singularly gripping musical experience, depending on your view, but what makes the so-called *White Album* interesting is its mess."

Regardless of various opinions on the album's consistency and overall quality, most listeners agree that The Beatles contains some deeply spiritual and self-reflective moments, and at times rocks hard. A perfect example of the playful and sometimes rougher sound of some tracks is "Everybody's Got Something to Hide Except Me and My Monkey." Its meaning remains vague — does "monkey" refer to drug addiction, or a term used by their spiritual guru the Maharishi Mahesh Yogi? No matter the interpretation, the track soars with John Lennon's screaming vocals and piercing lead guitar as well as McCartney's furious bass playing.

Principal songwriter Lennon composed the track in 1968; according to George Harrison, the Beatles' time studying under the Maharishi partially inspired the song's title. "Everybody's got something to hide" was the spiritual guru's frequent mantra, but Harrison once stated that he never knew what "except for me and my monkey" signified. In 1980, Lennon explained that the phrase referred to his blooming romance with Yoko Ono. "Everybody seemed to be paranoid except for us two, who were in the glow of love. Everything is clear and open when you're in love," he said. "Everybody was sort of tense around us — you know, 'What is SHE doing here at the session? Why is she with him?' All this sort of madness is going on around us, because we just happened to want to be together all the time."

However, McCartney posited a different scenario in Barry Miles' *Many Years from Now*. During the *White Album* period, Lennon began experimenting with harder drugs, particularly heroin. He would commonly use terminology familiar to heroin addicts such as "fixes" and "monkeys." McCartney added that the other Beatles were concerned about Lennon's heroin use, and "Everybody's Got Something to Hide" was written and recorded during this difficult period. However, McCartney admitted, "often that adversity and that craziness can lead to good art, as I think it did in this case." Lennon always denied this interpretation, although lyrics such as "the deeper you go, the higher you fly" could be read as a drug reference.

No matter how the track is analyzed, its beginnings derive from the Beatles' time in Rishikesh, India. While studying Transcendental Meditation from February until approximately April 1968, they also composed an astounding number of songs, only some of which made it onto the *White Album*. When they regrouped in London that May, all four came bearing notebooks chock full of these tracks, and they began recording demos at Harrison's Esher bungalow. As is evident in the original demo, the as-yet-untitled song originated as a slower, acoustic-driven track. The lyrics were also in their infancy, often filled with "come ons"; this was a typical feature of Lennon's early song drafts. He would fill still blank verses with repeated phrases or nonsense syllables.

Recording on "Everybody's Got Something to Hide" commenced

on June 26, 1968, although these initial sessions consisted of rehearsals. The next day they recorded six takes of the track; on the last take, they overdubbed two lead guitars, bells, and shaker. According to the *Beatles Bible*, a "reduction mix to free up spare tracks also resulted in the song being sped up from 3'07" to 2'29"; it would end up faster still following a later mix." The reduced mix resulted in speeding up the tempo and changing the key in addition to shortening the track's length. Refinements on take eight continued on July 1, when McCartney recorded an additional bass guitar part and Lennon laid down new lead vocals. By July 23, more backing vocals, the "come on, come on" ending, handclaps, and another bass part were all recorded.

Two more reduction mixes were made, which now made the latest version take ten. According to the *Beatles Bible*, these reductions made room for Lennon to redo his vocals. This take thus replaced his vocals recorded on July 1. Two more reduction mixes were made (takes 11 and 12), Lennon laid down another vocal track and more shouting, handclaps, another McCartney bass part, and additional percussion by Ringo Starr completed the session. Once these tasks were completed, "Everybody's Got Something to Hide" was mixed for mono, followed by the stereo mix on October 12.

Technical details aside, what makes "Everybody's Got Something to Hide" stand out? From the first thud of Starr's drums, the raucous tone immediately grabs the listener by the collar. After a brief, slower start, the band kicks into high gear by rapidly accelerating the tempo. "Come on is such a joy," Lennon almost shouts, raspiness coloring his voice. "Take it easy!" he cries, the rhythm pattern changing once again. After delivering the chorus, Lennon's guitar pierces through the noise, signaling another change in the track. He intones that the deeper one travels, the higher one may soar. Yet the higher one flies, the deeper one delves. These mysterious words remain ambiguous, allowing the listener to interpret their meaning.

By the time he reaches the next verse, he further obscures the words' meaning: "Your inside is out, and your outside is in; your outside is in, and your inside is out." These phrases perfectly illustrate Lennon's obvious love for wordplay, present in his writings (*A Spaniard in the Works*, *In His Own Write*, and *Skywriting by Word of Mouth*) as well as songs like "I Am the Walrus," "Come Together," "Revolution 1," and "Glass Onion," among many others. But even more importantly, the song simply rocks.

Their previous albums focused on their mastery of studio recording and creating fantastical imagery through their words. With the *White Album*, the group planned to return to their pure rock roots. "That was really all I wanted to do — make a very loud raunchy rock and roll record with the Beatles, which it is," Lennon once said. With tracks like "Everybody's Got Something to Hide" and "Helter Skelter" (inspired by the Who, who claimed they had just recorded the loudest, dirtiest song ever), the Beatles sought to reestablish their position as one of music's best, most dangerous bands. "*Sgt. Pepper* did its thing; it was the album of the decade — of the century, maybe," Starr stated. "It was very innovative, great songs — glad I was on it — but (on) the *White Album*, we ended up being more of a band again and that's what I always love. I love being in a band."

McCartney once said that the Beatles had one overreaching goal for the *White Album*: "We just tried to get it loud, guitars, can we have them sound louder, the drums louder." As the song fades out, the lead guitar screams through the speakers, the bass and rhythm guitars pound, and the joyful cries of the Beatles themselves linger: "Everybody's Got Something to Hide Except Me and My Monkey" embodies the spirit of the early Beatles, the young, hungry group who would stomp the floor and "mach schau" for jaded Hamburg patrons in seedy clubs. The Beatles' frantic cries of "come on" at the end of the track strongly echo their past, but the track also demonstrates how years of experience molded them into a totally original and unparalleled live band. Raunchy and loud? Mission accomplished.

Originally published September 7, 2012 at http://somethingelsereviews.com/ 2012/09/07/deep-beatles-everybodys-got-something-to-hide-except-for-me-and-my-monkey-1968/

"Savoy Truffle"
The Beatles (1968)

Many Beatles songs contain two key elements: wordplay and nods to their R&B roots. George Harrison is no stranger to either aspect, and few songs encapsulate these qualities like "Savoy Truffle," the *Beatles* (aka the White Album) track that salutes the sweet tooth. It also represents one of many times Eric Clapton influenced his songwriting.

In his autobiography *I Me Mine,* Harrison recalled writing the song as a good-natured jab at Clapton's penchant for sweets. Apparently Clapton suffered from multiple cavities, yet continued eating chocolate. "Once he saw a box he had to eat them all. He was over at my house, and I had a box of 'Good News' chocolates on the table and wrote the song from the names inside the lid," Harrison wrote. He added that the song features an unlikely collaborator: press officer Derek Taylor. After experiencing difficulties with the bridge, Harrison said, Taylor suggested the line "you know that what you eat you are." Overall, Harrison wrote the song to tease pal Clapton, whose dentist had warned him off of eating any more candy.

The "Savoy Truffle" sessions commenced at Trident Studios on October 3, 1968, minus John Lennon. According to the *Beatles Bible*, they recorded the basic track for lead guitar, bass, and drums in one take (it is possible that previous rehearsal footage may have been erased). Harrison returned to Trident on October 5 to lay down his lead vocal, with Paul McCartney on harmonies. Six days later, George Martin arranged and conducted the horn section (two baritone saxophones and four tenor saxophones) at Abbey Road.

All seemed well until Harrison decided he wanted distortion

added to the horns. Engineer Brian Gibson labeled the process "a real chore." He explained to Mark Lewisohn that the brass section played their parts perfectly; then Harrison told engineer Ken Scott that he wanted the horns to have a distorted sound. "So I had to plug-up two high-gain amplifiers which overloaded and deliberately introduced a lot of distortion, completely tearing the sound to pieces and making it dirty," Gibson said. According to the *Complete Beatles Recording Sessions*, Harrison apologized to the session musicians when they heard the playback: "Before you listen I've got to apologize for what I've done to your beautiful sound. Please forgive me — but it's the way I want it!"

More overdubs occurred on October 14; returning to Abbey Road, they recorded the second electric guitar, organ, bongos, and tambourine parts. This time Ringo Starr was absent as he had left for a family vacation. One debate still rages: did coproducer Chris Thomas play the organ — since he is not credited on the album — or did Harrison? Some reports have Harrison originally playing the electric piano, which was eventually replaced by Thomas's organ and piano parts. After the overdubbing, Martin and Scott completed the mono and stereo mixes. Audiophiles may note that the mono version (embedded below) differs slightly from its stereo counterpart; the mono features additional sound effects during the solo, and the guitar solo bleeds into the next chorus.

Internal strife aside, most of the group managed to produce a roaring tribute to rhythm and blues. The horn section sounds straight out of a New Orleans club, while the rollicking beat and piano pay homage to Fats Domino. Harrison made no secret of his love for soul music — he recruited Billy Preston to play with the Beatles and produced his Apple solo albums, and later penned "Pure Smokey," a tribute to idol Smokey Robinson. Yes, the horns sound filtered, but the distortion adds a harder rocking edge to a soul number. Starr also turns in a bravado performance with his furious, typically hard-charging drumming.

Like Lennon, Harrison loved playing with language and injecting humorous images into his lyrics; as mentioned earlier, Harrison begins by listing the contents of the Good News chocolate box: "Creme tangerine and montelimar, a ginger sling with a pineapple heart; a coffee dessert," he sings, slyly referring to the chocolate brand.

One can imagine the fun Harrison experienced further tweaking Clapton's penchant for sweets. Interestingly Harrison uses imagery more appropriate for drug withdrawal rather than simply giving up candy. He warns that one may not feel the candy withdrawal immediately, but once the pain arrives, he will experience the consequences of his sweets addiction. While these lines probably refer to Clapton's toothaches, they definitely have a double meaning. One senses that Harrison is talking about more than dessert cravings when he mentions sweating and shouting, the words sounding eerily reminiscent of Lennon's "Cold Turkey."

The bridge at first seems serious with the lines "You know that what you eat you are, but what is sweet now turns so sour," referring to Clapton's candy addiction but possibly addressing many other bad habits. In a particularly humorous turn, Harrison references another *White Album* song, "Ob-La-Di, Ob-La-Da," then adds the mysterious line asking whether the listener can't tell Harrison where he/she resides. The last verse faintly echoes the "what you eat you are" line, but is otherwise intentionally vague.

"Savoy Truffle" encapsulates Harrison's apparent glee in playing with language — his description of various candy immediately creates vivid images in the listener's head. At the same time, Harrison leaves room for interpretation, and double meanings invite speculation: Just why did he mention "Ob-La-Di, Ob-La-Da," a McCartney track Lennon openly detested? Regardless of meaning, "Savoy Truffle" stands a memorable, fun track that recalls the Beatles' R&B beginnings.

Originally published February 15, 2013 at http://somethingelsereviews.com/ 2013/02/15/deep-beatles-savoy-truffle-1968/

"Cry Baby Cry"
The Beatles (1968)

John Lennon may have called it "a piece of rubbish," but "Cry Baby Cry" symbolizes one of Lennon's more underrated compositions. Written while in India, "Cry Baby Cry" serves as a twisted nursery rhyme, and he would return to the motif years later on *Double Fantasy's* "Cleanup Time." The 1968 tune landed on The Beatles (aka the *White Album*), and still intrigues with its unusual instrumentation and cryptic lyrics.

As has been well documented, the Beatles' time studying under the Maharishi Mahesh Yogi in India also produced a wealth of new material. According to Hunter Davies' *Beatles* biography, Lennon's inspiration for "Cry Baby Cry" drew from a television commercial. "I think I got them from an advert — 'Cry baby cry, make your mother buy.' I've been playing it over on the piano. I've let it go now. It'll come back if I really want it," he told the author. Another probable source is the nursery rhyme "Sing A Song of Sixpence," which contains lines very similar to "Cry Baby Cry" such as "The king was in his counting house counting out his money; the queen was in the parlor eating bread and honey."

Finishing the track in India, Lennon brought it to George Harrison's Esher home in May 1968; there, the group laid down several demos which would ultimately make up much of the *White Album*. Returning to Abbey Road Studios on July 15, 1968, the Beatles began work on "Cry Baby Cry"; according to the *Beatles Bible,* they filled four 30-minute tapes with numerous rehearsal takes. Unfortunately, this material was wiped during two subsequent recording sessions.

The next day, the Beatles recorded ten additional takes — take one later surfaced on *Anthology 3*, and differed little from the final version. However, taken ten was deemed best, with Lennon on acoustic guitar, piano, and vocals, Paul McCartney on bass, and Ringo Starr on drums (Harrison did not participate in these sessions). Ultimately the group created two mixes of take ten, retaining the instrumentation but removing most of Lennon's vocals. Take twelve was finally selected as the basis for the final version.

By this time, longtime Abbey Road engineer Geoff Emerick had walked out of the *White Album* sessions in protest; thus Ken Scott replaced Emerick on July 18. Under Scott and Martin's guidance, Lennon performed new lead vocals while Martin added harmonium. McCartney laid down harmonies, Starr shook a tambourine, and Harrison rejoined them to play electric guitar and add sound effects. Mixing would not commence until October 15, when artificial double-tracking was implemented to strengthen the acoustic guitar section.

Interestingly, the *White Album* features a hidden coda to "Cry Baby Cry": a song fragment informally titled "Can You Take Me Back." An impromptu jam, the song derives from the September 16 "I Will" recording sessions. Not surprisingly, the percussion, acoustic guitar, and McCartney's gentle vocals all closely resemble the *White Album* ballad. "Can You Take Me Back" does not directly relate to "Cry Baby Cry"; as Alan Pollack writes in his "Notes On" series: "The album context of 'Can You Take Me Back' is ambiguous, the song not being singled out per se on the track listing. Are we to consider it as a trailer to 'Cry Baby Cry' or a curtain raiser to 'Revolution 9'?" An examination of the lyrics may provide some clues.

Lennon's vocals stand front and center throughout the relatively simple tune, with lines resembling the aforementioned "Sing A Song of Sixpence" in lyrics such as "The king of Marigold was in the kitchen cooking breakfast for the queen." He continues painting a precious or "twee" image of a royal family, heavily emphasizing childlike themes. While the king was picking flowers for a visiting friend, the queen was busy painting pictures for the children. As Lennon's breathy voice narrates this charming scene, he introduces two more characters: the Duke and Duchess of Kirkcaldy, who arrive late for tea with the picture-perfect royal family.

Woven throughout this seemingly serene and unremarkable moment is the chorus, with Lennon telling an unnamed person to cry and "make your mother sigh." While this may echo the advertisement Lennon mentioned in Davies' book, it also injects a sense of foreboding, as if something dark looms over this tranquility. The next eerie lines suggest as much, informing listeners that a séance will occur later that evening. This apparent supernatural element casts a shadow on the proceedings, although Lennon clarifies that the children may be pulling a prank on the grownups. Who is deceiving whom in this scenario? Note how Lennon portrays the duke and duchess as well as the king and queen as juvenile and simplistic. Their children do not play or paint — their parents do. Instead, the children become active only in order to fool the adults.

Indeed, "Cry Baby Cry" inverts the conventional nursery rhyme, suggesting turbulence in parent-child roles and relationships. Martin's harmonium only enhances the quaintness — and, perhaps, false peacefulness — of this domesticity. Starr's bombastic drums stress incongruity, that what lies beneath the surface of the quaint images may be something darker. Along with Lennon's haunting voice, and McCartney's descending bass lines, Starr's drums may be the most important ingredient of an unusual tune.

He may have dismissed "Cry Baby Cry" as "rubbish," but strangely he implemented a similar structure on the *Double Fantasy* song "Cleanup Time." Those lyrics reverse the gender roles in "Sing A Song of Sixpence" and strongly resemble "Cry Baby Cry." In "Cleanup Time," Lennon sang that the queen was counting their money while the king baked bread and honey in the kitchen. More can be said about the deeper meaning of "Cleanup Time," but that merits a separate column.

"Cry Baby Cry" may not receive as much attention as other *White Album* tracks, but it perfectly embodies a Beatles trademark: turning musical conventions upside down, lending their own interpretations to traditional forms through alternate arrangements and at times unsettling lyrics.

Originally published February 14, 2014 at http://somethingelsereviews.com/2014/02/14/deep-beatles-cry-baby-cry-from-the-beatles-1968/

"Hey Bulldog"
Yellow Submarine (1968)

Years after the Beatles recorded the *Yellow Submarine* track "Hey Bulldog," John Lennon casually described the song as "a good sounding record that means nothing."

Perhaps it does not contain deep meaning, but "Hey Bulldog" stands as an all-out rock workout that sounds like a *White Album* outtake; however, the group recorded it specifically for the *Yellow Submarine* film. According to engineer Geoff Emerick, it gained significance for another reason: it represents one of the Beatles' last group efforts, with each member contributing parts to the overall song.

"Hey Bulldog" evolved from an early 1968 demo by John Lennon; he had been working on a track tentatively titled "She Can Talk to Me," named after the rudimentary chorus. On February 11, the Beatles assembled at Abbey Road to film a video for their upcoming single "Lady Madonna"; so as not to waste time, multi-tasker Paul McCartney suggested that the four work on a new song while NEMS employee Tony Bramwell's cameras rolled. Lennon brought up the home demo, and McCartney began contributing additional lyrics. Lennon improvised the opening piano riff on the spot, and his fingerprints are all over the nonsensical lyrics.

Since Lennon mentions "bullfrog" at the song's start, the track started life as "Hey Bullfrog"; the duo's hysterical ad-libbing, however, changed the entire nature of the tune.

According to *Rolling Stone*, McCartney had played drums on a Paul Jones track entitled "The Dog Presides" just a few days earlier; apparently with dogs on the brain, he and Lennon mimicked that song's sound effects by enthusiastically barking and howling.

Legend has it that McCartney's misreading of the lyrics also altered the nature of the song in significant ways. He claimed that he misread the original lyric, "some kind of solitude is measured out in news" as "some kind of solitude is measured out in you"; Lennon preferred the word change, and the group left in the slip.

More importantly, as Lennon and McCartney improvise at the tune's outro, McCartney accidentally said "bulldog" instead of "bullfrog" (perhaps confusing the "bullfrog" and "sheepdog" references); again, Lennon enjoyed the new lyric. As McCartney told biographer Barry Miles, he and Lennon shouted back and forth as if egging each other on to new levels of insanity.

The instrumentation also underwent several changes. According to Hunter Davies' *Beatles* biography, Lennon originally wanted to play sitar on the track and sing in a Lancashire accent; obviously the group rejected the idea. The final version consisted of Lennon on piano and guitar; McCartney on bass and tambourine; George Harrison on guitar; and Ringo Starr, of course, on drums. They recorded the song in a ten-hour session, with take ten deemed the best.

According to the *Beatles Bible* website, the group then overdubbed more drums, fuzz bass, a guitar solo, Lennon's double-tracked lead vocals, and additional backing vocals from McCartney.

Two mono mixes were immediately made, with one given to King Features for the *Yellow Submarine* film. As the *Beatles Bible* notes, the tape machine ran slightly faster during the mixing, thus raising the pitch and tempo of "Hey Bulldog." On October 29, Emerick oversaw the stereo mixes; interestingly, "All Together Now," "All You Need Is Love," and "Only A Northern Song" also received remixing for the *Yellow Submarine* soundtrack album.

The footage of the Beatles recording "Hey Bulldog" was superimposed over the "Lady Madonna" single; thus viewers assumed the group was performing the latter for the song's video. But Harrison revealed the truth behind the clip to *Billboard* in 1999: "Neil Aspinall who found out that when you watched and listened to what the original thing was, we were recording 'Bulldog,'" Harrison explained. "This was apparently the only time we were actually filmed recording something, so what Neil did was, he put (the unused footage) all back together again and put the 'Bulldog' soundtrack onto it, and there it was!"

The restored video was part of the rerelease of the *Yellow Submarine* film and soundtrack, or "songtrack," as it was retitled. Another addition to the rerelease: the restoration of the "Hey Bulldog" sequence in the film, as it was deleted from American prints.

While never released as a single, "Hey Bulldog" remains an underrated rocker in the Beatles' oeuvre. McCartney's bass fascinates; the isolated track in the video above reveals the intricate lines that prove crucial to the song's pounding rhythm. While hotly debated whether Lennon or Harrison played the guitar solo (my guess is Harrison), it still cuts sharply through the background, lending a harder edge.

Indeed, the lyrics conjure silly images — a Lennon trademark — yet the instrumentation rescues the track from becoming a simple novelty. Hearing Lennon and McCartney shouting and laughing toward the end demonstrates that despite their growing differences, they loved recording together and never strayed far from their youthful Liverpool roots.

Originally published August 9, 2013 at http://somethingelsereviews.com/ 2013/08/09/deep-beatles-hey-bulldog-1969/

"Because"
Abbey Road (1969)

For the next several columns, I will closely examine the legendary *Abbey Road* medley, their 16-minute magnum opus comprised of numerous song fragments. Where did these short works come from? How did they fit together so flawlessly? "Deep Beatles" digs deeper to take apart their famous and (technically) final work.

The song that leads off the medley is the last song recorded for *Abbey Road*: "Because," a track notable not only for its lush harmonies but for Yoko Ono's increasing influence on John Lennon's craft.

Ono may be best known as an avant-garde artist, but she also was a classically trained pianist. One day in 1969, Ono and Lennon were lounging in their home when Ono began playing Beethoven's *Piano Sonata No. 14* in C-sharp minor, Op. 27, No. 2, otherwise known as the *Moonlight Sonata*. On a whim, Lennon asked her if she could play the chords backwards. Instantly he wrote the lyrics around the ensuing music; in 1980 Lennon seemed proud of the words: "The lyrics speak for themselves; they're clear. No bullshit. No imagery, no obscure references," he said.

Around the release of *Abbey Road*, Lennon stated that he anticipated writing many more songs with Ono. In a 1969 interview, Paul McCartney cited lines such as "Because the world is round it turns me on" as some of Lennon's best lyrics.

Recording began on August 1, 1969, with Lennon, McCartney and George Martin laying down 23 takes of the track. Lennon played electric guitar, Martin played the harpsichord, and McCartney plucked his usual bass; Ringo Starr added a hi-hat rhythm strictly for guiding purposes and was not on the final recording. After take 16 was judged best, Lennon, McCartney, and George Harrison painstakingly recorded their layered harmonies. Two more vocal tracks were added on August 4; the next day, Harrison performed a Moog part, which he recorded twice. The final product created a nine-part harmony effect due to the triple overdub.

"The harmony was pretty difficult to sing. We had to really learn it. But I think that's one of the tunes that will impress most people. It's really good," Harrison said in 1969, adding that "Because" was his favorite *Abbey Road* tune.

Apart from the lovely harmonies and Ono's part in composing "Because," the track remains significant for another reason: it was the last time all four Beatles recorded a song together.

Against the beautifully restrained chords, Harrison, Lennon and McCartney croon philosophical and mysterious phrases. In addition to the aforementioned lyrics, Lennon also penned the lines "Because the sky is blue, it makes me cry," the image being a popular one in his later tunes (most notably calling women "the other half of the sky" in the ballad "Woman").

McCartney told biographer Barry Miles that he suspected Ono suggested the images of nature, taking that the wind, sky, and earth were recurrent themes in Ono's book *Grapefruit*. However, another frequent trope appears, this one Beatles-centric: the power of love. They had previously sung "All You Need Is Love," and on *Abbey Road* would sing the immortal lines "And in the end, the love you take is equal to the love you make."

Here Lennon declares that love is both old and new, and it exists in the world and within individuals. Love encompasses everything, love is in all of us — these are heady themes for a rock song. Yet, "Because" succeeds at being deep yet accessible simultaneously.

While no demo seemingly exists, Lennon did briefly sing "Because" during his and Ono's 1969 Montreal bed-in. In 1996, the *Anthology 3* collection revived the song by eliminating the instrumentation, fully revealing those complex harmonies. The Cirque du Soleil show *Love* enhanced this version with some birds twittering in the background; audiences still cite the chilling effect "Because" occurs during the Las Vegas production.

No matter what version, "Because" represents the Beatles at their best lyrically and vocally, and perfectly introduces the intricate *Abbey Road* medley.

Originally published August 23, 2013 at http://somethingelsereviews.com/2013/08/23/deep-beatles-because-1969/

"You Never Give Me Your Money"
Abbey Road (1969)

"Deep Beatles'" look at the *Abbey Road* medley continues with "You Never Give Me Your Money," an obvious nod to the group's legal and financial woes from their ill-fated venture Apple Corps. The track is a mini-epic in itself, a three-movement song addressing anger, despair, frustration, and the desire to escape. It may be a "fragment" included in the magnum opus, but it stands as one of Paul McCartney's greatest performances and compositions.

McCartney began composing "You Never Give Me Your Money" as an angry reaction to new manager Allen Klein. As he told biographer Barry Miles: "This was me directly lambasting Allen Klein's attitude to us: no money, just funny paper, all promises and it never works out. It's basically a song about no faith in the person, that found its way into the medley on *Abbey Road*. John saw the humor in it." Klein had recently become the Beatles' manager, despite McCartney's objections. McCartney appears to express his conflicting emotions within the song, which accounts for the wistful beginning, rhythm and blues middle, and full-out rock at the end.

After composing the track, McCartney and the Beatles entered Studio One at Olympic Sound Studios on May 6, 1969, recording an astonishing 36 takes of "You Never Give Me Your Money." McCartney was on piano, John Lennon on distorted guitar, George Harrison on another guitar (the Beatles Bible site states the sound was fed through a revolving Leslie speaker), and Ringo Starr on drums. The group recorded the instrumental section live onto eight-track tape, with take 30 deemed the best. Since the Beatles and producer George Martin had yet to fit the track into the medley, the song abruptly ended after the nursery rhyme chant. At this point, McCartney had also recorded his guide vocal.

Almost two months passed before McCartney returned to the song, dubbing his lead vocals over take 30, according to the *Beatles Bible*. Two weeks later the group returned to Abbey Road Studios to add more vocals and instrumentation such as chimes. Interestingly, the Beatles then attempted to connect "You Never Give Me Your Money" to "Sun King," ultimately deciding on a long organ note and additional harmonies. The next day, these vocals were eliminated, and McCartney alone completed the song by playing bass and piano.

However, the transition to "Sun King" still needed work so, on August 5, McCartney brought in homemade tape loops containing effects such as bird and cricket chirps. After two more attempts on August 14 and 21, the crossfade was finally completed. While just a fragment of the medley, "You Never Give Me Your Money" was a complicated recording in that it required multiple days for takes, overdubs, and mixing sessions.

Lyrically, the track contains a clear theme: wanting to be rid of "funny paper" and petty squabbles, and to return to the Beatles' early days. The first section, introduced with restrained piano, apparently addresses Klein directly, accusing him of withholding money and causing rifts among the Beatles. Here he summarizes the anguish the entire band felt by rephrasing the last line as "I break down" in the next stanza. McCartney's quiet vocals emphasize the pain, his voice double tracked to add drama. The next stanza features Harrison and Lennon harmonizing with McCartney, suggesting that they all shared in McCartney's frustration.

Suddenly, the piano becomes strident, with Ringo Starr's drums thumping through the quiet. McCartney assumes his Fats Domino-like vocal, also present in such tracks as "Lady Madonna." The music rumbles as he reminisces about earlier times, when money hadn't entered the picture. He longs for the days when he was broke, unsure of the future, and had nowhere to go — all sentiments virtually everyone has experienced. While money may be short and jobs scarce, McCartney says, he loved that "magic feeling" of this uncertainty. In other words, he longs for the carefree days of youth; in his case, this may refer to the Beatles' early days in Liverpool and Hamburg.

Harrison, Lennon, and McCartney then harmonize wistfully, as if reveling in nostalgia.

The final section, the "sweet dream" part, advocates for escapism both physically and emotionally. McCartney's voice soars, allowing some grittiness to creep into his singing. His dream involves taking off in a limousine, adding devastating lines about wanting to jump in his car and escape. While those lines communicate freedom, they also express the prison that the group found themselves in during their final years together. Lennon and Harrison's guitars cut through this tension, the sonic bursts of energy emulating breaking free — a theme McCartney would revisit often on his subsequent albums.

Since this is just a dream, the music slows and gradually fades as McCartney repeats the line concerning a sweet dream coming true. Harmonies return as Harrison, Lennon, and McCartney chant the following nursery rhyme: "One, two, three, four, five, six, seven. All good children go to heaven." What does this have to do with the overreaching theme? McCartney may have longed for returning to childlike innocence, of life not corrupted by money and power. Since the three croon the lines as if singing a lullaby, it could be simulating that state where one falls into a deeper sleep. Indeed, their vocals fade out as the guitars also become softer, the tweeting and chirping effects eventually taking over, creating a dreamlike state.

"You Never Give Me Your Money" is a rich track in many respects. It features one of McCartney's finest vocal performances as well as the Beatles' unparalleled harmonies. The meaning is complex, with the theme both depressing and uplifting. As usual, Starr anchors the song with his strong drumming style, effectively changing the entire mood of the song from introspective to bombastic. McCartney continues performing this song on his many tours, and no wonder: "You Never Give Me Your Money" may comprise just one part of the medley, but its sophistication and density stand alone.

Originally published September 7, 2013 at http://somethingelsereviews.com/2013/09/07/deep-beatles-you-never-give-me-your-money-1969/

"Sun King"
Abbey Road (1969)

Next in the *Abbey Road* medley is one of the Beatles' most beautiful yet mysterious tracks, "Sun King." In later years, John Lennon dismissed "Sun King" as "a piece of garbage I had around," but its lovely harmonies and mystical lyrics transform it into an entrancing listening experience.

Supposedly the title came to Lennon in a dream, but some Beatles historians speculate that the phrase may have derived from the popular 1966 book *The Sun King*, a history of King Louis XIV. The chord progression originates from Lennon's composing tear during the group's 1968 India sojourn. Previously, Lennon brought in the piece during the 1969 *Get Back* sessions, and its chord progression closely resembles another Lennon composition from the period: "Don't Let Me Down."

However, another musical influence entered the studio — Fleetwood Mac. In 1968, the Peter Green-iteration of the band released "Albatross," a dreamy instrumental driven by Green's reverb-filled guitar solo and chords emulating the tide rolling in. In a 1987 interview, George Harrison revealed that the single inspired the Beatles to rework "Sun King." "At the time, 'Albatross' was out, with all the reverb on guitar. So we said, 'Let's be Fleetwood Mac doing "Albatross," just to get going,' Harrison said. "It never really sounded like Fleetwood Mac ... but that was the point of origin."

While "Sun King" may not exactly duplicate the track, the mellow quality of the song, created with melodic guitars and sound effects like chimes and use of cymbals, faintly echo "Albatross."

Soon after the Beatles abandoned the *Get Back* sessions, they returned to Abbey Road to record their final album. Paul McCartney revived "Sun King" for the medley; by this time, Lennon had changed the lyrics and titled the song "Here Comes the Sun King," perhaps a wink at Harrison's composition "Here Comes the Sun." Obviously, the moniker changed to avoid confusion between the two tracks. Next came the addition of the mysterious ending lines — what do they mean? Lennon and McCartney later admitted the words were pure gibberish, but in four different languages. While individual words were real, strung together they made little sense.

A Lennon interview aired during the *Anthology* documentary further explains:

> When we came to sing it, to make them different we started joking, saying "cuando para mucho." We just made it up. Paul knew a few Spanish words from school, so we just strung any Spanish words that sounded vaguely like something. And of course we got "chicka ferdi" — that's a Liverpool expression; it doesn't mean anything, just like "ha ha ha." One we missed: we could have had "para noia," but we forgot all about it. We used to call ourselves Los Para Noias.

Further evidence of Lennon's assertions can be found during the 1968 *White Album* sessions, most notably in the outtake "Los Paranoias." The Latin feel present in "Sun King" can be heard in this studio jam.

Recording began on July 24, 1969, with "Sun King" and "Mean Mr. Mustard" fused as one track. They taped 35 takes, with Lennon on rhythm guitar and guide vocal; McCartney on bass; Harrison on lead guitar; and Ringo Starr on drums. They returned to Abbey Road the next day to overdub vocals and piano, and added an organ part played by George Martin.

Finally, the group finished "Sun King" on Jul 29 by overdubbing more vocals, piano, organ, and percussion. According to engineer Geoff Emerick, Starr would drape tea towels over his drums to achieve a softer sound, hitting them with timpani mallets rather than drumsticks. Indeed, Starr's beautifully understated work is key to establishing the song's intimate atmosphere. His drums gain power abruptly before segueing into "Mean Mr. Mustard." Similar to "Because," Harrison, Lennon, and McCartney's seamless, triple-tracked harmonies still amaze.

"Sun King" remains an intriguing part of the medley. Its haunting quality — the chirping sound effects suggesting walking outside in the middle of the night — provides a soothing diversion from the intensity of "You Never Give Me Your Money" as well as the gradual build to the medley's climax. Lennon may have called it "a piece of garbage," but "Sun King" serves as a crucial part of *Abbey Road*.

For more evidence of its stunning quality, listen to the Cirque du Soleil Love version, which features the track backwards.

Originally published September 20, 2013 at http://somethingelsereviews.com/2013/09/20/deep-beatles-sun-king-from-abbey-road-1969/

"Mean Mr. Mustard"
Abbey Road (1969)

As "Sun King" quietly fades, a drum kickstarts this darkly humorous track: "Mean Mr. Mustard," a John Lennon composition dating to 1968. His own harshest critic, Lennon later labeled it a "piece of garbage." However, it contains a classic Lennon technique: creating eccentric characters who display outrageous — even offensive — traits.

"Mean Mr. Mustard's" origins trace back to the Beatles' stay in India. Although the Beatles were there to study transcendental meditation and spirituality, the trip also fueled their creativity. Each member brought numerous tracks for the *White Album* sessions, leaving the group with the unenviable problem of choosing the best tracks for the two-disc project.

One of those extra songs, "Mean Mr. Mustard" was inspired by a newspaper story; this would mark yet another time that Lennon drew from a news story for his songwriting. In a 1980 interview, he claimed that he'd read a story about "this mean guy who hid five-pound notes, not up his nose but somewhere else. No, it had nothing to do with cocaine."

The Beatles recorded a demo of the track at George Harrison's bungalow in Esher, Surrey in May 1968. This stripped-down take, above, features acoustic guitar and Lennon's double-tracked voice. Lacking harmonies, the early "Mr. Mustard" also contained no ending. Toward the end, Lennon starts repeating the title phrase and ad-libbing phrases like "such a dirty dirty Mean Mr. Mustard." Although frequently bootlegged, the demo later surfaced on the *Anthology 3* collection.

The group returned to the track in January 1969 during the infamous *Get Back* sessions. In this version, embedded below, Lennon's electric piano prominently features, while Harrison contributes new guitar licks. Note that one lyric differs here; in *Anthology*, Lennon explains that "I said 'his sister Pam' — originally it was 'his sister Shirley' in the lyric. I changed it to Pam to make it sound like it had something to do with ['Polythene Pam']." Frequently Lennon ad-libs in a similar manner to the 1968 demo, along with a bit of scatting. Clearly, the Beatles were still playing with the track, unsure how to end it.

After the *Get Back* project was shelved, the group reunited for the *Abbey Road* album and fused the fragments for the medley. On "Mean Mr. Mustard," Lennon played guitar, maracas, and sang lead; McCartney provided crucial harmony vocals, bass, and perhaps piano (it is unclear whether he or Lennon played this); Harrison contributed lead guitar; and Ringo Starr, of course, played drums and tambourine. They completed 35 takes of the rhythm track on July 24 — take 35 was deemed the best — then finished overdubs July 25 and 29.

Now comes a crucial point in Beatles history: originally "Her Majesty" was to have been sandwiched between "Mean Mr. Mustard" and "Polythene Pam." Ultimately, McCartney vetoed the idea, believing the sequence just did not work. So-called "outfakes" that later emerged recreated this order, demonstrating the jarring effect. However, before making this decision, they altered the ending of "Mean Mr. Mustard" to smoothly transition into "Her Majesty." In the July 1969 version, embedded below, listen for the drum crash at the end of the track. The crashing chord at the beginning of "Her Majesty" derives from this early experiment with the medley sequence.

In Alan Pollack's excellent "Notes On" series, he classifies "Mean Mr. Mustard" as a bridge of sorts, a way to link two disparate songs. "Following on the heels of the more substantial and self-contained previous two songs this one critically needs to pick up the pace and get the show on the road, medley-wise," he posits. "The short track length, incomplete form, and the tighter, smoother coupling of the track at both ends to the songs that surround it seem as a group of factors to work out just right." Initially the tempo recalls "Sun King," but ultimately speeds up to introduce "Polythene Pam."

Lyrically, the song reflects Lennon's unique gift for portraying outsiders, sometimes with unattractive traits (see "Nowhere Man," "Sexy Sadie," "A Day in the Life," and "Dr. Robert," among many others). He points listeners to a homeless man who "sleeps in a hole in the road." While he supposedly saves money to buy clothes, the phrase "keeps a ten bob note up his nose" suggests gluttony and greed. In contrast, his sister Pam is employed, a "go-getter," and higher class.

She tries exposing her brother to the elite by taking him out to see the Queen, but he fails to emulate her civility. Instead, Mr. Mustard yells something "obscene," proving that he will forever dwell in his den of iniquity. He's "such a dirty old man," "such a mean old man," and remains so despite his sister's best efforts. It would have been interesting if Lennon had fleshed out the rest of the song; would he have changed the Pam character? As in his later work, would he have criticized her for working too hard, wearing blinders to the world around her?

In 1994, McCartney discussed the track, calling it "very John. I liked that. A nice quirky song." While quirky, it also stands as a chugging rocker that contains tight harmonies and memorable lyrics. "Mean Mr. Mustard" serves as a crucial transitional tool to merge two disparate songs — "Sun King" and "Polythene Pam" — in a way that only the Beatles could execute.

Originally published October 5, 2013 at http://somethingelsereviews.com/ 2013/10/05/deep-beatles-mean-mr-mustard-from-abbey-road-1969/

"Polythene Pam"
Abbey Road (1969)

One of John Lennon's more underrated compositions, "Polythene Pam" fits perfectly with the preceding *Abbey Road* fragment "Mean Mr. Mustard." Like "Mr. Mustard," Lennon created a composite character, a combination of several women who enjoyed kinky sex. Its hand-clapping rhythm and hard-driving guitars rock as Lennon sings in a deliberate scouse accent, stressing the seediness of the song's topic.

As a side note, unlike past columns, this edition of "Deep Beatles" may need a PG-13 rating, due to the song's backstory!

The genesis of "Polythene Pam's" lyrics merit their own novel. In a 1980 interview, Lennon explained that the words derive from a 1963 incident with English beat poet Roston Ellis. After crossing paths in 1960, the Beatles and Ellis remained friends. During the Beatles' tour, Ellis invited Lennon to his apartment to meet his new girlfriend. Lennon arrived with his own girl, and the couple soon learned that Ellis' latest interest enjoyed dressing in all polythene. "She didn't wear jackboots or kilts, I just sort of elaborated. Perverted sex in a polythene bag. Just looking for something to write about."

Ellis recalled the incident differently — if more graphically — in Steve Turner's seminal book *A Hard Day's Write*. He stated that he and his friend Stephanie invited Lennon back to their apartment, and the three decided to experiment with having sex while wearing polythene. "We all dressed up in them and wore them in bed. John stayed the night with us in the same bed. I don't think anything very exciting happened and we all wondered what the fun was in being 'kinky,'" he said.

Yet another explanation is offered in *A Hard Day's Write* through Pat Dawson, a Liverpool fan who courted infamy through her, um, interesting love of polythene. Dawson first befriended the group in 1961, and they would often offer her a ride home after certain concerts. "It was about the same time that I started getting called Polythene Pat. It's embarrassing really. I just used to eat polythene all the time. I'd tie it in knots and then eat it. Sometimes I even used to burn it and then eat it when it got cold," she said. "I had a friend who got a job in a polythene bag factory, which was wonderful because it meant I had a constant supply." It would not be surprising that Lennon would draw inspiration from such a figure, as he enjoyed writing about quirky characters.

After composing the song in 1968, Lennon and the Beatles recorded a demo at George Harrison's Kinfauns home in Esher. This early version eventually appeared on the *Anthology 3* collection, sporting several different lyrics (most notably "well it's a little absurd but she's a nice class of bird" instead of "she's the kind of a girl that makes the News of the World") and chord variations. Originally considered for the *White Album*, "Polythene Pam" was then left on the shelf until the 1969 *Get Back* sessions. After abandoning the project, they revisited the tune for inclusion on *Abbey Road*, deciding to combine it with Paul McCartney's "She Came in Through the Bathroom Window." According to the *Beatles Bible* website, it marked the only time that two separate songs by Lennon and Paul McCartney were recorded as one track.

Sessions began for both tunes on July 25, 1969. In a 12-hour marathon, the group recorded an astounding 39 takes of the instrumental track, featuring Lennon on acoustic guitar, McCartney on bass, Harrison on lead guitar, and, of course, Ringo Starr on drums. On this day, Lennon and McCartney initially laid down guide vocals, soon replacing them with permanent lead vocals.

They also rerecorded drum and bass parts; three days later, they returned to the studio to overdub more lead vocals, acoustic guitar, electric guitar, tambourine, cowbell, electric piano, and acoustic piano. Overdubs were completed on July 30, the same day when the Beatles finalized the medley running order and finished mixing, editing, and crossfading.

"Polythene Pam" features Lennon at his most playful, gleefully telling the raunchy story of a possible transvestite. Like "Get Back," the song describes the heroine as attractive but masculine, sometimes dressed in drag, dressed in a "polythene bag." Apparently referring to Ellis' girlfriend, he paints a lurid picture of her "in jackboots and kilt," stressing her promiscuity by calling her essentially a pinup girl, featured in the tabloid *News of the World*.

Essentially labeling her a centerfold in a British tabloid, Lennon emphasizes the sleaziness of the topic by singing in a deliberate scouse accent. The "yeah yeah yeah" refrain faintly echoes "She Loves You," perhaps a gentle parody of their earlier, more innocent love songs.

The instrumentation also stands out, particularly Harrison's piercing lead guitar, Lennon's relentless rhythm guitar, and Starr's intricate percussion (proving that you indeed cannot have too much cowbell in a song). The group's harmonies on the "yeah yeah yeah" refrain are tight, and Lennon's gleeful vocal adds a humorous dimension to an otherwise seedy subject. Right before "She Came in Through the Bathroom Window," Lennon laughs as he yells "look out," expressing joy in writing and singing a naughty track.

When establishing the medley's final running order, the Beatles proved ingenious in combining "Polythene Pam" and "She Came in Through the Bathroom Window." Both describe adventurous women, but with a wink and a healthy dose of Liverpudlian humor. Lyrics aside, "Polythene Pam" illustrates why the the Beatles rank among the best rock and roll bands due to their tightness and musicianship.

Originally published October 18, 2013 at http://somethingelsereviews.com/2013/10/18/deep-beatles-polythene-pam-from-abbey-road-1969/

"She Came in Through the Bathroom Window"
Abbey Road (1969)

The next entry in the *Abbey Road* medley continues the naughtiness of "Polythene Pam." While John Lennon told the story of a sexually adventurous and androgynous figure, "She Came in Through the Bathroom Window" is loosely based on an overzealous McCartney fan.

This time, McCartney's lyrics are opaque, veering from the title phrase to an unusual tale of a somewhat scandalous woman. Even George Harrison admitted in 1969 that it was "a very good song of Paul's, with good lyrics. It's really hard to explain what they're about." No matter the vagueness, the track rocks hard with stellar McCartney bass, Ringo Starr's heavy drums, and the group's usual outstanding harmonies.

"She Came in Through the Bathroom Window" dates back to the *Get Back* sessions, when McCartney brought the song to the band in January 1969. According to several sources, the story stems from an incident regarding fans breaking into McCartney's home. A group of women informally dubbed "Apple Scruffs" by Harrison would congregate outside the Beatles' homes, Abbey Road Studios, and Apple headquarters, hoping to catch a glimpse of their idols. Most of these fans were benign — some were invited into the Beatles' homes, while two were even recruited to sing backup on a version of "Across the Universe."

However, a few Apple Scruffs decided to break into McCartney's house by taking a ladder from his garden, leaning it against his home, and crawling through the bathroom window to obtain some "souvenirs" such as clothing and photographs. Other versions involve McCartney learning of a groupie climbing through a bathroom window to sleep with a member of the Moody Blues; band members told the Beatle of the incident the next day, inspiring McCartney to compose the track.

Lennon offered yet another explanation of the lyrics in a 1980 interview, stating that McCartney composed the lyrics while the duo were promoting their newly formed Apple Corps. in New York during a 1968 visit. "That's Paul's song. He wrote that when we were in New York ... and we first met Linda. Maybe she's the one that came in the window. I don't know; somebody came in the window," he recalled. This seems unlikely, as McCartney first met future wife Linda Eastman in 1967, when *Sgt. Pepper's Lonely Hearts Club Band* was released.

In Barry Miles' biography *Many Years from Now*, McCartney said that he composed the "so I quit the police department" section while returning home from New York. While sitting in a cab bound for New York's JFK airport, he noticed the driver's license on the dashboard. Above the cabbie's name and photo were the words "New York Police Dept.," instantly inspiring McCartney to begin the song's final lyrics with that line.

As the Beatles gathered for the tension-filled *Get Back* (later *Let It Be*) sessions in January 1969, they began work on the track. *Anthology 3* and numerous bootlegs illustrate how "She Came in Through the Bathroom Window" started life as a slower, bluesier song. Listening to the Twickenham Studio recordings, it is evident that the Beatles struggled with the tune, attempting to integrate guitar and establish the tempo. Typical of the *Get Back* sessions, the group would lessen frustration by joking around, intentionally singing words in cartoonish ways. As has been well documented, the Beatles soon shelved this material and focused on recording their final studio album, *Abbey Road*.

Not surprisingly, "Polythene Pam" and "She Came in Through the Bathroom Window" were recorded together. On July 25, 1969, they recorded 39 takes of the basic track at Abbey Road Studios. McCartney played bass, Lennon strummed 12-string acoustic rhythm guitar, Harrison assumed lead guitar, and Starr played drums. At first Lennon and McCartney recorded guide vocals; later that day they added lead vocals and rerecorded the drum and bass parts. Three days later, they returned to the track, laying down a variety of overdubs; according to the Beatles Bible, these additions included more vocals, electric and acoustic guitar parts, more percussion, and electric as well as acoustic piano.

Interestingly, many of these changes were not implemented in the final mixes. The Beatles finished the recording on July 30 by overdubbing yet more percussion and guitar. George Martin and engineers Geoff Emerick and Phil McDonald completed most of the edits, crossfades, and mixes of the track on August 14.

As Lennon yells "look out!" at the end of "Polythene Pam," "She Came in Through the Bathroom Window" crashes in, McCartney immediately singing the title phrase. While an Apple Scruff may have been the original inspiration, the lyrics quickly veer from that theme. The line "protected by a silver spoon" may suggest an upper-class woman, but he then infantilizes her, adding that she sits by the banks of a lagoon and sucks her thumb. What the latter line means is open to interpretation, or perhaps McCartney is daring listeners to decipher the meaning themselves — a pastime in which fans are admittedly all too willing to engage.

Harrison, Lennon and McCartney harmonize powerfully in the chorus, asking if anyone saw this unusual woman. Some interpret the next lines, "Sunday's on the phone to Monday; Tuesday's on the phone to me" as his neighbors phoning the police after seeing fans break into his home. The lyrics echo "Lady Madonna," personifying the days of the week. Like Lennon, McCartney occasionally returns to tropes such as these in his songwriting.

As Harrison's guitar pierces through the instrumentation, McCartney suddenly changes his characterization of the woman. She may have an upper class background, but she claims she was a dancer who worked at multiple clubs (presumably an exotic dancer). Perhaps she has more in common with "Polythene Pam" than previously thought. In his imaginary conversation with her, he said that the girl thought he would tell her the answer, but somehow he lacked the words to express his thoughts. Again, the content of this unspoken question and answer is left to the listener's imagination.

The aforementioned "police department" section signals the impending conclusion, but also contains, in my opinion, one of the best lines in the Beatles catalog, that "she could steal — but she could not rob." Harrison, Lennon, and McCartney cannot resist wordplay, and the latter line exemplifies this technique. The terms "steal" and "rob" may be considered synonyms, but here McCartney suggests subtle connotations. The *Oxford English Dictionary* defines "steal" as "to take without permission or legal right and without intending to return it," while "rob" is listed as "to take property unlawfully from (a person or place) by force or threat of force." In other words, the unnamed woman can surreptitiously confiscate goods, but not through violence.

Is this another reference to the woman being "protected by a silver spoon," implying privilege? In other words, is McCartney stating that the woman can commit a crime behind one's back, but not in front of the person? Whether he is stressing weakness or a general lack of character is anyone's guess. Regardless of meaning, McCartney demonstrates his mastery over composing cryptic lyrics that somehow still make sense.

Besides the mysterious lyrics, "She Came in Through the Bathroom Window" excels because of pure teamwork. McCartney's complicated bass lines, prominent in the early mix below, prove crucial to Starr's hard-driving beat. Harrison's tasteful solos perfectly punctuate the words, while Lennon provides essential harmonies and rhythmic guitar that further accents the percussion. All of these ingredients comprise two minutes of sheer rock and roll, illustrating how despite their personal issues, they were still at the top of their game.

Originally published November 1, 2013 at http://somethingelsereviews.com/ 2013/11/01/deep-beatles-she-came-in-through-the-bathroom-window-fromabbey-road-1969/

"Golden Slumbers"
Abbey Road (1969)

One of the most tender and moving sections of the *Abbey Road* medley, "Golden Slumbers" features Paul McCartney at his best. His gift for melody, along with his clear vocals and skilled piano, shines in this modern adaptation of a very old lullaby.

The lyrics' origins date back long before the Beatles. In 1603, English dramatist Thomas Dekker, along with coauthors Henry Chettle and William Haughton, published a play entitled *Patient Grissil*, loosely based on the character Griselda from Geoffrey Chaucer's *Canterbury Tales* (specifically "The Clerk's Tale"). Translated into modern English, the original poem reads as follows:

> Golden slumbers kiss your eyes,
> Smiles awake you when you rise;
> Sleep, pretty wantons, do not cry,
> And I will sing a lullaby,
> Rock them, rock them, lullaby.
> Care is heavy, therefore sleep you,
> You are care, and care must keep you;
> Sleep, pretty wantons, do not cry,
> And I will sing a lullaby,
> Rock them, rock them, lullaby.

As McCartney later recalled, he had visited his father's Liverpool home and noticed sheet music on his piano. Stepsister Ruth had left her songbook on the stand; curious, McCartney leafed through it and stumbled upon Dekker's "Golden Slumbers," now better known as a stand-alone lullaby. Since McCartney could not read music and had forgotten the original melody, he decided to write his own tune, slightly editing the lyrics. *Anthology* suggests that McCartney had previously composed "Carry That Weight," and rewrote the original "Golden Slumbers" poem to better fit his other song.

Recording commenced on July 2, 1969; John Lennon was absent from these sessions, as he and Yoko Ono were recovering from injuries sustained from a car accident in Scotland. No guitar part occurs, therefore the lineup slightly differs from typical Beatles records. McCartney played piano and sang lead; George Harrison took over on bass; and as usual, Ringo Starr played drums. Unknown classical musicians added violins, cellos, violas, double bass, horns, trumpets, trombone, and bass trombone. Lennon humorously commented on this section in a 1969 interview:

> I personally can't be bothered with strings and things, you know. I like to do it with the group or with electronics. And especially going through that hassle with musicians and all that bit, you know, it's such a drag trying to get them together. But Paul digs that, so that's his scene. It was up to him where he went with violins and what he did with them. And I think he just wanted a straight kind of backing, you know. Nothing freaky.

In *Many Years from Now*, McCartney recalled honing his vocals for maximum effect. He rehearsed the lead vocal endlessly, wanting to achieve strength yet tenderness in his voice. Helmed by producer George Martin and engineers Geoff Emerick and Phil McDonald, the first session consisted of 15 takes of "Golden Slumbers" and "Carry That Weight," recorded together. Takes 13 and 15 were judged best, so these backing tracks were edited together the next day. According to the *Beatles Bible* website, they recorded additional overdubs on July 4, but the specifics are unknown. McCartney returned to lay down lead vocals on July 30 and 31, and the orchestral section was added on August 15. The 30-piece orchestra (conducted by Martin) played on an astonishing five tracks that day: "Golden Slumbers," "Carry

That Weight," "The End," "Something," and "Here Comes the Sun."

After the bawdiness of "Polythene Pam" and "She Came in Through the Bathroom Window," "Golden Slumbers" represents a radical change of pace. After a brief pause, the piano enters, followed by McCartney's initially low-key vocals. Before referring to the "Golden Slumbers" poem, he adds lyrics evoking images of home and hearth, announcing that he will sing a lullaby. Rather than lulling listeners to sleep, however, McCartney wants to energize, increasing the volume and intensity of his voice. The lyrics differ slightly from the original poem — he substitutes "kiss" with "fill," and not surprisingly sings "pretty darling" rather than "pretty wantons." Because of this last change, he eliminates "rock them, rock them, lullaby" since he now addresses one person.

How does "Golden Slumbers" relate to "Carry That Weight?" McCartney leaves this open to interpretation. "Golden Slumbers" seeks to soothe, albeit in an unusually passionate sense, while "Carry That Weight" suggests coping with seemingly overwhelming problems. Considering the internal strife the Beatles experienced at that time, it is not difficult to envision them working out their turmoil through song. "Golden Slumbers" clearly references childhood, while "Carry That Weight" segues into adulthood. However, the beginning lyrics about returning home intrigue — is McCartney yearning for a return to innocence, to simplicity, similar to his desires in "You Never Give Me Your Money"?

"Golden Slumbers" signals the beginning of, literally, "The End," the climax of the medley. McCartney's adaptation of Dekker's lullaby symbolizes the bottom of the hill, the start of a slow climb toward the top and, ultimately, the denouement of the medley, album, and the Beatles' own story. The song is a creative way of preparing fans for an emotional and musical release.

Originally published November 15, 2013 at http://somethingelsereviews.com/2013/11/15/deep-beatles-golden-slumbers-from-abbey-road-1969/

"Carry That Weight"
Abbey Road (1969)

Continuing the melancholic mood set by "Golden Slumbers," "Carry That Weight" further stresses the turmoil the Beatles were experiencing by 1969. A brief reprise of "You Never Give Me Your Money" underscores this tension.

In a typical instance of understatement, John Lennon commented on the track in 1980: "That's Paul. Apparently he was under strain at that period." More accurately, all four members were struggling with money and contract issues, family commitments, and their growing artistic independence. Indeed, they were carrying several weights, and this section of the *Abbey Road* medley packs a corresponding emotional punch.

Paul McCartney composed "Carry That Weight" in reaction to the band's various troubles. In *Many Years from Now*, McCartney told author Barry Miles that drugs combined with Klein's demands and the group's arguments made him feel as though a weight were on his shoulders.

McCartney, George Harrison, and Ringo Starr entered Abbey Road Studios on July 2, 1969 to record "Carry That Weight" and "Golden Slumbers" together. Lennon was still recovering from a car accident in Scotland, but would rejoin them about a month later. They recorded 15 takes of both tracks with Harrison on bass, Starr on drums, and McCartney on piano and lead vocal. Takes 13 and 15 were deemed best, and George Martin, Geoff Emerick, and Phil McDonald edited both versions together. July 3 and 4 saw McCartney overdubbing lead vocals and rhythm guitar, while Harrison laid down his lead guitar part. All three then sang the "carry that weight a long time" line; Lennon then returned to the studio July 30 to add his vocals. Lennon continued this work the next day, while Starr overdubbed more percussion.

The group completed work on August 15, when the orchestral section was recorded (12 violins, four violas, four cellos, string bass, four horns, three trumpets, trombone, and bass trombone, according to the *Beatles Bible*). In general, the final version of "Carry That Weight" contains two unusual elements: first, the chorus features all four Beatles' voices. Second, the "You Never Give Me Your Money" reprise did not contain multi-member harmonies, but McCartney's voice multi-tracked.

As McCartney croons the word "lullaby," Starr's drums crash through to signal the next section of the medley. Strings give way to the foursome chanting the line "carry that weight" lyric, with Starr's voice particularly distinctive here. The horns and Harrison's guitar recall the melody from "You Never Give Me Your Money," and McCartney's multi-layered vocals reprise that song, ending with the crucial lines that in the midst of the celebrations, trouble still looms.

The "breakdown" has a short life, however, as the Beatles resume chanting — almost shouting — the title words, adding that the narrator will carry this unnamed weight for a long time. Harrison's guitar returns, sounding distorted, almost underwater, as he slightly recalls the "Money" melody.

Read in tandem, the lyrics resemble a dialog, either literally between two people or an inner debate. The narrator in "Money" still despairs over breakdowns in communication; here he appears alone despite being in a room filled with people. Contrast that stanza with the "carry that weight" segment, where "I" becomes "you." A Greek chorus of sorts sympathizes with the previous speaker, telling him he will have to carry the burden of his depression. In other words, it may take a while before the sun reappears (to paraphrase another *Abbey Road* track) Anyone wanting to know the state of the Beatles at that time need only listen to this song — the pain and disintegration are dramatized musically and verbally.

"Carry That Weight" leads to the final lap of the *Abbey Road* medley. Will there be a resolution to this tension and anguish? Stay tuned for the next song.

Originally published November 29, 2013 at http://somethingelsereviews.com/2013/11/29/deep-beatles-carry-that-weight-from-abbey-road-1969/

"The End"
Abbey Road (1969)

The final section of the *Abbey Road* medley also symbolizes the Beatles winding down their careers. Ringo Starr's furious drum solo; the epic guitar "battle" between Paul McCartney, John Lennon, and George Harrison; the tight harmonies; and the legendary final verse lead up to "The End." With this track, the Beatles went out at the top of their game, providing fans with a perfect summary of the 1960s spirit.

Evidence points to McCartney as the main composer, as Lennon famously disliked the *Abbey Road* medley — even though he contributed some tracks. In 1980, Lennon dismissed "The End" as: "Paul again, the unfinished song, right? Just a piece at the end. He had a line in it [sings] 'And in the end, the love you get is equal to the love you give [sic],' which is a very cosmic, philosophical line. Which again proves that if he wants to, he can think." Obviously Lennon misquoted the final line, but he clearly recognized the simple elegance of that lyric. McCartney later told biographer Barry Miles that he wanted to end the album on a couplet to add meaning to the medley.

McCartney also wanted to give all four of them a turn in the spotlight; Starr, however, hated solos and remained skeptical. "Ringo would never do drum solos. He hated drummers who did lengthy drum solos," McCartney recalled in 1988. "But because of this medley I said, 'Well, a token solo?' and he really dug his heels in and didn't want to do it. But after a little bit of gentle persuasion I said, 'it wouldn't be Buddy Rich gone mad,' because I think that's what he didn't want to do. … anyway we came to this compromise, it was a kind of a solo. I don't think he's done one since."

In a 2009 interview with *MusicRadar*, sound engineer Geoff Emerick added "the thing that always amused me was how much persuasion it took to get Ringo to play that solo. Usually, you have to try to talk drummers out of doing solos! (Laughs.) He didn't want to do it, but everybody said, 'No, no, it'll be fantastic!' So he gave in — and turned in a bloody marvelous performance!" As for the ending guitar jam, Emerick recalled it as a spontaneous decision, although Harrison supposedly needed extra encouragement to participate.

Recording began on "The End" — now bearing the working title "The Ending" — on July 23, 1969. They taped seven takes of the track, with Starr slightly altering his drum solo each time. The group selected the final take as the best backing track. According to the *Beatles Bible*, the song originally clocked in at 1:20; the Beatles soon lengthened it to 2:20 with extra overdubs, including the orchestral section. Once they completed the backing track, the group did not return to "The End" until August 5, when they laid down the vocal tracks.

Additional drums, bass, and guitar were recorded August 7 and 8, the former date being most significant. On this day, Lennon, McCartney, and Harrison played their guitar solos live. As Emerick remembered it: "The order was Paul first, then George, then John, and they went back and forth. They ran down their ideas a few times and before you knew it, they were ready to go. Their amps were lined up together and we recorded their parts on one track." The emotion one hears in the track was sincere. "You could really see the joy in their faces as they played; it was like they were teenagers again. One take was all we needed. The musical telepathy between them was mind-boggling," Emerick told *MusicRadar*. According to the *Beatles Bible*, the trio was supposed to play for 22 bars, but an additional edit extended the section to 28. On the same day, the three also recorded the "love you" chant.

To complete most of the instrumental track, the orchestra entered Abbey Road to lay down their section on August 15. In Mark Lewisohn's *The Complete Beatles Recording Sessions*, engineer Alan Brown marveled at the size and cost of this session. "The orchestral overdub for 'The End' was the most elaborate I have ever heard: a 30-piece playing for not too many seconds ... and mixed about 40 dBs down. It cost a lot of money: all the musicians have to be paid, fed and watered; I screw every pound note out of it whenever I play the record!" The final addition to "The End" took place on August 18, when McCartney overdubbed the piano notes introducing the "and in the end" line.

Judging by the *Anthology 3* version, the Beatles and George Martin experimented with editing and other effects. One can hear McCartney, Harrison, and Lennon "warming up" their guitars, with (presumably) Harrison playing an additional solo. Starr performs slightly different drum fills at the beginning. The orchestra also figures more prominently, with horns resounding over the final "love you" chants. A sustained chord, very similar to the never ending "A Day in the Life" piano chord, lingers after the song ends.

The Beatles placed "The End" at a perfect place in the medley, and not simply because it signals the apparent end of *Abbey Road*. After the angst expressed in "Carry That Weight" and the "You Never Give Me Your Money" reprise, "The End" injects pure adrenaline and joy into the proceedings. Even though the group has experienced strife and money woes, they argue, they remain four musicians who love to perform together. As Starr's drums and blazing guitars crash into the medley, interrupting the downward spiral of "Weight," McCartney asks in his best rock and roll voice whether the listener will be in his dreams that evening. This style recalls his vocals on "Helter Skelter" and even earlier cuts like his cover of "Kansas City/Hey-Hey-Hey-Hey." Through his singing, McCartney demonstrates that the Beatles never lost sight of their R&B roots.

Then comes one of the best moments: Starr's powerful solo. It might not be as technical or sophisticated as Buddy Rich, but it anchors the track and adds excitement. To enhance this unbridled enthusiasm, McCartney, Harrison, and Lennon unleash their dueling solos Each has their own sound and style, reflective of their personalities. One can imagine the three of them in the studio, thinking that this would be the last time they would perform together, and deciding to go out with a sonic boom. They unquestioningly accomplish this goal, jamming as they probably did in their earliest days as Beatles. The three chant "love you" in the background, their harmonies subtle but tight. Interwoven in this audial blast is the orchestra, and all reach a climax again suggestive of "A Day in the Life."

The music briefly drops out to just McCartney and his piano, serving as the prologue to the Beatles' philosophy: "And in the end, the love you take — is equal to the love you make." Harrison and Lennon join in the last two lines, then the three sing an ascending note as the orchestra and band rises, eventually reaching the conclusion.

Throughout the medley, the Beatles dramatize their highs and lows, and illustrate how they had grown as musicians. "The End" effectively summarizes their career trajectory as well as the end of the 1960s. Their "All You Need Is Love" message resounds, and by inserting it as the final line to the medley and the entire *Abbey Road* album, they argue that love is the message the group wants to send to fans. Most of their songs addressed love — some romantic, some platonic, some paternal, some otherwise familial — in some form. The '60s counterculture movement also promoted the issue through protests, sexual liberation, and music, and the Beatles helped shape that era. For those reasons as well as representing the final days of the Beatles, "The End" serves as more than a mere final track to an album. McCartney further explained these intentions in 1994:

> We were looking for the end to an album, and 'In the end the love you take is equal to the love you make' just came into my head . . . I can't think of anything much better as a philosophy, because all you need is love. It still is what you need . . . So, you know, I'm very proud to be in the band that did that song, and that thought those thoughts, and encouraged other people to think them to help them get through little problems here and there. So ... we done good!

Originally published December 13, 2013 at http://somethingelsereviews.com/ 2013/12/13/deep-beatles-the-end-from-abbey-road-1969/

"Her Majesty"
Abbey Road (1969)

Concluding our walk through the *Abbey Road* medley is the brief, secret coda "Her Majesty." At only 23 seconds, it stands as the shortest song in the Beatles catalog. However, it exemplifies composer Paul McCartney's gift for melody, and provides a cheeky ending that winks at the audience. Her Majesty may not have had a lot to say, but the song and its formation speaks volumes.

The track began life as a song fragment that McCartney brought to the *Let It Be* sessions at Twickenham Studios. Written during a Scotland holiday, he introduced "Her Majesty" to the other Beatles on January 9, 1969. His initial effort featured McCartney playing piano while humming some of the yet-to-be-completed lyrics.

About two weeks later, the group returned to the track, this time back at Apple Studios. By then, McCartney had slightly revised the lyrics, although he seemed to be playing with the words in the embedded recording here. In this January 24 version, McCartney remained on piano and sang in falsetto; John Lennon joined in on slide guitar; and Ringo Starr can be heard trying out drum patterns. While George Harrison's guitar cannot be heard in this outtake, his voice is present — he repeatedly calls out for band assistant Mal Evans.

Interestingly, "Her Majesty" took on a country twang in an earlier demo version, quite different from the minimalist arrangement of the final take.Once the Beatles decided to shelve the *Let It Be* sessions (at this point still called the "Get Back Tapes"), they did not return to the work-in-progress "Her Majesty" until July 2, when McCartney recorded the final version of the track at Abbey Road Studios. He laid down three takes, with the third judged the best.

The initial version featured a full ending, as heard in the clip at bottom.

At this point, the band intended to fit the song fragment within the medley, sandwiched between "Mean Mr. Mustard" and "Polythene Pam." Evidence of this plan exists at the beginning and end of "Her Majesty" — the crashing chord stems from the ending chord of "Mean Mr. Mustard" (probably taken from a previous mix), while the abrupt end was meant to segue into "Polythene Pam." Once completed, McCartney joined Harrison and Starr to record "Golden Slumbers/Carry That Weight." Lennon did not participate in these sessions, as he was still recovering from a car accident. When McCartney heard the proposed medley edit, with "Her Majesty" inserted in between "Mean Mr. Mustard" and "Polythene Pam," he decided the songs did not mesh together well. Judge for yourself by listening to a recreation of this proposed medley, which follows.

After hearing this version, McCartney ordered engineer John Kurlander to remove "Her Majesty" from the lineup. According to Mark Lewisohn's *Complete Beatles Recording Sessions*, Kurlander did so but forgot to remove that final stray note at the end of the track. He then secretly kept the fragment and, without McCartney's knowledge, later appended it to the conclusion of medley. After hearing the revised medley the next day, which now featured "Her Majesty" as a "hidden track," McCartney approved the change. "The Beatles always picked up on accidental things. It came as a nice little surprise there at the end, and he didn't mind. We never remixed 'Her Majesty' again, that was the mix which ended up on the finished LP," Kurlander told Lewisohn.

In 1969, McCartney explained that he wrote the song "as a joke." Indeed, the lyrics are sassy and suggestive, poking good-natured fun at the monarchy. At first he softly sings how Her Majesty is a pleasant woman, but has little to say and is moody. He wants to break through this aloofness, but he needs to build his courage by drinking great amounts of wine. Appearing before the Queen while drunk reinforces the Beatles' rebellious attitude toward societal conventions, and even typical Liverpudlian humor, also known as "taking the mickey" out of someone. McCartney concludes with the desire to make her his own someday. Now the track has taken another turn, this time away from simple irreverence and more toward affection. He has softened the blow, illustrating how the Beatles deftly skirted around the edges of censorship; they could challenge norms yet retain their accessibility and ultimate commercial force.

McCartney's acoustic guitar fretwork also stands as an under-appreciated aspect of the song. Similar to tracks such as "Blackbird," he demonstrates an impressive ability to play delicate yet intricate chords and notes, establishing rhythm and melody in his understated style. As both a bassist and guitarist, McCartney deserves to be ranked among rock's best all-around musicians.

"Her Majesty" may last less than 25 seconds, yet it serves as a fitting coda not only for the *Abbey Road* album, but for the Beatles' career. They gave fans one more taste of their humor, lightening the intense emotion expressed in "The End." Their wit, playfulness, and tuneful qualities are wrapped up in one song fragment that came close to remaining on the cutting room floor.

Originally published January 17, 2014 at http://somethingelsereviews.com/ 2014/01/17/deep-beatles-the-beatles-her-majesty-from-abbey-road-1969/

"Dig a Pony"
Let It Be (1970)

A classic example of John Lennon's love of wordplay, the *Let It Be* track "Dig a Pony" features some mysterious lyrics, raw Paul McCartney-Lennon harmonies, and crunching guitars.

Interestingly, the song divides fans. A sampling of comments on music blogs and YouTube reveals how fans either love or hate this track. Alan Pollack's "Notes On" series refers to this division: "An admittedly non-scientific poll of my acquaintances reveals that some people just don't like this song because of this sloppy, while over-the-top intensity," he writes. Typical of Lennon's harsh assessments of his work, he dismissed it as "another piece of garbage" in a 1980 interview.

Is "Dig A Pony" deserving of such scorn?

Lennon's only major contribution to *Let It Be*, "Dig a Pony" was one of the earliest tracks recorded during the *Get Back* sessions. The version that was released, however, originates from the rooftop concert. Lennon first brought his new composition (originally titled "All I Want Is You") to Twickenham Studios on January 2, 1969, when the Beatles were rehearsing material for a planned concert. As the group worked on arrangements on January 7 and 13, a film crew documented their every move for a planned film. The story is well known: The cameras exacerbated existing tensions, leading to George Harrison temporarily quitting the group. He eventually returned, but only after asking his bandmates to agree to certain terms, including recording at Apple Studios rather than the sterile movie set.

The Beatles resumed work on "Dig a Pony" on January 22, recording several versions (one of which surfaced on *Anthology 3*).

Two days later they revisited the song, playing it several more times. This time they selected a take for the planned *Get Back* album. Still making adjustments on January 28, they ran through it yet again in preparation for the planned concert.

Finally, "Dig a Pony" made its public debut on January 30; after a brief rehearsal and a false start, the Beatles performed the entire song live. As McCartney stated in *Anthology*, "We decided to go through all the stuff we'd been rehearsing and record it. If we got a good take on it then that would be the recording; if not, we'd use one of the earlier takes that we'd done downstairs in the basement." Originally produced by George Martin, an edited, Phil Spector-produced version would ultimately appear on *Let It Be* a year later.

Interestingly, Spector chose to edit out the repeated "All I want is you" phrase at the beginning and end of the track; Harrison sang backup on those sections of this rendition of "Dig a Pony." Yet another version exists: on *Let It Be ... Naked*, an edit of the rooftop performance and another version recorded on a different date is included. Billy Preston's gospel-tinged piano can be heard more clearly in the *Naked* version as well.

The ambiguous lyrics challenge the listener, an intentional move on Lennon's part. Asked to explain "Dig a Pony" in a 1972 interview, Lennon responded "I was just having fun with words. It was literally a nonsense song. You just take words and you stick them together, and you see if they have any meaning. Some of them do and some of them don't." Clearly, he wanted fans to decipher the words. As the *Beatles Bible* points out, some clearer references exist — such as "pick a moondog" (a possible nod to a previous band moniker for the Beatles, "Johnny and the Moondogs") and "I roll a stoney" (a reference to pals the Rolling Stones?).

The lineup included Lennon on lead vocals and rhythm guitar; McCartney on harmony vocals and bass; Harrison on additional harmony vocals and lead guitar; Ringo Starr on drums; and Preston on keyboards. Preston's tasteful but passionate piano perfectly complements the deep guitars and bass, while Starr's drumming is understated but effective. The harmonies emphasize key lines, particularly the climactic "all I want is you" lyric.

Pollack discusses how Lennon assumes two voices in "Dig A

Pony"; he labels them the "Exhorting Prophet" and the "Love Obsessed Screamer." These simplistic categorizations beg for an alternative reading, namely a sequel to "Nowhere Man." Lennon mocks someone who claims to possess rare knowledge. He calmly sings the lyrics, communicating seemingly philosophical statements.

Unlike "The Word" or "All You Need Is Love," however, these words mean nothing. "I dig a pony; well, you can celebrate anything you want," he begins, soon followed by head-scratching lines like "you can syndicate any boat you row." The verse "you can imitate anyone you know" may be another clue that the narrator is wearing a mask, spouting rhetoric he may have heard someone else say. Yet, as Lennon discussed in later interviews, the words are largely nonsense.

The only time his voice rises in passion is when he yells how much he desires his beloved. In 1969 he and Yoko Ono were in the early days of their romance, with love consuming the singer/songwriter. He further explored the theme in another *Let It Be*-era track, "Don't Let Me Down," as well as *Abbey Road's* "I Want You (She's So Heavy)."

While the "Love Obsessed Screamer" label may be true, another persona emerges. His raspy voice, increasing in volume and intensity, rises above his previously inhibited delivery only during these lines. Unlike the pseudo-philosophy spewed forth in previous lyrics, only the his desire holds truth and power for the narrator. For him, his love for Ono supersedes everything else, rendering other words meaningless.

Lennon and McCartney then harmonize on the word "because," signaling a change in direction and tone. From that moment, Lennon resumes his false philosopher pose, only breaking through when discussing love and lust. In other words, he fluctuates between the "Nowhere Man" and a wiser, more emotional, and less inhibited John Lennon.

"Dig a Pony" may seem unpolished in contrast to *Abbey Road* album tracks, thus has been dismissed as a throwaway. Yet the lyrics contain complexity beneath the surface, and the rumbling guitars, gospel-tinged piano, skilled drumming, and tight harmonies elevate the song from *Let It Be* curiosity to a prime example of Lennon's sophisticated wordplay.

Originally published October 17, 2014 at http://somethingelsereviews.com/ 2014/10/17/deep-beatles-dig-a-pony/

"I've Got a Feeling"
Let It Be (1970)

Volumes have been written on the Lennon/McCartney dynamic, after point/counterpoint exchanges graced "We Can Work It Out," "Getting Better," and "She's Leaving Home." One of their finest moments as a duo occurred during the troubled *Get Back* sessions.

Like many of the tracks that would surface on *Let It Be*, "I've Got A Feeling" has a complicated history, but its sheer power and engaging blending of Paul McCartney and John Lennon's perspectives makes it an unforgettable moment in the band's catalog.

Like "A Day in the Life," "I've Got A Feeling" consists of two separate songs combined; McCartney penned the section referring to the title, while Lennon contributed a song initially dubbed "Everyone Had A Hard Year," a track he previously brought to the *White Album* sessions. The lyrics could refer to the turmoil in Lennon's life, as he was recovering from a divorce, heroin addiction, Yoko Ono's miscarriage, and an infamous drug bust. Clearly Lennon originally intended the song to be a tender ballad, very much in the vein of "Julia." Another version, where Lennon and Ono croon the song fragment together, even contains a guitar riff similar to "Julia."

Other reports claim the song also derives from a January 14, 1969 jam session, recorded at Twickenham Studios. Due to a dispute, George Harrison had briefly quit the band, so McCartney replaced him on lead guitar at this time. The resulting song, "Watching Rainbows," resembles the structure and feel of what would eventually become "I've Got A Feeling"; several bootleg compilations contain "Watching Rainbows," including the *Black Album*.

Meanwhile, McCartney used his own life experience for his

composition, as he was in the throes of his relationship with future spouse Linda Eastman. He and Lennon thus interwove all these songs, completing the writing at McCartney's home on Cavendish Avenue. They took a brief stab at rehearsing the song on January 10, but tensions were too high after Harrison stormed out of the Twickenham Studios sessions.

Recording commenced on January 22 at Apple Studios; by this time Harrison had returned to the group, and he had invited singer/pianist Billy Preston as a guest artist. They recorded an astonishing 29 versions of "I've Got A Feeling" that day; for the next four days they would continue refining the track. A take from January 23 would later emerge on Anthology 3, while a version from the 24th was originally pegged for inclusion on the eventually aborted Get Back album. Finally the moment of truth arrived on January 30, 1969: the day that the Beatles performed in public for the last time, on top of the Apple building's rooftop.

On a bitterly cold day, the Beatles (plus Preston) performed some of their new tracks for 42 minutes, according to the *Beatles Bible*. Deep in the basement studio, producer George Martin, engineer Glyn Johns, and tape operator Alan Parsons were recording the concert. As with "Get Back," "Don't Let Me Down," and "Dig A Pony," the Beatles performed "I've Got A Feeling" twice; the first take appeared on the *Let It Be* album and in the film, while a combination of the two versions surfaced on the *Let It Be … Naked* disc.

Martin and Johns completed the stereo mix of "I've Got A Feeling" on February 5, although this mix was never used. Their second attempt on March 13 was intended for inclusion on the *Get Back* album, but soon Lennon would reject the proposed LP, and the tapes were shelved. A year later, Harrison and Lennon lobbied for "Wall of Sound" producer Phil Spector to sort through the material, remix the songs, and release the best tracks as the *Let It Be* album. The rest is history: McCartney famously hated Spector's treatment, finally remastering and releasing his vision of the album as 2003's *Let It Be…Naked*.

Why does "I've Got A Feeling" remain an underrated Beatles rocker? First, a distorted rhythm guitar crunches through the mix, adding a harder edge to the track. The lead guitar sharply pierces through the noise, and it particularly soars during the descending note solo. Ringo Starr's hard-drumming style propels the track, emphasizing the harder sound. McCartney's bass booms in the mix, while Preston's piano lends a soulful tone, furthering stressing the Beatles' R&B roots.

What consistently thrills, however, is Lennon and McCartney's give-and-take lyrics. McCartney's words are optimistic and celebratory: he has a feeling that he cannot mask, but must share with the world. While he sings these lines in a clear and straightforward voice, he almost unintelligibly screams the track's most romantic themes. After years of wandering the earth looking for the right person, he finally finds "the one" and laments that he did not find her sooner. The music then drops out, leaving Harrison's guitar to guide the listener back from this highly emotional moment.

Entering into this mix is Lennon's world-weary point of view; he acknowledges experiencing difficult times, but suggests that humankind can overcome obstacles. In typical Lennon fashion, he enjoys experimenting with language and pairing apparent opposites, contrasting "good year" and "hard time," then adding naughtiness by announcing that everyone had a "wet dream" as well as seeing the shine and letting go of their inhibitions. The song's two sections have no explicit connection, although they both generally address love and happiness. In other words, we can all identify with these feelings and desires to achieve happiness and freedom.

The Beatles never released "I've Got A Feeling" as a single, but McCartney revived it during his 2004 European summer tour. Since then the tune has become a staple of his shows, with drummer Abe Laboriel, Jr. and guitarist Rusty Anderson subbing for Lennon. While the song may not sound quite the same without Lennon's subtle, gritty vocals, "I've Got A Feeling" remains one of *Let It Be's* best tracks, and an example of how a band in strife can pull together to create stirring music.

Originally published February 1, 2013 at http://somethingelsereviews.com/ 2013/02/01/deep-beatles-ive-got-a-feeling-1970/

"For You Blue"
Let It Be (1970)

Unlike many bands, the Beatles' B-sides were often just as good, if not better, than the A-side single. Case in point: "For You Blue," the B-side to the hit single "The Long and Winding Road." While "Long and Winding" certainly contained great emotion, "For You Blue" represents pure George Harrison, a man who enjoyed blues and country just as much as rock. In *I Me Mine,* Harrison described this fun tune as "a simple 12-bar song following all the normal 12-bar principles, except that it's happy-go-lucky!" Indeed, Harrison's many asides and chuckles during the track demonstrate how much fun he was experiencing while recording it. This optimism is remarkable considering the origins of "For You Blue": the infamous *Get Back* sessions.

Reportedly then-wife Patti Boyd once again served as Harrison's muse, with him penning lyrics such as "Because you're sweet and lovely girl, I love you" in her honor. After writing the song in late 1968, Harrison presented it to the Beatles in January 1969, when they were deep into the *Get Back* sessions (later compiled into the *Let It Be* album). The Beatles rehearsed the track 15 times at Twickenham Studios, according to Beatles researcher Robert Fontenot; much of this footage can be found on bootlegs such as *Thirty Days.*

Unlike other tracks, "For You Blue" did not vary greatly from take to take, except for Harrison later substituting "it's true" to avoid repeating "I love you" and "I do" too many times. *The Beatles Bible* reports the band recording the song in six takes on January 25, 1969, the last being deemed the best version.

"For You Blue" contains what would become a trademark of

Harrison's songs: slide guitar. Therefore, many listeners assume that Harrison plays lead throughout the track. Surprisingly, it was John Lennon who performed the solos on lap steel guitar, using a shotgun shell as a slide. The long out-of-print *Let It Be* film shows Lennon executing the solos, leaning over the guitar while laboriously executing the notes. Harrison can be heard encouraging Lennon in the endeavor, yelling "Go, Johnny, go!" and "Elmore James' got nothing on this baby," a reference to another slide guitar master. While a blues track, Harrison sings in falsetto, his voice floating over the guitar, piano, and shuffling drum beat. One gets the sense of the four sitting in a living room, just jamming for fun. Harrison's ad-libbed lines of "same ol' twelve bar blues" and the final line, "I'm living the blues," add to the song's charm and upbeat spirit.

As is well-known, the Beatles would soon abandon the sessions, later regrouping for the *Abbey Road* album. At Lennon's urging, the band turned over the *Get Back* session tapes to producer Phil Spector, who would salvage the best tracks, add more production (or overproduction, depending on one's opinion), and release the album as *Let It Be*. To further refine "For You Blue," Spector called in Harrison to contribute a new lead vocal, which he did over January 4 and 8, 1970.

In true eccentric Spector fashion, he experimented with the track by creating a 16-second loop of the instrumental break, inserting snippets of dialogue from the *Let It Be* movie. Wisely he later abandoned the idea, retaining only Lennon saying "Queen says no to pot-smoking FBI members," which strangely introduces "For You Blue" on the original *Let It Be* soundtrack.

Subsequently on May 11, 1970, the Beatles released "The Long and Winding Road" as a U.S. single, with "For You Blue" gracing the B-side. The McCartney-composed track reached No. 1, and Billboard listed "For You Blue" on its charts as well, per its then-policy of listing the A and B sides of a 45. But "For You Blue" was never considered a "true" No. 1 — as Fontenot correctly points out, the song was excluded from the 2000 *1* compilation. However, the bluesy track should not be overlooked, as it features some exquisite guitar playing, and demonstrates how Lennon is often underrated as a guitarist.

True to many Beatles tracks, "For You Blue" is available in several versions. One of the six takes from January 25, 1969 is included on the *Anthology 3* compilation, and the take included in the film graces the *Let It Be...Naked* album. As a solo artist, Harrison revisited the track, performing it during his ill-fated 1974 Dark Horse tour. During the 2002 *Concert for George*, McCartney performed a spirited version as a tribute to his friend.

Which version of "For You Blue" is superior — the original, *Anthology*, or *Naked* version? That question remains open for many fans, as all these takes possess great qualities. What remains constant, however, is Harrison's lovely, light vocals and Lennon's twangy guitar, and both drive this unjustly overlooked song.

Originally published November 3, 2012 http://somethingelsereviews.com/ 2012/11/03/deep-beatles-for-you-blue-1970/

"Free as a Bird"
Anthology 1 (1995)

The anniversary celebrations abound everywhere: 50 years ago, the Beatles first reached American shores, debuted on the *Ed Sullivan Show*, and officially kicked off the Beatlemania era. However, another event occurred at the Rock and Roll of Fame ceremony 20 years ago: On January 19, 1994, Paul McCartney inducted John Lennon into the Hall of Fame, a significant event in itself. But what happened offstage proved even more important: that night, Yoko Ono handed McCartney cassette tapes containing four Lennon demos.

Out of this moment came the "Threetles" sessions, or the virtual Beatles reunion that would cap off the 1995 *Anthology* project. The first single, "Free as a Bird," was based on an unfinished 1977 composition that indicated how Lennon was experimenting with his sound and clearly finding renewed inspiration.

So, the story begins 17 years before that fateful Rock and Roll Hall of Fame meeting, back when Lennon was slowly returning to writing and recording. He and Ono had repaired their faltering marriage and were enjoying parenting two-year-old Sean. Lennon famously became a "house husband," caring for Sean while taking an extended break from music. Inspiration slowly returned, and he finally began composing songs. As part of this creative spurt, he recorded various demos at the Dakota apartment, often featuring partially completed lyrics.

One such track, "Free as a Bird," was recorded on cassette with Lennon's vocals and piano. *The Reunion Sessions* site states Lennon may have recorded three takes of the song, with Lennon repeating the title phrase, a few key lines, and the unfinished lyric beginning with "whatever happened to" along with generic vocal fills. Apparently Lennon abandoned the song, as he never officially recorded it for *Double Fantasy* nor did it appear on the posthumous collections *Milk and Honey* and *Menlove Ave.*

Flash forward to 1994, when the surviving Beatles debated recording new material together for the *Anthology* documentary. After briefly considering creating just "incidental" or background music for the film, they decided it would be more meaningful to reunite as much as possible to lay down new material. Stories vary as to whether McCartney or Harrison first approached Ono with the idea of working from Lennon demos, but in the end Ono handed over tapes for "Free as a Bird," "Real Love," "Grow Old with Me," and "Now and Then."

In an interview promoting *Anthology*, McCartney recalled the emotion everyone experienced when first hearing these unfinished Lennon tracks. "I played these songs to the other guys, warning Ringo to have his hanky ready. I fell in love with 'Free As A Bird,'" he said. "I thought I would have loved to work with John on that. I liked the melody, it's got strong chords and it really appealed to me. Ringo was very up for it, George was very up for it, I was very up for it."

After choosing to work on "Free as a Bird," however, various challenges arose. First, the tape's condition was not optimal, as Lennon had recorded the song on a home tape recorder. Second, despite modern technology, it was impossible to separate Lennon's vocals from the piano without sacrificing even more sound quality. Finally, original Beatles producer George Martin could not helm these sessions, as his hearing loss forced him to largely retire. George Harrison solved one problem by recommending his friend Jeff Lynne, the former Electric Light Orchestra mastermind who had produced Harrison's comeback album Cloud Nine and the subsequent Traveling Wilburys discs. This decision drew controversy from fans and even McCartney, as all feared Lynne's distinctive production stamp might overshadow the delicate ballad. Debates rage on to this day.

Lynne later admitted that the technical challenges were daunting. He and his production team spent weeks utilizing ProTools and every other piece of editing software to sharpen the sound and remove as much tape hiss as possible. By February 1994, Lynne had finally created a "dummy" or rough draft version to play for Harrison, McCartney, and Starr for their final decision. They convened at McCartney's home studio, the Mill, to work on "Free as A Bird" as well as the other demos. After experiencing even more difficulties (including that Lennon's demo did not keep strict time), they were forced to isolate Lennon's vocals as much as possible so that the three could play guitar, bass, piano, and drums, and add their own voices.

Another issue occurred when Harrison and McCartney appended lyrics to Lennon's line starting with "Whatever happened to." As McCartney later explained, "When we were working on 'Free As A Bird' there were one or two little bits of tension, but it was actually cool for the record. For instance, I had a couple of ideas that [Harrison] didn't like and he was right. I'm the first one to accept that, so that was OK."

The rest, of course, is history: those who watched the first installment of the *Anthology* documentary in 1995 well remember the countdown clock that appeared during the closing credits, which led to the premier of the song and its "Easter egg"-filled video. The song itself included even more winks to longtime fans, with the ukulele at the end and a backwards loop of Lennon apparently saying "made by John Lennon" (actually Lennon muttering "turned out nice again") Billed as the first Beatles single in years, "Free as a Bird" peaked at No. 6 on the *Billboard* Hot 100 and No. 2 on the UK Singles Chart.

"Free as a Bird" met with mixed reaction from critics and fans, some expressing disappointment at the seemingly depressing tone of the track. Others criticized Lynne for hijacking the song to sound like an ELO cut. Regardless of opinion, it gave the "Threetles" an impetus to record together again. It also indicates how Lennon would have expanded his sound, as the chord changes and Lennon's falsetto departed from his previous material. Despite the plodding rhythm and the predominance of minor chords, the lyrics suggest Lennon emerging from darkness into light. Being free as a bird is wonderful, but he also points out that a homing bird will fly but return to the safety of home.

These words correlate with Lennon's "nesting" stage, finding happiness with family. However, he uses the bird image as the embodiment of freedom: What kind of freedom is he espousing? Here, home is sanctuary, a place to return for emotional and physical shelter. Clearly, however, he yearns for a kind of freedom; based on his "Lost Weekend" years and well-chronicled battles with depression, he could mean liberty from his previous darkness. As with many Lennon lyrics, he leaves them to individual interpretation so anyone can relate to the emotion expressed within the words.

Harrison and McCartney's added lines create further obfuscation. They ask what happened to their previous lives, asking if they can really be free and completely independent. The duo's appended words suggest that freedom also means connection, that isolation leads to an emotional prison. Living with and loving each other — in other words, emotional connection — leads to freedom from darkness. It is interesting to speculate what Lennon intended with the "whatever happened to" line. Was he reflecting on past relationships, or the camaraderie he once felt with his former bandmates? Obviously we will never know the truth, but once again, Lennon leaves the meaning to individual speculation. Whether he would have approved of Harrison and McCartney's composition is also an open question.

While Lynne's production is in the forefront, "Free as a Bird" does incorporate key Beatles sounds such as Starr's powerful drumming, Harrison's wailing slide guitar, and McCartney's piano. Hearing Harrison and McCartney's vocal parts also thrills, their voices undimmed by time. Unfortunately their harmonies are buried under the heavy-handed production, and technical limitations lessen the power of Lennon's voice.

Nevertheless, "Free as a Bird" provides an epilogue, albeit imperfect, to the Beatles' story. Twenty years ago, the surviving Beatles entered the studio to experience their chemistry one more time, and "Free as a Bird" serves as a permanent record of their improbable reunion.

Originally published January 31, 2014 at http://somethingelsereviews.com/2014/01/31/deep-beatles-free-as-a-bird-from-anthology-1-1995/

Who Has the Biggest Selling Album of the Decade?

December always brings out the end-of-the-year retrospectives and top ten "best of" lists. This year has inspired decade recaps, and, inevitably, debates as to which albums best encapsulate the spirit of the 2000s thus far. Recently Nielsen Soundscan released its list of the top-selling albums of the decade, which includes very familiar names (*NSYNC, Britney Spears, Eminem) and a newcomer who earned critical and commercial success (Norah Jones). So who ranks as number one — Beyonce? Jay Z? Usher?

The Beatles.

No need to recheck your calendars — The Beatles are the biggest selling act of the past decade. According to Soundscan, the 2000 hits compilation *1* sold a staggering 11,499,000 copies; the runner up, *NSYNC's *No Strings Attached*, moved 11,112,000 units. *1* also set a record for the fastest-selling album ever, with million copies sold in its first week, and 12 million units sold in the third week (see CNN's 2000 report). No wonder *Rolling Stone* named the Beatles the "World's Hottest Band" on its March 1, 2001 cover, even at a time when Spears, 'NSYNC, the Backstreet Boys, Christina Aguilera, and other bubblegum pop acts were ubiquitous.

These figures continue to astound — after all, the material (27 number one hits) was already available in various forms. Many fans probably owned the songs on vinyl, tape, or the original 1987 CDs. In addition, the band broke up almost 40 years ago; why is there continued interest?

Perhaps the convenience factor played a major part in sales. Casual fans who simply wanted the major hits could purchase one CD instead of the entire catalogue. To this day, fans cannot buy individual tracks from iTunes or other online music stores. In addition, back in 2000 and 2001, some of my friends purchased *1* to play for their kids. After hearing the songs, their children would sing along in the car or at home; therefore *1* successfully introduced the Beatles' legendary music to younger generations.

But what do Soundscan's figures say about our current musical landscape? After all, we're still experiencing extended Beatlemania with the recent, much-hyped releases of the remastered catalogue and the Rock Band video game. Surely sociologists could research why the Beatles continually pervade popular culture. Perhaps, though, the answer is simple: the music's timelessness.

Instead of sounding dated, The Beatles' messages still resonate today. Many of their songs dealt with two universal themes — love and peace. Everyone can relate to songs that tell of first true romance ("I Want to Hold Your Hand"), love lost ("Yesterday") and possible reconciliation ("We Can Work It Out") and commitment ("Something"). Love of a different sort figures into "All You Need Is Love" — that of respect for fellow human beings. Even love for a mother ("Let It Be") and a son ("Hey Jude") are addressed. In addition, other songs inspire listeners to just enjoy good, old-fashioned rock, such as "Get Back" and "Lady Madonna." Not all of their songs dealt with cheerful topics — "Eleanor Rigby" eloquently addresses loneliness, while "Help" suggests desperation and depressions. However, these emotions all comprise the human experience.

Of course, the bottom line is that The Beatles made fantastic, groundbreaking music. Today their songs remain fresh both sonically and lyrically. While degrading current music hardly encourages further artistic development, few can argue that anyone has matched The Beatles' skill for addressing universal themes. Judging from Soundscan's figures, listeners still crave music that speaks to them, that articulates emotions that are difficult to express in words alone. It's about listening to George Harrison's, John Lennon's, Paul McCartney's, and Ringo Starr's music and lyrics, nodding and saying "I know what they're talking about. I've felt that way." The

1 album's ranking as the biggest-selling album of the decade proves that good music fulfills this role in society, and perhaps exemplifies the old adage: the more things change, the more they stay the same.

Originally published at Blogcritics, December 14, 2009 at http:// blogcritics.org/ who-has-the-biggest-selling-album

PART THREE

SELECT SOLO ALBUMS AND TRACKS

"Flaming Pie" - Paul McCartney
Good Evening New York City (2009)

This Paul McCartney track perfectly exemplifies how live recordings often improve upon studio versions. Some artists use concerts as an occasion to play deep album tracks that may have been unfairly overlooked, and McCartney took that opportunity in 2009 by including "Flaming Pie" on his Summer Live '09 Tour setlist.

His energetic performance of the 1997 tune was captured on the CD/DVD *Good Evening New York City,* which chronicled his 2009 three-night gig to inaugurate the new Citi Field.

Before discussing the live version, a brief history of "Flaming Pie" is necessary for fully appreciating the track. During 1995, McCartney was riding high on the success of *Anthology*, a multi-part documentary intended to serve as a definitive history of the band. As a bonus for fans, the surviving Beatles reunited to record new songs, two of which would be officially released: "Free as a Bird" and "Real Love," two John Lennon compositions. Since he had recorded demos of both songs, his voice was used on the final versions. Electric Light Orchestra (ELO) founder and frequent George Harrison collaborator Jeff Lynne was tapped to helm the project, a huge task due to the poor sound quality of the Lennon demos. The two singles became big hits, and the documentary garnered huge ratings in the UK and US.

Feeling nostalgic after the experience, McCartney decided to incorporate Beatles history in his upcoming solo album. He recruited Lynne to co-produce the project, and Beatles producer George Martin also took part in some sessions.

Perhaps the most telling connection to McCartney's past was a quirky track he composed (which would become the album's title): "Flaming Pie," a title he borrowed from a Lennon joke. When first asked how the Beatles got their moniker, Lennon told the legendary Liverpool paper *Mersey Beat* in 1961:

> Many people ask what are Beatles? Why Beatles? Ugh, Beatles, how did the name arrive? So we will tell you. It came in a vision–a man appeared in a flaming pie and said unto them "From this day on you are Beatles with an A." "Thank you, Mister Man," they said, thanking him.

Lennon would tell variations of this story throughout the Beatles' early days, probably in response to the often tedious questions reporters posed to the group. When this anecdote resurfaced in *Anthology*, McCartney decided to compose a song based on the words "flaming pie."

Using a healthy dose of Lennon-esque word play, he wrote some of the most offbeat lyrics of his career, with memorable lines such as "I took my brains out and stretched 'em on the rack; now I'm not so sure I'm ever gonna get 'em back." The original midtempo track featured unusual piano breaks played Fats Domino style and a pounding drumbeat reminiscent of Starr's unique style.

When released in 1997, the album *Flaming Pie* netted McCartney with great critical acclaim, even though the three released singles ("The World Tonight," "Young Boy," and "Beautiful Night") failed to significantly impact the US charts. Perhaps considered too eccentric, the title track was never released as a single.

When McCartney undertook his 2009 tour, he apparently decided to throw his diehard fans a few bones by including lesser-known Beatles and solo tracks in his setlists. "Flaming Pie" made a delightfully surprising return after sporadic appearances over the years, and the live version almost supersedes the studio original.

The *Good Evening New York City* version worked seamlessly with the rest of the heavier-leaning tracks. Drummer Abe Laboriel, Jr.'s enthusiastic style added a harder-edged sound, while guitarists Rusty Anderson and Brian Ray laid down a gritty-sounding cushion for McCartney's still-intact voice. As he plucked his famous Hofner bass, McCartney's clear vocals emphasized the loopy fun of the lyrics, consistent with Lennon's original goofy wordplay. Paul "Wix" Wickens perfectly replicated the rollicking piano sections, but this was not simply a retread of the original version: instead, McCartney and his band breathed new life and energy into an already stellar tune.

As McCartney continues his current "Out There" tour and celebrates his recent Bonnaroo performance, he has demonstrated that at 71 he still loves to rock. He remains a compelling live performer, and has the unique distinction of not only playing beloved songs, but continually improving upon them.

Originally published June 21, 2013 at http://somethingelsereviews.com/2013/06/21/deep-beatles-paul-mccartney-flaming-pie-from-good-evening-new-york-city-2009/

"Coming Up" - Paul McCartney Live at Knebworth '90

No retrospective of vintage live Paul McCartney would be complete without his popular tune "Coming Up." Since this column is entitled "Deep Beatles," however, we want to explore a different version than the 1979 "Live at Glasgow" hit. Instead, we dig deeper to reveal the dance-oriented treatment from the *Knebworth '90* concert. With his stellar all-star band in tow, McCartney kept the crowd on its feet by incorporating touches of hip hop with a dash of disco. This may sound like a risky move, but McCartney has frequently dabbled in the dance music realm.

As any McCartney fan knows, "Coming Up" first surfaced on 1980's *McCartney II* album; like the other tracks, it maintained a robotic sound that McCartney experimented during that time. The song gained further attention with its humorous (and technically advanced for its time) video, where McCartney and wife Linda portrayed all members of the fictional band the Plastic Macs. McCartney and Wings debuted the song during their 1979 UK tour (he also performed the track with slightly different lyrics as part of a 1979 benefit concert for Kampuchea), with a version recorded during their Glasgow, Scotland performance.

While "Coming Up" became an immediate hit in the UK, the studio single stalled in the US until some DJs began airing the live version–the flip side of the "Coming Up" 45. Interestingly his label, Columbia, wanted to include the live version on *McCartney II*; McCartney vetoed the idea, citing his desire for *McCartney II* to be a true solo album without any Wings presence.

"Coming Up (Live at Glasgow)" helped propel the single to the top of the US charts; for the first twelve weeks on the chart, *Billboard* listed the studio version (including three weeks at number one); during the remaining nine weeks, the magazine changed the listing to the live recording.

Flash forward ten years: McCartney was undergoing his first tour under his name alone, and his first in a decade. One stop on the highly successful venture was the June 30, 1990 Knebworth Festival, an all-star music fest on the grounds of Knebworth House, near the village of Knebworth in Hertfordshire, England. McCartney was part of an impressive lineup, headlining with Dire Straits, Elton John, Eric Clapton, Genesis, and Pink Floyd. Due to his long absence from the road–as well as his rock royalty status–he wowed the crowd with a setlist featuring a John Lennon tribute medley, a handful of Beatles tunes, and a few solo tracks. His touring band consisted of music industry pros: ex-Average White Band member Hamish Stuart on guitars and vocals; onetime Pretenders member Robbie McIntosh on guitar and vocals; top studio drummer Chris Whitten; and keyboardist and singer Paul "Wix" Wickens, who still performs in McCartney's band.

With Linda as second keyboardist and background vocalist, McCartney tore into a very danceable version of "Coming Up." This being 1990, he apparently decided to update the track by adding a sample and stronger disco beat. "Get on up! Get into it!" chanted a sampled voice while Whitten pounded on the drums. Keyboards and bass immediately dominated, establishing the song's rhythm. Using a much gruffer voice than on the studio recording, McCartney growled the opening lines asking if one wants an everlasting love. Throughout the track, Stuart echoed McCartney's lines, harmonizing with him on lyrics urging people to stay with him to learn the secret to lasting love. Wickens played an important role, as his keyboard riffs laid down the track's melody.

In this live version, an extended drum break allowed a drum machine to briefly take over the beat, with another sample of a voice repeating "yo, check this out man!" accenting the tempo. Throughout the performance, McCartney and his bandmates frequently exchanged smiles, seemingly enjoying themselves. Linda, in particular, worked hard to maintain the crowd's energy.

In general, "Coming Up" served as the perfect attention-getting opener to McCartney's Knebworth set.

"Coming Up" accomplishes what McCartney intended: it establishes a party atmosphere, blending pop with some R&B. He would go on to explore dance music further, whether through remixes, his side project The Fireman, or tunes he cut specifically for dance markets ("Goodnight Tonight," "Ou est le Soleil"). Ultimately concerts are about having a good time celebrating the artist's music, and the Knebworth '90 version of "Coming Up" certainly accomplishes that goal.

Originally published June 7, 2013 at http://somethingelsereviews.com/ 2013/06/07/deep-beatles-paul-mccartney-coming-up-knebworth-1990-version/

"Bluebird" - Paul McCartney and Wings
Rockshow (1976)

Sellout crowds. Onstage marriage proposals. Grasshopper infestations. Paul McCartney's latest world tour has been eventful, finding him presiding over a successful marriage proposal and fending off insects pelting him as he performs "Hey Jude." After kicking off his "Out There" tour in Brazil with these memorable incidents, McCartney has begun the American leg of concert dates. In addition, the latest release in the Paul McCartney Archive Collection, *Wings Over America*, hits stores next week.

Due to this McCartney media blitz, "Deep Beatles" will spend the next few weeks saluting some of his best — and lesser-known — live performances of his extensive catalog. What better way to begin this examination than to start with his first major American tour as a solo artist: the triumphant 1976 "Wings Over America." While he has included the song periodically in subsequent set lists, "Bluebird" remains an underrated gem filled with McCartney trademarks: lovely harmonies, timeless lyrics, and a distinctive melody.

"Bluebird" dates back to the *Band on the Run* album, supposedly written during a Jamaican vacation. McCartney, along with wife Linda and bandmate Denny Laine, began laying down the track in Lagos, Nigeria, eventually finishing recording at George Martin's AIR Studios in London. The group acquired two temporary members during the latter session: Howie Casey, a top session musician who played the essential saxophone solo; and Remi Kebaka, an African percussionist. While Casey also lent his talents to "Jet" and "Mrs.

Vanderbilt," his history with McCartney dated back to Liverpool. A former member of the band Derry and the Seniors, he and his group performed side-by-side with the Beatles at the famed Cavern Club.

Along with being a *Band on the Run* album track, "Bluebird" also appeared as the B-side of the "Mrs. Vanderbilt" single in 1974. Americans did not experience the song as a single, however, as it was released only in Australia and mainland Europe. Therefore it must have been a pleasant surprise for audiences when McCartney resurrected the song for Wings' first major world tour. It appeared as part of the concert's "unplugged" section, a segment McCartney still includes in tours today. Sitting side-by-side on stools, wielding acoustic guitars, Laine and Wings bandmate Jimmy McCulloch join McCartney and Linda on this quiet track. Casey recreates the sax solo, and a rhythm box sets the Latin-tinged tempo (enhanced by Joe English and other percussionists).

"Bluebird" gives McCartney and Wings the opportunity to show off their tight harmonies, and their perfect vocal blend is used to particular effect during the live version. The stripped down arrangement lets the romantic lyrics shine through. McCartney uses the bird symbol to represent freedom, similar to his previous composition "Blackbird," but this time he clearly references love and how it transcends reality. He alternately calls his lover and himself bluebirds, ending the song by pronouncing them bluebirds together. Referencing nature, he describes that they will fly through the night sky, across the sea, and achieve ultimate freedom. Tropical images soon follow, placing the lovers on a desert island, living as birds in the trees. He paints charming pictures of love and how it can create feelings of liberation and invincibility.

The live version of "Bluebird" equals and even surpasses the studio original through added guitars and deeper, multilayered harmonies. Somehow the *Wings Over America* and *Rockshow* renditions lent the song more energy that never detracted from the track's basic delicacy. Critics of that time may have dismissed McCartney for writing "Silly Love Songs," but this performance proves that his gift for composing emotional and memorable ballads that resonate with audiences remains unrivaled.

Originally published May 25, 2013 at http://somethingelsereviews.com/2013/05/25/deep-beatles-paul-mccartney-bluebird-1976-rockshow-edition/

"Little Willow" - Paul McCartney
Flaming Pie (1997)

Since Christmas is right around the corner, I planned on writing about the Beatles' Fan Club Christmas records. However, last week's mass shooting in Newtown, Connecticut, has halted the usual festivities, teaching us that life is fragile.

When such a tragedy occurs, music can be a source of comfort, a way to somehow make sense of unfathomable truth. Throughout their group and solo careers, the Beatles wrote about difficult subjects, forcing listeners to open their minds to new ideas, enact change, or grieve for those suffering from injustice. Paul McCartney's 1997 composition "Little Willow" exemplifies this tradition; while not calling for revolution, he gives voice to those experiencing the loss of a loved one.

McCartney was inspired to write this delicate song in 1994, when Ringo Starr's first wife Maureen Cox Starkey died of cancer. McCartney and wife Linda had remained close with Maureen and her children with Starr, and expressed great sadness at the news. As McCartney explained in 1997 interviews promoting the album *Flaming Pie*, he wished to write a song to comfort her kids and help himself work through the grief. The "little willow" mentioned in the lyrics refer not only to Maureen, but to anyone who has passed away from illness or an accident. In *Flaming Pie's* liner notes, he explained that "I wanted to somehow convey how much I thought of her. For her and her kids. It certainly is heartfelt, and I hope it will help a bit."

The recording of *Flaming Pie* commenced after the completion of the 1995 *Anthology* documentary, and featured Jeff Lynne at the helm. Due to Linda's own cancer struggles, the album sessions spanned two years. Lynne, the Electric Light Orchestra frontman who had previously worked with George Harrison and the so-called "Threetles" for the *Anthology* tracks "Free as a Bird" and "Real Love," used a fairly light touch with McCartney, avoiding swamping the songs with overproduction. "Little Willow" typifies this new approach, although the typical ELO sweeping harmonies accent McCartney's lilting voice.

Recording at his Essex home studio the Mill, McCartney and Lynne began working on the track on November 21, 1995, according to the *MACCA-Central* site. He was juggling several other projects at the time, including the symphonic work *Standing Stone*, a one-off performance with Elvis Costello, and various tracks that surfaced after *Flaming Pie*. Yet "Little Willow," as well as the entire album, does not have a rushed feel. Instead, it sounds intimate, as if he were simply playing in a small room with — and for — a select audience. As on albums like *McCartney* and *McCartney II*, he plays most of the instruments on the track: bass guitar, acoustic guitar, Spanish guitar, electric guitar, piano, harpsichord, harmonium, mellotron, and percussion. Lynne provided assistance on backing vocals, electric spinette, and harpsichord. Appropriately enough, longtime Beatles engineer Geoff Emerick presided over the session, adding another Beatle-esque touch to the proceedings.

Over a simple arrangement slightly reminiscent of chamber music, McCartney's voice lies in the forefront of the mix. The lyrics concern coping with trying circumstances, meeting life's challenges, and dealing with the fact that we have little control over events. While he appears to address the loved one, he indirectly refers to those left behind after she is gone. Only time will heal their wounds.

Several heartbreaking lines lie within the tender ballad, both comforting the family but empathizing with their grief. Who cannot relate to the feeling that life is too short and can end suddenly? But he assures listeners that despite these challenges, nothing can remove or obliterate biggest gift: love. In other words, life may seem unbearable upon losing someone dear, but enduring love will remain and overcome sorrow.

In these challenging times, such a message deeply resonates: It expresses our agony, but also consoles us. When something as inexplicable as the Sandy Brook school tragedy occurs, music can help us make sense of the world; at the very least, it makes us feel like we're not alone in our sadness. "Little Willow" may have described one person's death, but its impact reaches much further.

Originally published December 21, 2012 at http://somethingelsereviews.com/ 2012/12/21/deep-beatles-paul-mccartney-little-willow-1997/

Ringo Starr Plays Philosopher in 1992's "Weight of the World"

The 1980s proved to be a tumultuous decade for former Beatle Ringo Starr. He suffered the critical and commercial disappointment of 1983's *Old Wave* album and grieved for bandmate John Lennon. He had remarried, this time to actress Barbara Bach, but in 1988 they entered rehab for alcoholism. Despite the turmoil, he did not disappear completely from the public eye. He narrated the UK children's TV show *Thomas the Tank Engine*, later portraying the conductor on the US spinoff *Shining Time Station*. In addition, he appeared in numerous commercials for Pizza Hut and (unfortunately, considering his issues) Sun Country Classic Wine Coolers. But after exiting rehab, Starr decided to rebuild his life and career. After a successful 1989 tour with the first All Starr Band (which included legends Billy Preston, Clarence Clemons, Dr. John, and Joe Walsh, among many others), he signed with the Private Music label in 1991 and began sessions for *Time Takes Time*, which would produce one of his best singles: "Weight of the World."

Wanting to create a strong comeback album, Starr recruited stellar producers and friends Don Was, Joe Walsh, Jeff Lynne, and Phil Ramone. Was, also Ringo Starr known as part of the group Was (Not Was), produced "Weight of the World," a song containing lyrics accurately reflecting Starr's transformation from potential rock casualty to sobriety. Despite its deeply personal words, Starr did not pen the tune, relying on songwriters Brian O'Doherty and Fred Velez. With guitars sounding like a fusion of The Byrds, The Traveling Wilburys, and, yes, The Beatles, the song retains a lighthearted feel that cloaks some very serious lyrics. Indeed, Starr sings of letting go of the past, shedding yourself of emotional baggage that weighs you down and prevents you from truly living.

The first verse involves Starr counseling a woman to reconcile with her troubled past. Her father may have been distant and her mother just coping, but those days have passed, Starr argues. She must rid herself of whatever is holding her back, before it's too late.

Interestingly, Starr uses the first person in addressing his own problems, admitting that he may not always have supported the person. He has his own pain and struggles, and he believes the unnamed woman is transferring her pain onto him, also forcing him to carry her burdens as well as his. So what must we choose? According to Starr, you have to let go of the past or you will be bidding farewell to the future. Letting go of this weight will allow us to "fly so high," but for now it is simply a weight that must be removed. He concludes the song by stressing that we all have burdens and troubled pasts, that "we've all been abused," but we must reconcile our pain in order to have a future.

It may seem surprising that Starr chose "Weight of the World" as *Time Takes Time's* first single. Some fans may have been puzzled by its intensely personal lyrics and serious subject matter. But the sunny, upbeat music underlying the words — as well as an overall positive message — remains very consistent with Starr's other work. To me, it stands with some of his best songs, ranking up there with "Photograph," "It Don't Come Easy," "Back Off Boogaloo," "Wrack My Brain," and another Time Takes Time track, "Don't Go Where the Road Don't Go," among others. Unfortunately the track barely squeaked in at number 74 on the British charts in 1992.

Starr obviously performed the song during his subsequent 1992 All Starr Band tour, but deleted it from the setlists afterward. After making *Time Takes Time*, he partnered with longtime collaborator Mark Hudson for *Vertical Man*, *Ringo Rama*, and *Choose Love*, all of which critics and most fans hailed as Starr's true "return to form." But "Weight of the World" should not be an overlooked entry in the Starr catalog, as it represents a turning point in his life, not only professionally but personally. Deeper meanings aside, it also exemplifies delectable pop and remains a finely crafted, memorable single. Starr and his band are performing in the UK this summer;

here's hoping that he may reintroduce the song and demonstrate what an engaging performer — and thoughtful singer — he can be.

"Weight of the World" is also available on the excellent 2007 collection *Photograph: The Very Best of Ringo Starr*.

Originally published as part of my "Cutout Bin" column on Blogcritics, June 20, 2011, http://blogcritics.org/ringo-starr-plays-philosopher-in-1992s/

Remembering John Lennon's Lesser-Known Songs

In marking what would have been John Lennon's 70th birthday, artists, critics, friends, and family have tried to describe his legacy. Some articles, such as a recent *Vanity Fair* piece, have speculated on what Lennon might have been like at 70. While no one may ever be successful in fully encapsulating his complex life and personality, one indisputable fact remains: Lennon was a first-class singer and songwriter. Everyone knows "Imagine," "Instant Karma," and "(Just Like) Starting Over," among many other hits; digging through his catalog (much of it remastered as part of a box set, individual CDs, and new compilations) reveals some lesser-known treasures. This list is limited to official releases, although many quality bootlegs exist.

"Isolation": *John Lennon/Plastic Ono Band*, otherwise known as the "primal scream album," featured highly confessional songwriting in tracks such as "Mother," "God," and "Working Class Hero." His anguished, bare-bones vocals transform listeners into eavesdroppers, as if Lennon is inviting the audience to share his doubts, insecurities, and pain with him. While the aforementioned tracks are all standouts, my favorite song from the album remains "Isolation." Few other songs have captured the essence of loneliness and feelings of helplessness like this one does in its lyrics. The first words grab the listener's attention, stating that while they may appear to lead a charmed life, they feel fear just like everyone else. Perhaps referring to his work with Yoko Ono, he sings of "a boy and a little girl" who want to change the world. During the bridge, Lennon addresses an unknown nemesis. He does not expect the person to understand his struggles, but he ultimately forgives this indifference, as the person is simply human and "a victim of the insane." When Lennon holds the note while singing the word "isolation," his voice rises to almost a scream, enabling everyone to experience his anguish. "Isolation" may be a heartbreaking track, but it represents Lennon's unique ability to express blunt honesty in a brutal yet beautiful way.

"I Don't Want to Be a Soldier Mama I Don't Want to Die": Choosing a particular song from Lennon's masterpiece *Imagine* poses a challenge. The album contains no filler tracks; they are all artfully crafted works. But "I Don't Want to Be a Soldier Mama" receives less attention than other songs such as the title track, "Jealous Guy," and his jab at Paul McCartney, "How Do You Sleep?" However, "I Don't Want to Be a Soldier Mama" stands out for its unusual rhythm, biting slide guitar, and Lennon's drawling vocal performance. The shuffling percussion, amplified by Phil Spector's resonant production, differs greatly from the album's other tracks. George Harrison's slide guitar adds just the right amount of anger to the politically charged song. At the beginning of each line, Lennon draws out the words "well" and "I," further enhanced by Spector's echoing effects. The effect lends an angry but uneasy air to the song, with Lennon expressing uncertainty at following society's expected roles. The line that resonates with me is how he does not want to end up a failure. Again, Lennon infuses his lyrics with honesty, using strong words like "failure" to demand that everyone listen.

"Bless You": Lennon recorded the album *Walls and Bridges* during a tumultuous time in his life. Separated from Ono, he moved to Los Angeles with his girlfriend, May Pang, and embarked on what he would later term the "Lost Weekend" (which lasted 18 months). While struggling with demons, particularly excessive drinking, he still managed to record a solid album. "Bless You" reveals Lennon's tender side, which occasionally surfaces in his work with the Beatles as well as solo material such as "Woman" or "Beautiful Boy." The song also represents a departure from Lennon's normal sound, as the chord progressions reflect jazz more than rock. His voice takes on a softer tone, presumably addressing Ono in lines such as "Still we're deep in each other's hearts." This underrated track contains lyrics that describes love's complications, and ends on a hopeful note, that their love will last forever no matter where their relationship takes them.

"What You Got": Rock with just a touch of soul, the song features an uptempo beat and a popping bass line. The horns lend a hint of southern soul. But underneath the party atmosphere, with lines suggesting he is ready for fun, undercurrents of regret and a willingness to change exist. Lennon's voice is in full rock and roll mode, hoarseness evident in lyrics begging for one more chance. He may like to party, but inevitably the fun ends and he must return to the tedium of everyday life. In the chorus, he concludes "you don't know what you got, until you lose it," clearly referring to his troubled relationship with Ono. *Walls and Bridges'* "What You Got" is a multi-layered track in terms of meanings and musical styles, which results in a compelling listening experience.

"Beef Jerky": John Lennon, funky? Indeed, this rare instrumental pays tribute to Stax soul. The only instrumental in his official catalog, "Beef Jerky" contains a guitar riff inspired by McCartney's "Let Me Roll It." The bass line and the horns contribute to the funky sound, with Lennon paying tribute to his soul and blues background. Anyone who believes Lennon could not jam or disliked R&B should hear this fun track off of *Walls and Bridges*.

"Peggy Sue": To be honest, Lennon's *Rock 'n' Roll* album has always been slightly disappointing for me. Like *Walls and Bridges*, it was recorded during a turbulent period, and it shows through his sometimes shredded vocals and the album's overproduction. Lennon possessed one of the greatest rock voices in music; thus I feel he deserved better than this effort. Still, it includes some great moments (such as "Stand by Me" and "Slipping and Sliding"), and Lennon clearly enjoyed singing material close to his heart. When brainstorming names for his band, he was partially inspired by Buddy Holly and the Crickets in deciding on the name "Beatles." One of his first recordings with McCartney was a cover of "That'll Be the Day."

Obviously Holly influenced Lennon, and thus he pays tribute to the legend with his cover of "Peggy Sue." Lennon evidently wanted to emulate Holly's unique vocal style, and he succeeds admirably. Just listen for the hiccups and slight nasal quality Lennon's voice takes on; listeners can immediately appreciate the deep respect he had for Holly's singing and songwriting. Lennon's joy shines through his enthusiastic performance.

"Real Love" (original guitar version): During the *Beatles Anthology*, McCartney, Harrison, Ringo Starr, and producer Jeff Lynne elaborated on Lennon's rough demos of "Real Love" to create the virtual Beatles reunion single in 1996. But the song first emerged in 1988, when the sixth take was included on the *Imagine* documentary soundtrack. I love the song's simplicity, as Lennon recorded it only as a home demo. He sings in a gentle manner, utilizing his voice's higher ranges. Featuring slightly different lyrics than the 1996 version, "Real Love" benefits from the lack of production (unlike the overproduced *Anthology* track) and allows him to display his gift for writing elegant, romantic songs.

"I'm Losing You" (Cheap Trick version): While the official *Double Fantasy* track "I'm Losing You" is likable, this rendition, included in the *John Lennon Anthology* box set, simply blows the album version away. During the *Double Fantasy* sessions, producer Jack Douglas suggested bringing in members of Cheap Trick to play on some of the tracks. Minus lead singer Robin Zander, the group recorded a blistering version of "I'm Losing You," amping up the rock guitar. The cutting guitar riffs enhance Lennon's obvious frustration in lyrics asking what he should do to repair the relationship. The softer version on *Double Fantasy* sounds apologetic; the Cheap Trick rendition adds bite and anger to the song, thus enhancing the lyrics. Why this version did not make the final cut is a total mystery.

"Dear Yoko" (acoustic version): Lennon played rhythm guitar with the Beatles, but this home demo of the *Double Fantasy* track "Dear Yoko" features his considerable lead guitar skills. Like "Real Love," this version (available on *John Lennon Acoustic*) lacks any production; it simply presents Lennon singing and playing to himself, fine-tuning the track. He strikes up a strong rhythm that closely resembles the final version, but his enthusiastic vocals demonstrate the affection he had for the song. When he sings "I'm never, ever, ever, ever, ever gonna let you go," listeners can hear his conviction and love for his wife. For the deft guitar work alone, the acoustic version of "Dear Yoko" is well worth finding.

"Borrowed Time": Released posthumously on the collection *Milk and Honey*, "Borrowed Time" makes for a bittersweet listening experience. His new-found contentment shines through lyrics describing his joy over his current stage in life, yet he would not change the past. He looks back on his youth, admitting he was "living illusion of freedom and power" but actually experiencing confusion and despair. While he felt uncomfortable not knowing the answers as a teenager, now he knows that the more he sees, the less he understands. However, he has clearly grown accustomed to this uncertainty, that he understands he is indeed "living on borrowed time" and should focus on the present, not dwell in the past or worry about the future.

Every time I hear this song, it brings a smile to my face; his voice exudes happiness and new-found joy, and he embraces the future. Of course, these lyrics also inspire sadness, as Lennon never got to experience the middle age years and revel in his contentment. Still, the reggae-infused song shows Lennon at his happiest, and hints at how he would have experimented with his sound by incorporating other genres.

Originally published at Blogcritics, October 9, 2010, at http://blogcritics.org/remembering-john-lennons-lesser-known-songs/

Want to Hear Paul McCartney's Most Adventurous Album? Just *Press to Play*

"Oklahoma was never like this!" Paul McCartney proclaims on *Press to Play*, and certainly the 1986 album contains perhaps some of the strangest songs of McCartney's illustrious career. Fans remain divided on the work — some view it as one of McCartney's weakest efforts, while others maintain that it includes some hidden gems. Even McCartney has yet to perform any of *Press to Play's* songs live. Regardless of this debate, the album features some his most ambitious work, and deserves a second listen.

Looking for a new direction, McCartney hired producer Hugh Padgham, who had previously worked with Genesis, Peter Gabriel, and the Police, to name a few artists. McCartney also gained a new writing partner — Eric Stewart, best known as a member of 10cc ("I'm Not in Love"). Initially producer Phil Ramone took part in early sessions; while he recorded numerous tracks with McCartney, the most notable one being "Spies Like Us" from the 1985 film of the same title. Special guests such as Phil Collins, Pete Townshend, and Stewart also contributed to *Press to Play*. On paper, the combination of this talent would seemingly result in a massive hit, but the album peaked at number 30 on the *Billboard* charts, making it one of the worst-selling albums of McCartney's career.

Did *Press to Play* deserve this chilly commercial reception? Granted, some of the songs are downright weird. "Pretty Little Head" features almost mystical lyrics, such as "Hillmen come down from the lava / Forging across the mighty river flow." At various points McCartney chants The cut "Talk More Talk" begins with a warped voice talking of "sleazy instruments, half talked, half baked ideas," then McCartney engages in intriguing wordplay: "Digital organ, finishing stretch / Instrumentation, analogue gretsch." While these songs' meanings remain a puzzle, one has to give him credit for experimenting with different sounds and images.

The album does contain some rockers — "Stranglehold" slowly builds into a catchy chorus, while the roaring "Angry" shows that McCartney could sound gritty as well as smooth and romantic. Like other *Press* tracks, "Move Over Busker" contains strange words, conjuring images of Mae West "in her sweaty vest," but he delivers the lyrics with a wink while wielding a blaring guitar. He also fuses two seemingly different tunes together: "Good Times Coming / Feel the Sun." The former reggae-tinged song rings of nostalgia, reflecting on a "golden summer" from the past, while the latter track uses the sun to symbolize optimism and the healing power of love. The result is a clever and contagious groove fusing two song fragments together seamlessly. Another track, "Write Away," has its own charm, its foot-tapping beat and playful synthesizer parts sounding as if he recorded the song at his home, a la the homespun quality of *McCartney* or *McCartney II*.

Press to Play's two highlights were released as singles, although surprisingly did not chart very high. This is a mystery, as both songs exemplify McCartney's gifts as a pop songwriter and performer. The first, "Press," contains a chugging beat and an enthusiastic rock vocal. He instructs he lover to use a secret sign or code when she desires affection — just tell him to "press." Next comes the bizarre line "Oklahoma was never like this."

Again, the song's meaning remains vague, but the beat, hot guitar riffs, and McCartney's slightly raspy vocals add to the tune's appeal. In my opinion, the video for this song is one of McCartney's best, simply showing him riding the tube and interacting with delighted passengers.

From his time with the Beatles to his solo career, McCartney has demonstrated that he is a superior ballad craftsman. Nowhere is this more evident than on "Only Love Remains," a gorgeous slow number with the singer/songwriter doing what he does best: sitting at the piano and singing simple lyrics straight from the heart. He describes how he will always desire her, and bring "a happy ending to our song." With his usual skill, McCartney's words beautifully imagine creating a special memory when they are alone. This is a mature, deep love he is examining — after all the noise of life, as the title states, "only love remains." Unlike many other *Press to Play* tracks, "Only Love Remains" boasts a spare arrangement, giving it a timeless quality. While the song found a home on adult contemporary radio, it inexplicably never became a huge hit.

Yes, *Press to Play* contains synthesizers and electronic drums, two staples of '80s music. And yes, these elements date some of the songs. But as with many McCartney albums, some hidden treasures lie amongst the track list. In addition, he should be acknowledged for taking risks and trying to expand his repertoire. *Press to Play*, along with *McCartney II*, arguably laid the foundation for his future musical experiments under the name The Fireman (particularly the first two albums, *Strawberries Oceans Ships Forest* and *Rushes*). Hopefully McCartney will someday authorize the album to be released on iTunes and other online music stores so listeners can discover the avant-garde side of the rock legend.

Originally published as as part of my "Cutout Bin" column at Blogcritics, April 22, 2010, http://blogcritics.org/want-to-hear-paul-mccartneys-most

Giving George Harrison's *Thirty-Three and 1/3* Another Spin

When people hear the name "George Harrison," two thoughts come to mind: his work with The Beatles, and his masterpiece *All Things Must Pass*. Obviously the latter album stands the test of time, boasting a staggering number of quality singles: "My Sweet Lord," "Isn't It a Pity," "Wah Wah," and "What Is Life," just to name a few. However, Harrison released several other solo albums; while some were uneven, most contained at least a few gems. One such album that has received surprisingly little attention is 1976's *Thirty-Three and 1/3,* a stellar effort that features beautiful ballads, his trademark humor, and just a touch of soul.

The album came at an interesting time in Harrison's career: he had just formed his custom label, Dark Horse, and **Thirty-Three and 1/3** would be the label's debut release. In addition, he was recovering from a painful lawsuit, having been found guilty of plagiarizing The Chiffons's "He's So Fine" for his song "My Sweet Lord." His last album for EMI/Capitol, 1975's *Extra Texture (Read All About It)*, had not performed well on the charts; adding to the aggravation was negative reviews he received for his accompanying North American tour. Considering these problems, the album's content astounds with its positive and romantic outlook.

Kicking off the album with a funky beat is "Woman Don't You Cry for Me," featuring Willie Weeks's popping bass line, Harrison's signature guitar, and Tom Scott's deep saxophone adding some punch. Harrison appears in fine voice, exploring its upper ranges. Changing gears is "Dear One," a track that could have been an extra song from *All Things Must Pass*. Featuring church organ from Billy

Preston, the tune beautifully reveals Harrison's spiritual side: he pleads with the "Dear One" to show him grace, to allow him to become closer to spirituality. "Dear One" serves as a lovely hymn, a proclamation of his beliefs.

Perhaps expanding on this spiritual theme is "See Yourself," a song that calls upon the listener to look deeply at one's strengths and faults. A gentler version of John Lennon's "Crippled Inside," Harrison sings that telling a lie is easier than admitting the truth and that criticizing others is much easier than facing one's one faults. These blunt lyrics are accompanied by piercing guitar, as if to emphasize these points. Like "Dear One," "See Yourself" urges people to look beyond the surface to explore more profound issues.

George Harrison's well-known sense of humor emerges in two songs: "This Song" and "Crackerbox Palace." The former answers his critics from the "He's So Fine" lawsuit, stating the tune doesn't "infringe on anyone's copyright" and that his "expert" assured him that the lyrics were legal. Preston's rocking piano and Scott's screeching sax add to the song's fun, and Harrison's buoyant solo shows his enjoyment in skewering those involved in the trial. Listen closely for a brief cameo from *Monty Python's* Eric Idle during the bridge.

"Crackerbox Palace" contains surreal images and sly wit: when a song begins with the line proclaiming that he was "so young when I was born," it signals the absurd theme. Featuring Harrison's slide-guitar and a synthesizer that sounds as if it were being played underwater, the track is simply a delightful romp that illustrates Harrison's love of wordplay.

Another standout, "Pure Smokey" serves as Harrison's tribute to legendary Motown star Smokey Robinson. Since The Beatles covered "You Really Got a Hold on Me" in their early days and consistently cited their love of soul music, Harrison's obvious adoration of Robinson's music comes as no surprise. The gentle acoustic guitar and lush synthesizer set a soft, romantic tone, reminiscent of Robinson's records. "Clearly Harrison had great affection for the soul star, and this track beautifully recalls that silky soul sound.

My favorite song, "Learning How to Love You," is simply a gorgeous ballad that exudes emotion. The chord changes are unusual yet beautiful, and the band gels together to produce a laid-back sound. Harrison's almost fragile voice soars over the keyboards. His picking style in the bridge demonstrates Harrison's skills as a guitarist.

Interestingly, the lyrics can be read in a romantic or religious sense. He chronicles his struggle with "learning how to love you," that his goal is to "Love you like you may have never seen." These lyrics can be read as a man learning how to properly love a woman, yet he also states that he is "waiting on the light," an obvious nod to spirituality. No matter which interpretation you choose, it remains an example of Harrison's exquisite talents as a lyricist and musician.

While *Thirty-Three and 1/3* fared well on the charts in 1976, it is often overlooked in Harrison career retrospectives. Even Rolling Stone's website skips over the album, and the All Music Guide contains a very brief synopsis, dismissing the work as "slight." But *Thirty-Three and 1/3* deserves a special place in the Harrison catalog, as it illustrates his exemplary gifts and shows how music can be both uplifting and thought provoking.

Originally posted as part of my "Cutout Bin" column at Blogcritics, November 11, 2009 at http://blogcritics.org/giving-george-harrisons-thirty-three-and/

PART FOUR
THE 2009 REMASTERS
—

*The following section includes a special series
I wrote for Blogcritics marking the 2009 release
of the Beatles CD remasters.*

Meet the Beatles Again Through Their Remastered Catalog

09/09/09.

Chances are you've seen these mysterious numbers in the media of late, and those digits represent a special occasion. In addition to The Beatles: Rock Band game release, the date marks the debut of The Beatles digitally remastered catalog. After over 20 years of complaints concerning the original 1987 CDs, music fans will finally hear the Fab Four's iconic songs in their clear, crisp glory, as close to the original masters as possible.

A team of Abbey Road Studios sound engineers have spent the past four years painstakingly listening to the original reel-to-reel tapes, vinyl masters, the 1987 CDs, and finally the newly remastered CDs, making sure that the sound represents the best quality possible and omits any tape hiss, pops, or distractions. Finally, the packaging vastly improves upon the original CDs, including detailed booklets describing the making of each album as well as the entire original album artwork.

Consumers have several choices in purchasing the Beatles remastered catalog. Two box sets are currently available: the stereo set and the limited edition mono set. In addition, the stereo remasters may be purchased separately. The following is an overview of the stereo CDs and box set, the mono box set, as well as a look back at the original 1987 CDs, and a discussion of why these remasters matter.

The Stereo CDs and Boxed Set

The stereo set includes the 12 U.K. albums, the American issue of the *Magical Mystery Tour* soundtrack (which, according to the Beatles' multimedia corporation Apple Corps.'s official press release, became part of the catalog upon the 1987 CD release), and one disc combining the *Past Masters, Volumes One and Two* collections. As the press release states, the remasters mark the stereo debut of the first four Beatles albums, in their entirety, on CD. Totaling 16 CDs, the set also includes brief documentaries on the making of each album, all comprising one DVD which may be played on any DVD or Blu-Ray player. The CDs may also be purchased separately, with the documentaries included as Quick Time files on each album, viewable only on computer. These mini-films were directed by Bob Smeaton (writer and director for the *Anthology* documentary), and include rare archival footage, photographs, and studio chat. While the DVD will continue to be included in the boxed set, the Quick Time versions on the separately sold stereo CDs will be available for only a limited time.

Each CD booklet details recording information as well as historical notes, with reproductions of the original album art. Beatles historians Bruce Spizer and Matt Hurwitz gave the August 2009 Chicago Fest for Beatles Fans audience a sneak preview of the remasters, stating that Kevin Howlett (who wrote the liner notes for the *Beatles Live at the BBC* CDs) and Allan Rouse, Abbey Road engineer and chief project coordinator, wrote the historical and recording notes, respectively. All original liner notes are present on the CDs as well.

Below is the complete list, according to Apple (all except *Past Masters* also include the Quick-Time mini documentaries. The boxed set includes a separate DVD containing all the documentaries):

- *Please Please Me* (CD debut in stereo)
- *With The Beatles* (CD debut in stereo)
- *A Hard Day's Night* (CD debut in stereo)
- *Beatles for Sale* (CD debut in stereo)
- *Help!*
- *Rubber Soul*
- *Revolver*
- *Sgt. Pepper's Lonely Hearts Club Band* (includes 1987 liner notes, updated, and new introduction written by Paul McCartney)

- *Magical Mystery Tour*
- *The Beatles (aka The White Album)*
- *Yellow Submarine* (includes original US liner notes)
- *Abbey Road*
- *Let It Be*
- *Past Masters* (Vols. 1 and 2 combined onto one disc, contains new liner notes)

The Mono CD Boxed Set

Intended for serious collectors, the mono boxed set encompasses only the albums that were originally mixed in mono. It contains 10 such albums, plus two more discs of mono masters which, according to Spizer and Hurwitz, includes all mono singles not previously available on the albums. To be included in the compilation, the singles had to be originally issued in mono; thus the single version of "Let It Be" is not present, as it was never mixed for mono. In addition, this set includes two further mixes of *Help!* and *Rubber Soul* — the original 1965 studio mixes, which have never been released on CD (producer George Martin remixed both in stereo for the 1987 releases). Perhaps sporting the ultimate in Beatles packaging, the albums are encased in mini-vinyl CD replicas of their original inner sleeves, which incorporate their original inserts and label designs. Like the stereo boxed set, the CDs include historical notes, and a Howlett-penned essay about the mono mixes' significance. Unlike the stereo CDs, the mono versions are not sold separately, but rather solely as part of this set.

Why would collectors be interested in the mono mixes? Unlike the stereo versions, these mixes are as close to the original masters as possible. No techniques such as limiting or loudness adjusting were used, making the mono mixes perhaps the "purest" of the remastered releases. In addition,the mono versions are seen as the definitive record of their music, as the Beatles themselves, together with Martin, mixed those recordings. Stereo mixes were often conducted as an afterthought, with The Beatles typically having no involvement (see the *Los Angeles Times* overview "Meet (and be) The Beatles"). Kenneth Womack, professor of English at Penn State Altoona and Beatles scholar, explains that "these albums must be experienced in their mono format in order to receive the text, if you will, as the Beatles and George Martin originally crafted it. In many ways, the upcoming release of the mono versions will provide us with the closest approximation to the Beatles' original artistic intentions, and I'm pretty excited about that indeed!"

Another attraction: the mono boxed sets are being produced as a limited run. Once production runs are ceased, no further sets will be manufactured. The stereo boxed set and individual stereo CDs will continue to be sold.

In addition, frequent Beatle Brunch radio show and *Beatlefan* contributor Tom Frangione notes various key differences between the mono and stereo mixes. "For example, on *Sgt. Pepper*, the song 'She's Leaving Home' is noticeably slower in stereo (not faster in mono, as many people think), so much so that it is a semi-tone lower in pitch," he states. Fans hearing the mono mix of the White Album may be in for a surprise: "many folks who may be hearing the *White Album* in mono for the first time may end up scratching their heads wondering where the coda of 'Helter Skelter' (with Ringo famously shouting 'I got blisters on my fingers') went. Well, that fade part was not part of the 'official' mono mix!"

Below is the mono boxed set list, according to Apple:

- *Please Please Me*
- *With The Beatles*
- *A Hard Day's Night*
- *Beatles for Sale*
- *Help!* (CD also includes original 1965 stereo mix
- *Rubber Soul* (CD also includes original 1965 stereo mix)
- *Revolver*
- *Sgt. Pepper's Lonely Hearts Club Band*
- *Magical Mystery Tour*
- *The Beatles*

Overall, as *Beatlefan* Editor-in-Chief Bill King explains, "when you hear The Beatles in mono, you're hearing their best effort. Stereo was an afterthought. Also, since the mono mixing was done separately from the stereo, some differences between the two pop up. So for completists, having the mono mixes is important."

1987 Compact Discs: The "Rushed" Releases

Fans may remember the publicity blitz surrounding the debut release of the Beatles catalog on compact disc. First the public grumbled that the initial four CDs would be issued in mono only, and then "purists" complained that George Martin had remixed *Help!* and *Rubber Soul* to improve stereo sound quality. Letters to such fan publications as *Beatlefan* claimed that the bass channels had been switched as well as other sounds. Ultimately, the CDs were rushed into stores, adversely affecting sound quality. Beatles producer Martin admitted as much in a February 23, 1987 interview published in the *New York Times;* as he told writer Allan Kozinn, EMI "really consulted me out of old fashioned courtesy — saying, you know, 'don't you think we've done rather a good job?' And when I heard what they'd done, I thought they were dreadful." Martin further stated that *A Hard Day's Night* and *Beatles for Sale* were issued in mono for "expediency" rather than trying to exactly duplicate the sound quality of the original albums.

Womack adds that the CDs were "mere duplications of the master tapes, in most cases, with very little effort in the way of taking advantage of the digital possibilities of their reproduction...In some cases, the material is absolutely subpar– *Beatles for Sale*, for example, sounds like it was recorded from an old eight-track. It lacks the original album's luminosity." Steve Marinucci, creator of the authoritative Beatles news source *Abbeyrd's Beatles Page*, summarizes the dismay of many '80s music buyers: "[The stereo mixes of the first four albums] should have been done originally and I know I'm not alone."

In the 1987 interview, Martin discussed the difficulties of recreating a four-track mix onto a CD. "The mixes that I did in 1964 were fine for vinyl, issued in 1964. When you hear them on CD, they're not fine...you hear a wider frequency range on CD, and you're hearing things that I never intended you to listen to in the first place, in 1964." Forming an argument that also applies to the remasters, he added that "the mixes I did then, when they're heard in the form they were done then were fine; but if you're hearing them as CDs, they should be different in order to be the same. "

Defending his *Help!* and *Rubber Soul* remixes, Martin told Kozinn that from 1962-1967, he and the Beatles created only mono records. By 1967's *Sgt. Pepper's Lonely Hearts Club Band*, though, he had experimented with enough techniques to record the entire album in stereo. "I was experimenting. I was putting voices on one side or the other, I was trying all sorts of different things," he said. "And some of those experiments didn't work out well.The Beatles And in fact, Help! in particular was a very rushed album, because of the pressures of the film...I just want it to be a bit better than it was." *Rubber Soul* involved similar experimentation, and EMI's stereo mix sounded "very woolly" to him. "I went back to the four-tracks on those and actually did remix them — not changing anything, but hardening up the sound a little bit, and cutting down a little background noise," Martin explained.

Despite Martin's misgivings, the Beatles catalog was issued on CD in 1987, and remained in that form for over 20 years.

Fans Protest the "Thin" '80s CDs, Get Teasers of What Remastering Sounds Like

As with most technology, digital remastering improved greatly in the 20 years since the 1987 releases. Software such as Cedar Audio and Pro Tools make eliminating tape hiss, raising the volume, and clarifying murky sound even easier. While controversy accompanies these methods — audiophiles often protest any alteration of original recordings, similar to editing historical documents — they can be used to impressive effect. Nonetheless, Apple Corps. consistently ignored fan requests for a complete overhaul of the catalog. As Frangione explains, listeners have proclaimed the 1987 CDs "a bit harsh or brittle," particularly in light of current technology (Frangione points out, however, that in 1987 the Beatles CDs were seen as "state of the art" in sound). *Beatlefan* Executive Editor Al Sussman expresses the frustration felt by many fans: "The '87 CDs came out pretty early in the digital age, when record companies were taking all sorts of short cuts to get CD versions of popular albums onto the market and EMI certainly did that with the first four CDs, which were all in rather dull, little-high-end mono," he states. "They didn't sound great in '87 and certainly don't sound any better now and the CD booklets, with no new liner notes, were hideous."

In *TONEAudio Magazine's* review of the remasters, *Sgt. Pepper's Lonely Hearts Club Band* is cited as a classic example of the original CDs' terrible sound. The 1987 CD sounds "tinny, lifeless, shrill, flat, and canned — to the extent where listeners are forced to mentally fill in parts they think (and know) should be present." After all, according to *Mojo's* review of the remasters, "the best Beatles music (and that, of course, is most of it) is a federation — not a union — of elements, with the individual contributions so discrete and characterful that any time spent drawing them out is well-rewarded."

Then in 1999, Beatles fans received their first clue of what a remixed, remastered Beatles album could sound like — the *Yellow Submarine* soundtrack. The album boasted remixes, which entails manipulating separate tracks to create altered vocals and instrumentation, according to Edna Gundersen's *USA Today* report). The sound engineers remixed each track from the original multi-track tapes, creating a stereo update of the tunes (for a detailed recounting of the original recordings and remixes, visit *Norwegian Wood's Yellow Submarine Songtrack* page).

2003's *Let It Be...Naked*, remixed and remastered under the direction of Paul McCartney, provided another example of what modern sound engineering could do. McCartney famously despised Phil Spector's 1970 production on the original *Let It Be* album, so he stripped the album of all Spector traces, then had Abbey Road engineers Paul Hicks, Guy Massey and Allan Rouse (who are also involved in the current remasters project) essentially create a new album from the original 1969 recording sessions. This digital tinkering resulted in a bare bones, sonically balanced album that serves as an interesting counterpoint to the 1970 original.

The ultimate tease — and perhaps the final straw for many listeners — occurred in 2006, with the release of the soundtrack for Cirque du Soleil show *Love*. Although not a true remastered Beatles album — producers George and Giles Martin created mash-ups of various Beatles songs — *Love* revealed how incredible and fresh the familiar songs could sound with new technology. McCartney's driving bass line on "Get Back" made the floor vibrate, while Ringo Starr's drumming thundered anew on "Within You Without You/

Tomorrow Never Knows." If the mashed-up *Love* songs could sound that vibrant, imagine what a complete audial makeover of the entire Beatles catalog could do. After fan protest dramatically increased, Apple finally announced the release of the remastered Beatles catalog in 2009.

Why Do the Remasters Matter?
Now that all 12 original Beatles albums have finally been remastered — as well as the American-issued *Magical Mystery Tour* soundtrack (which became part of the core catalog in 1987) and *Past Masters* CD — one question remains: why do the remasters matter? In other words, hardcore fans and collectors have been crying out for these recordings for over two decades — why should casual fans invest in them?

Sussman opines that "if, as I always say, the Beatles catalog is the Rolls-Royce of pop music catalogs, then that Rolls has been taken in for a complete tuneup, but not an overhaul, and a thorough cleaning/washing." The technology and the fact that the same engineering team lead the entire remastering process (in contrast to the 1987 releases, where Martin was brought in from *Help!* onward) also sounds promising, he adds. Marinucci states that while he disagrees with the idea that the 22-year wait is justified by great advancements in technology — "I think this should have been done sooner and done again," he adds —he expresses satisfaction in one element: "One thing they did, even if they didn't remix, was listen to the fans." Sussman also describes the remasters as the ultimate fan experience: "The remastered CDs will have a clarity and immediacy that the '87 CDs simply don't have, especially the early albums. Paul McCartney has said that it's like being in the studio with the Beatles. So I'm looking forward to putting on my headphones and hearing if all that is true."

Another reason for the publicity surrounding the remasters: money. The music industry hopes that the Beatles' multi-generational appeal will translate into big sales. As music critic George Varga writes, the remasters could be the last time that albums in physical form could garner millions of dollars. According to Varga, since 1991 the Beatles have sold 51 million albums in the United States alone. 1995's *Anthology 1* moved 450,000 copies on its first day of release, and the 2001 compilation *1* sold 31 million copies worldwide. *Beatlefan's* King notes that these releases may attract younger listeners as well as first-generation fans: "It means a better way to hear the music, which is always welcome. But I think maybe the big picture is that it means more to younger or newer fans, who might be put off by the inferior quality of the 22-year-old CDs." Not surprisingly, Vega explains, "expectations are so high now for the band's golden touch to reinvigorate the record business, if not spark a new round of Beatlemania."

Finally, the biggest reason for the massive interest lies in the Beatles themselves. "Simply put, this is the greatest catalog of music ever recorded," says Frangione. "It is the defining music of our time, and deserves to be heard in the best possible presentation." Womack, who teaches a course on the Beatles at Penn State, describes the continuing influence the group has on younger generations: "While my students know very little about Watergate or postwar history, they know the Beatles backwards and forwards," he explains. His students' interest in the Beatles, he adds, results from "their own efforts to seek out great music for themselves. It's as if they discover the Beatles–and Pink Floyd and Led Zeppelin, to name but a few–through a kind of trial and error natural selection."

Perhaps Womack best summarizes the massive interest surrounding the remasters: "With this massive and continually growing fan base, the Beatles have continued to dominate the marketplace even forty years after their disbandment, which is remarkable in and of itself."

Originally published September 8, 2009 at http://blogcritics.org/meet-the-beatles-again-through-their/

"Every Sound There Is": Comparing the Beatles' 1987 CDs and Remasters

Now that the Beatles remastered CDs are flying off store shelves, one major question remains: how good do these albums sound? Are they worth they money? To answer these questions, I conducted a very unscientific A/B audio CD comparison, examining the remastered stereo CDs against the 1987 albums (the only exception being the *Yellow Submarine* album, which I compared to the 1999 "songtrack," a remixed version of the original soundtrack). First, I selected several songs that contain certain elements that could be identified: bass, drums, other percussion, guitar, vocals, and various sound effects. Through headphones, I then listened to the 1987 versions, then the remasters, noting similarities and differences. In general, this experiment demonstrates that remastering resembles cleaning a dirty windshield: once the grime is wiped away, clear vision is restored. The Abbey Road engineers' digital remastering reveals the intricacies of various classics, allowing fans a new perspective on some very familiar songs.

The following list contains song titles, albums, years, reasons songs were chosen (drums, vocals, etc.) and the A (1987 CDs) and B (2009 remasters) comparisons. Again, since this is a largely unscientific listening experiment, the track list represents a very small portion of songs I most looked forward to hearing anew. The list contains a disproportionate number of harder rocking songs, as they contained some of most easily identifiable sound elements to compare.

"Please Mr. Postman" (*With The Beatles,* **1964, drums and**

vocals): Version B features a thumping backbeat, and John Lennon's vocals have never sounded clearer or more vibrant. While his appropriately raspy rock voice shines, Ringo Starr impresses here with his steady yet exciting drumming. The background harmonies of Paul McCartney and George Harrison stand out more from the instrumentation, as are the handclaps toward the end. Version A starts at a very quiet volume, and the sound is flat and treble-heavy. Ringo's drumming barely makes a dent, and overall the track sounds like it was transferred from a third-generation tape. Version B positively rocks, and it offers the listener a glimpse into what their raucous Hamburg and Cavern shows sounded like.

"And I Love Her" (*A Hard Day's Night*, **1964, guitar and percussion):** This classic tune greatly benefits from remastering. Version A sounds much softer and muffled, while B encompasses a fuller, louder sound. The double-tracked voices are clarified, and flow together in a smoother manner. Hearing the tremble in Paul's voice during the "dark is the sky" lyric will amaze, and George's guitar solo rises from the instrumentation. An interesting note: Paul slightly hums right before the final guitar solo, which I had never noticed before.

"Mr. Moonlight" (*Beatles for Sale*, **1964, vocals):** A much-maligned song, "Mr. Moonlight" features one of John's rawest vocal performances (listen to him scream "Mr. Moonlight" at the song's beginning). Studying Version A, I found the harmonies distorted, and John's voice sounded too muted. Version B increases the volume, but not to the point of sacrificing sound quality. John, Paul, and George's harmonies are more distinct — in particular, Paul's voice can be heard quite clearly. The gentle percussion stands out, although the organ solo (which they should have eliminated originally; it adds a corny touch) briefly drowns out the instruments, so the leveling should have been adjusted. However, the overall clarity is impressive — listen for extra harmonizing during the fadeout.

"You're Going to Lose That Girl" (*Help!*, **1965, vocals, guitar, bass, percussion):** While Version A sounds one-dimensional, the remastering cleans up the vocals and instrumentation to render this classic *Help!* track three-dimensional. The 1987 CD mutes Paul's bass, and George's guitar solo sounds tinny in the right channel. Ringo's bongo-playing fares the best in Version A. Version B places the vocals at the forefront, and raises the general volume. The bongos really jump out in the right channel — I detected rhythm patterns I never noticed before. The bridge vocals blend together smoothly, creating fuller harmonies. In addition, the remasters eliminate the previously tinny guitar solo, letting fans experience the full-bodied sound of George's guitar. Amazingly, the digital cleanup makes the track sound as if it could have been recorded today.

"Nowhere Man" (*Rubber Soul*, **1965, vocals**): Does leveling really matter? This song best demonstrates how raising the volume can dramatically improve sound quality. Version A sounds too quiet, with George's guitar sounding extremely muffled, as if he were playing in a distant room. His middle solo appears very distorted and flat. As for the harmonies, the one-dimensional mix makes it virtually impossible to distinguish among John, Paul, and George's separate voices. This has the effect of dulling the vocals cushioning John's smooth, emotional. As soon as Version B begins, the introductory harmonies jump out from the speakers. George's guitar sounds fuller again, with the high note at the end of his solo ringing out loud and clear. The harmonies are fully fleshed-out, with the double-tracking effect on John's voice perfectly audible. I looked forward to hearing that final high vocal harmony at the end of the song, and the remastering did not disappoint. Paul's high note can be fully appreciated at last.

"If I Needed Someone" (*Rubber Soul*, **1965, vocals, guitar, percussion**): Version A sounds muted, with the guitar buried deep in the mix, which detracts from the entire song. The riff powers the track, as does the drumming, which also appears quite muted here. The vocals aren't as distorted as on the other 1987 CDs, but could be clearer. Version B, however, vastly improves upon the master, with the volume significantly higher. George's vocals, vastly clarified, are fully featured, and the guitar-driven melody is slightly louder and more detectable in the left channel. Ringo's drumming pounds through the left channel, and the middle eight fully reveals George's complicated yet delicate solo (which is virtually indistinguishable in Version A). If the listener desires an instant education in the intricacies of The Beatles' harmonizing, listen closely to this remastered track.

"Taxman" (*Revolver*, **1966, bass, vocals, guitar, drums**): I admit that this classic *Revolver* track is one of the remasters I most looked forward to hearing. Paul's elaborate bass line and distorted guitar solo, as well as Ringo's funky drumming, are key to the cynical lyrics' cutting undertone. The guitar solo should simply slice through the song, which is fairly detectable in Version A. Version B, however, finally reveals Ringo's percussion (including a cowbell), and John's raspy voice assisting in the harmonies. Now *this* is why I bought the remasters!

"Tomorrow Never Knows" (*Revolver*, **1966, bass, vocals, percussion, sound effects**): Another true test of the remasters' quality is playing this song, which requires the listener to indeed "turn off your mind" by donning a pair of quality headphones, closing the eyes, and immersing oneself in this sonic carnival. Version A largely buries the backwards looped tapes, with the bridge's reversed guitar solo barely make an impression. The distorted vocal effects (particularly during the first verse) barely register, which would surely disappoint John, a proponent of experimenting with voice alteration. Clearly he desired to sound as different as possible, as evidenced by the he way he draws out the "-ing" syllable in lines like "it is not dying" and "of the beginning." But Version B rectifies all these problems; by raising the volume, the trippy effects immediately draw in the listener. Ringo's drums relentlessly pound, and the looped tapes (along with the backwards guitar loop) immediately stand out. Unlike the 1987 CD, the remaster fully exposes John's distorted voice. Of all the songs I tested, "Tomorrow Never Knows" benefit most dramatically from the digital cleanup. The superb remastering at last allows the listener to completely "surrender to the void."

"She's Leaving Home" (*Sgt. Pepper's Lonely Hearts Club Band*, **1967, vocals**): One aspect of this song has always bothered me: Paul's wobbly vocals. They sound as if they were originally slowed down to fit the song's tempo, but not very well; John's counterpoint also appears shaky. Version B largely corrects these problems, with Paul and John's steadier vocals sitting front and center in the mix. The strings come through clearly, displaying the beauty of the melody. The song's climax, Paul and John's exchange from the lead character's and parents' perspectives packs more of a sonic punch. While the improvements may be more subtle, they add to the song's emotion and dramatic storyline.

"**Sgt. Pepper's Lonely Hearts Club Band Reprise**" (*Sgt. Pepper's Lonely Hearts Club Band,* **1967, bass, vocals, percussion, guitar):** Obviously the first version opens the album on a rocking note, but I've always thought the faster reprise is just as good. On Version A, the harmonies sound muffled, although Ringo's driving drums emerge fairly well in the mix. Some of the crowd noise may be heard, but not significantly. Version B raises the overall volume, clarifying Ringo's drumming and even John saying "bye" at the track's beginning. Another welcome addition is the crowd noise, which lends to the rock concert-like atmosphere. John's voice is clearly heard in the harmonies, and Paul's bass drives even harder at the end.

"**A Day in the Life**" (*Sgt. Pepper's Lonely Hearts Club Band,* **1967, sound effects, vocals, drums):** No *Sgt. Pepper* review is complete without examining "A Day in the Life," one of music's most ambitious recordings. In Version A, Ringo's drums sound muted, and John's legendary vocals could be better highlighted. The swell of the orchestra, the song's climax, should burst through the speakers, but does not in the 1987 version. Paul's voice in the solo sections, coming through the right channel, seems murky.

Finally, the last piano chord (supposedly representing the end of the world) sounds distorted, not pounding in order to stress the dramatic tone. In Version B, the piano sits higher in the mix, as does Paul's voice and John's acoustic guitar. The remastering really brings out John's chilling singing, and Ringo's drums contain more bottom. The orchestra, particularly the horn section, bursts from the speakers. Paul's "woke up, got out of bed" singing is much louder, along with the fuller bass, drums, and piano. Interestingly, right after the bridge, I could detect a cough or sigh during John's "ah" section that I had never heard before. The orchestra buildup at the end sounds breathtakingly full and loud, as does the final crashing piano chord. This is more like it!

"**I Am the Walrus**" (*Magical Mystery Tour,* **1967, bass, vocals, sound effects, drums):** For years I've felt this track could have better bass, as I really wanted to hear that drum in addition to John's dreamlike voice. In Version A the bridge sounds thin, as if the bass drops out and John's voice becomes flatter. The strings should have a deeper tone, and the sound effects are buried to the point of being somewhat indistinguishable from the rest of the instruments. Version B solves many of these issues, even reducing some tape hiss from Version A. Ringo's drums have much more bottom, and John's voice sits up front, louder but not losing any of the distorted effect. In addition, the horns right before "I'm crying" really break through.

John's voice benefits most from the makeover; through headphones, I could hear every facet of his singing, including the slightly popped "p's." The weird background effects emerge from the sonic layers, with the "goo goo g'joob" ad libbing and the cacophony of voices, static, and other sounds assaulting the ears. Ringo's furious drumming at the end also deserves singling out.

"I Will" (*The Beatles*, **1968, vocals, guitar, percussion):** The differences between Versions A and B are slight on this beautiful ballad, although Paul's vocals on Version A seem distorted, like the 1987 leveling process was substandard. Not only are Paul's vocals clearer on Version B, but he can also be heard singing along with his bass. His "do dos" add to the song's charm, as do the clopping percussion noises.

"Everybody's Got Something to Hide (Except Me and My Monkey)" (The Beatles, 1968, vocals, drums, bass, guitar): Another song I was anxiously awaiting, "Everybody's Got Something..." remains a classic "crank it up" song. However, the 1987 version leaves the listener feeling that the song could rock out even more. Version A sounds too inhibited, with the bass, guitar, and drums too quiet and Johns incredible rock vocals strangely thin and buried. Version B corrects most of these mistakes, with guitar parts, along with handclaps and general screaming in the background, much louder. My favorite part, the duel between the bass and guitar, rocks even more in the remasters. In fact, I played this part at top volume several times!

"While My Guitar Gently Weeps" (*The Beatles*, **1968, vocals and guitar):** Like "Everybody's Got Something..." I always thought this George masterpiece should have been more powerful. George and Eric Clapton's guitars, Ringo's drumming, the bass — everything should have been more resonant on the 1987 CD. Ringo's drumming seems oddly sterile as well.

Interestingly, Version B eliminates the strange sound that accompanied the very beginning of the track, and fully expands the guitar and bass sound. Ringo's drums finally get a sonic boost, and the number of audible guitar riffs (including the acoustic rhythm guitar) seems to have increased. The harmonies are at the forefront of the remastered version, which is a welcome development. Overall the remaster is fuller, louder, and definitely rocks out more, like it should. I heard bass lines I previously missed, and I could even hear some extra George vocals where he imitates the wailing of the guitar. Put on headphones and listen to this track for some hidden gems.

"Hey Bulldog" (*Yellow Submarine*, **1968, vocals, guitar, bass,drums; note that A is the 1999 songtrack):** Even though the 1999 *Yellow Submarine Songtrack* remixed the original soundtrack, the vocals and general volume are flat. The remix did boost the volume of the guitars, but not enough to match the song's raucous tone. In Version B, the piano crashes and the bass thunders, the latter demonstrating Paul's considerable skill as a bassist. The harmonies really emerge from the instrumentation, particularly during the "you can talk to me" chorus. Ringo's powerful drumming nicely balances the searing guitar solo, and the digital cleanup reveals John and Paul clowning around in the background. While the bass volume could have been lowered slightly, "Hey Bulldog" still benefits greatly from remastering, bringing out the exuberance of the original track.

"Something" (*Abbey Road*, **1969, vocals, drums, guitar):** *Abbey Road* is perhaps The Beatles and George Martin's best-sounding production, so it seems as though the remastered stereo version could improve little on the original album. Can Version B possibly enhance Version A? Listening to the two versions back-to-back reveals small but significant improvements. The differences reside in Paul's bass and George's voice, with both sounding clearer and louder in Version B. Interestingly, Version B slightly reduces the echo on George's lead singing. By upping the volume, the bridge comes through more powerfully, rocking a little harder than the original. Ringo's simple yet powerful drumming really pops in the remaster.

"Carry That Weight/The End" (*Abbey Road,* **1969, guitar, drums, vocals, bass):** I always thought Version A's "Carry That Weight/The End" sounded one-dimensional and at too low a volume. After all, this song represents The Beatles' last hurrah, and needs to sound like it. Interwoven with "Carry That Weight" is a reprise of "You Never Give Me Your Money"; while it features their breathtaking harmonies, Version A mostly buries them deep in the mix. On "The End," Ringo's iconic drum solo should burst through the speakers, and the guitar duel at the end should pierce the senses. Does Version B deliver on these points? Most definitely — the sound is robust, the bass is heavy, the "Money" harmonies leap from the speakers, and Ringo's drumming positively thunders. This sounds like a true grand finale, complete with booming, majestic horns accenting the very end. Even the strings fade out a bit more slowly as the song ends.

"Two of Us" (*Let It Be,* **1970, percussion, guitar, bass, vocals**): Since *Let It Be* was recorded in stereo, Version B is not dramatically different from Version A. However, while Phil Spector's original production still sounds decent, I always felt that Ringo's drums needed more bottom. Version B does sharpen the previously murky-sounding drums, acoustic guitar, and bass, and John and Paul's seamlessly blended vocals sound clearer — to the point where their voices are more easily distinguishable from each other.

Conducting this admittedly unscientific A/B comparison reveals the obvious — and at times subtle — improvements that remastering can accomplish. Songs like "Yesterday" have remained in the public consciousness so long that it seems nothing new can be discovered about such iconic tunes. As The Beatles sing on the *Revolver* track "And Your Bird Can Sing," "you tell me that you've heard every sound there is." However, the remasters prove that, when digitally cleaned, The Beatles' classic catalog contains hidden sonic gems just waiting to be discovered.

Originally published September 12, 2009 at http://blogcritics.org/every-sound-there-is-comparing-the/

What Does "Remastering" Mean, Anyway?

Original Remastered Recording. Expanded and Remastered Remastered and Definitive Edition. So many variations of the term "remastered" have appeared on CD titles, the newest occurrence being on the Beatles remastered CDs. But what exactly does the term "remastered" mean? The word has appeared so many times as to render it almost meaningless. Exploring the Abbey Road engineers' journey in restoring the pristine sound of the Beatles catalog provides an overview of the often mysterious process.

Abbey Road Engineer/Project Manager Allan Rouse described remastering to the L.A. Times as "a much more subtle approach, as opposed to remixing," since "mastering is very limited; you can only do so much." Indeed, remixing involves manipulating separate tracks to create altered vocals and instrumentation, according to Edna Gundersen's *USA Today* report. Remastering involves taking an original source and cleaning up any sound imperfections, not adding new elements. The *All-Experts Encyclopedia* uses a familiar analogy to explain remastering: "For example, a vinyl LP originally pressed from a worn-out copy tape many tape generations removed from the 'original' master recording could be remastered and re-pressed from a better condition tape."

In the case of the Beatles remasters, Rouse explains, each track was dealt with individually in order to determine which flaws, if any, needed to be addressed. The remasters are derived from the original '60s mono and stereo mixes created by Producer George Martin and the Beatles as well as sound engineers Norman "Hurricane" Smith, Geoff Emerick, Ken Scott, Phil MacDonald, and Glyn Johns.

In an interview posted on Amazon, Rouse and Chief Engineer Paul Hicks discuss the entire process, which occurred in three phases over a four-year period. Phase one involved listening to the master tapes, vinyl LP, and 1987 CDs, noting any obvious flaws (bad edits, microphone pops, and sibilance, or whistling and lisping sounds due to poor microphone placement or recording technique, for example). However, certain quirks such as the squeaky chair at the end of "A Day in the Life" were retained. Once the engineers generated the errata, phase two entailed correcting these mistakes and adjusting the EQ, all without damaging the original recording.

After making these changes, the engineers compared the masters, vinyl, 1987 CDs, and the newly restored versions, deciding whether to keep the revisions. Finally, phase three entailed the team of engineers finalizing changes and presenting them to Rouse, who would suggest additional alterations.

During each phase, according to the Apple press release, the engineering team (which also included engineers Guy Massey, Sean McGee, Sam Okell, Mike Heatley, and Steve Rooke, alongside Audio Restoration engineer Simon Gibson) would listen to the remastered versions in Abbey Road's studio three, where any further EQ adjustment could be made in the mastering room. The team then rechecked the revised versions in another location until they were satisfied with the results. The final remasters were then presented to Apple Corps. for final approval.

During the entire process, Rouse and Hicks emphasize, keeping the original material as pure as possible ranked as the top priority. No remixing took place — *Let It Be…Naked* and *Love* were remixes, not remasters, they point out. However, digital technology had vastly improved since the original 1986 transfer from tape to CD. As Hicks told *Variety*, the catalog was originally transferred to CD "flat," with little equalization (EQ) adjustment. Hicks states that they listened to the masters on the original quarter-inch reel-to-reel machines, then used Cedar Audio's Cambridge restoration software to "keep it as pure as possible," he states. Gibson demonstrated in a recent presentation that the software visualizes the "temporal and spectral content of the sound they wish to treat," according to the Cedar Audio website.

Once these sounds are isolated visually, they can be "eliminated, replaced, moved, copied, or even remixed seamlessly with the surrounding signal," without altering all other audio. Massey also told *Variety* that "our goal was to represent the master tape as strongly as we could, in the best light possible, to bring a fresh perspective to it. But if that fresh perspective destroyed or had an imbalance anywhere, we'd take it back a step."

According to the Apple press release, the engineering team used "state of the art recording technology alongside vintage studio equipment, carefully maintaining the authenticity and integrity of the original analogue recordings." By listening to the original reel-to-reel tapes alongside the LPs and '80s CDs, engineers were able to produce "the highest fidelity the catalogue has seen since its original release."

Interestingly, original producer George Martin had experimented with stereo during the first two albums by recording on a two-track machine so he could blend harmonies at a later stage. Two-track was defined as "stereo" until the 1967's multi-tracked *Sgt. Pepper's Lonely Hearts Club Band* (see the site *The Beatles Index* for more detailed production notes). The only exceptions to the process was *Help!* and *Rubber Soul*, where the 1986 digital tapes were used instead of the original reel-to-reel masters. During the original tape-to-CD transference, Martin expressed great disappointment with the stereo mixes of both albums; thus he remixed them himself on digital tape. These became the masters for the remastering project, although the original masters are included in the mono boxed set.

In addition, unlike the 1987 CDs, the remasters were transferred at 192 Mhz/24 bit, which was unable to be detected on previous technology. This change results in a fuller sound, satisfying fans who complain about, as Kozinn writes, the "harsh and brittle" quality of the original CDs. Each track was individually copied from analog master tapes onto the digital medium, using a Pro Tools workstation. While the original tapes had not suffered major damage, they had a small buildup of dust, which was removed from the tape machine heads before transferring each album.

Although reducing tape hiss and other annoying sounds seems logical, it can produce undesirable results. Kozinn points out that noise-reduction methods can "slice away the high frequencies of a recording, dulling the treble sound (in return for eliminating tape hiss)."

Obviously this problem is nothing new — The Beatles' first engineer, Norman "Hurricane" Smith (who passed away in 2008), once said that because the material was transferred from tape to acetate, certain frequencies were distorted. "Instruments like the sitar were terribly, terribly difficult to record, due to the range of sound frequencies — the meter would be bashing over into the red, and so you didn't get any value for money," he told Richard Buskin of *Sound on Sound*.

Another concern in remastering is loudness, particularly in the iPod era. Typical playlists include songs from various periods, thus they vary in sound level. Fans complain that the 1987 CDs sound quiet in comparison to modern recordings, so adjusting the sound level became a necessity. This technique is controversial, as raising the sound level can distort the original recording. Dubbed the "loudness wars," the method still inspires heated debate among sound engineers. As *Uncut Magazine* puts it, some engineers and fans argue that "music is being 'brickwalled': compressed to headache-inducing levels in order to give albums an ersatz loudness." Aware of this controversy, Rouse and Hicks stress how they used loudness adjustment, often called "peak limiting," sparingly.

In general, limiting, according to *Sound on Sound's* online glossary, is controlling "the gain of a signal so as to prevent it from ever exceeding a preset level." If limiting is used incorrectly, one such result is "clipping," or distortion which occurs "when a signal attempts to exceed the maximum level which a piece of equipment can handle," according to *Sound on Sound*. "Anything that has a high tenor to it will be reduced, which can affect the sound. We did this as little as possible," says Hicks, who estimates that limiting comprises about five out of the 525 minutes comprising the entire Beatles catalog. After much discussion, Hicks adds, they decided to use limiting "to compete with what's out today...so the sound level is about the same as other albums." No level limiting was used on the mono collection.

While the term "remastering" can be applied broadly in sound engineering, the painstaking process restores an already stellar music catalog to its full sonic potential.

Originally published September 8, 2009 at http://blogcritics.org/what-does-remastering-mean-anyway/

Controversies Surrounding the Beatles Remasters

Customarily new Beatles product never lacks controversy, and the remastered catalog is no exception. The 1987 CDs remained a sore point for many Beatles fans for over 20 years, with many complaining about their inferior sound quality and producer George Martin's stereo remixes of *Help!* and *Rubber Soul* and his insistence on keeping the first two albums in mono.

Purists believe that no aspect of Beatles music should be tampered with, that the original recordings contain history that should never be altered. The long-awaited 2009 remasters, not surprisingly, also inspire controversy, with debate surrounding several key issues.

To honor the 9/9/09 release date, here are nine questions concerning the remasters:

1. Does it make sense to purchase the remasters in yet another format, and is the CD already endangered?
As Dr. Warren O'Boogie, Beatles expert and contributor to *Beatlefan* magazine, argues, "the ultimate question is, how many times will we have to buy this 'catalog' before we get the 'ultimate listening experience'?" If remastering technology further develops, "will we still be alive when they try to resell this catalog to us again, possibly in 2012?" asks O'Boogie.

Beatlefan Editor-in-Chief Bill King expresses concern that "basically...five years down the road we'll all have to shell out again to buy the entire catalog in 5.5 surround-sound! I'm cynical about why they didn't go ahead and do it now." However, frequent Beatle Brunch radio show and *Beatlefan* contributor Tom Frangione argues that "it's ridiculous that anyone could dismiss this by asserting that the catalog had already been remastered over two decades ago. The technological advances alone render this argument moot. Far less significant catalogs have been remastered several times in the period since the Beatles CDs appeared."

2. How much digital cleaning techniques did the recording engineers use? Did they remove any important sounds?

As Abbey Road Project Coordinator Allan Rouse told *AbbeyRd's Music Page* founder Steve Marinucci, "removing tape hiss from the mono and stereo remasters was rarely attempted, and when it was, it was used subtly and only to reduce the level of the noise, not to remove it. Less than 1% of the catalog was treated." *Beatlefan* Executive Editor Al Sussman expresses confidence in the Abbey Road engineers: "The team was determined to remaster the albums but retain the records' integrity, which might not have been the case if they had remixed them. The [art restoration] team cleaned and polished the Mona Lisa, but didn't put lipstick and eye liner on her."

3. Should CDs have been issued as "two on one," or having the stereo and mono versions on one CDs instead of two separate packages?

"There were rumors originally that the discs would include both stereo and mono mixes," says Marinucci, creator of the authoritative Beatles news source *Abbeyrd's Beatles Page*. "I can understand why they did the mono box — to keep the two separate and not overwhelm people — but I wish it could have been different." Allan Kozinn agrees, stating that the first seven albums contain only 25 minutes of music each. Thus "the mono and stereo versions of each — collectors prize both because of anomalies like different vocal takes, instrumental lines or effects — could have fit on a single CD with room to spare."

4. Were the tracks adjusted for loudness?

This issue brings up the current "loudness war," the current battle for listeners' ears. According to *Rolling Stone's* recent article "The Death of High Fidelity," producers and engineers often raise sound levels to make the music sound more exciting, or at the very least stand out from the crowd. As Rip Rowan states in his article "Over the Limit," loudness issues can produce shudders in longtime fans. Take, for example, the first CD issue of George Harrison's groundbreaking *All Things Must Pass*: "quite literally, it sounded like it was dubbed from a cassette. And a "big" sounding recording like that transferred terribly," Frangione explains. However, Marinucci says, the slightly louder results are powerful: "I took the *Abbey Road* disc in the car and my mouth literally dropped at the drum solo [from 'The End']. It sounds absolutely stunning."

5. Are the remasters worth the high price tag?

The stereo boxed set retails at $259.98; mono boxed set, $298.98 for the mono boxed set; and the individual stereo CDs retail at $18.99 each (prices do vary on different online stores, so comparison shopping is vital). In his 2009 review, *Chicago Tribune* music critic Greg Kot writes that the costs do not merit the features: "The sonic improvements in the stereo releases, while welcome and in some instances discernible on even mediocre playback devices, will be appreciated (for the most part) only by the die-hards who are familiar with every Mellotron flourish and French-horn riff."

6. Are certain quirks retained in the remasters?

Kenneth Womack, professor of English at Penn State Altoona [at the time of original publication] and a renowned Beatles scholar, explains his chief concern: silence spaces. "I'm hoping that the remastering personnel have taken the appropriate measures to replicate the lengthy silence preceding 'Her Majesty,' for example," he posits. "As the band's later albums demonstrate, the Beatles were meticulous about the presentation of their material, and these silences are integral to the representation of their art." Marinucci thinks that minor mistakes may have been repaired. "As for the sound question, there were little mistakes here and there that should have been fixed years ago but weren't. But I'm not for a complete restructuring and from what I've heard, they haven't done that," he says. Preview CDs show promise: in the *Chicago Tribune's* recent article "Maniacs Coming Together to Critique The Beatles' Reissues," listeners expressed joy at hearing the familiar, imperfect crack in Paul's voice during "If I Fell."

7. Why were George Martin's 1987 remixes of *Help!* and *Rubber Soul* used instead of the original masters?

"I suspect they felt they wanted to make the '86 remixes the mixes of record since the stereo CDs will be the new Beatles CDs in the marketplace," theorizes Marinucci. "So be it." Frangione, however, expresses some concerns. "This was actually the main thing I found incongruous in the current campaign, as these "remixes", which were in stereo, are being tacked on as (effectively) bonus material in the mono box," he explains. "While these mixes were authorized (and very good, by the way) it is a radical departure form the uniform presentation angle Apple seemed to be pursuing in this go 'round."

While the stereo and mono boxed sets include three versions of *Help!* and *Rubber Soul*, Marinucci concedes, mono "fold-downs" (remastering from stereo to mono) of *Yellow Submarine* and *Abbey Road* would have provided more context for listeners. "At least this way, the mono and stereo boxes would "mirror" each other. And hey — it would be something truly 'new' for collectors, to whom the set is geared anyway!" On Steve Hoffman's Music Forums. Rouse responded to this criticism: "This was not the mastering team's decision...this was made higher up than us...George Martin remixed these two albums back then at his own studio AIR."

8. Why are the remasters available (as of this writing) only on compact disc?

In *TONEAudio Magazine's* review of the remasters, it is said that "if the Beatles remasters signify the last great hurrah of the compact disc, at least the format is going out in style." The ongoing negotiations between Apple Corps. and iTunes has been well documented, and rumors swirl that the catalog may soon be available online *(note: the Beatles made their iTunes debut a year later)*. But will younger audiences purchase "outdated" CDs, now that they listen to music through iPods and computers? After all, as Beatles historian Martin Lewis told *Variety*, a Capitol survey commissioned after the release of the first *Anthology* album revealed that about 40% of album sales were to consumers aged 40 and under.

9. Why weren't original tracks remixed, similar to the 1999 *Yellow Submarine Songtrack* CD or *Let It Be...Naked?*

"With those early albums, simple remastering can only do so much, particularly in stereo, because of the extreme separation of the primitive stereo mixes they're working with," says King. "I have to admit I felt that way at one time, but I think now I'd rather have the original mixes get the benefits of the new technology, which is exactly what's happening," states Marinucci. "I don't think what's happening precludes future releases with remixes and, in fact, just guessing now, we'll see them one at a time in various special projects."

Originally published September 8, 2009 at http://blogcritics.org/controversies-surrounding-the-beatles-remasters/

Bought the Beatles Remasters? Try These CDs to Complete Your Beatles Library

You may have purchased either the remastered boxed set or individual CDs, but your Beatles collection is far from complete. Several special compilations and remixes exist that further illustrate the Fab Four's artistry and creative process. The following are key supplements to any Beatles library:

Live at the BBC: Any doubts that The Beatles could rock live are put to rest through this collection. Previously unavailable on official releases, these BBC radio performances showcase the band at their best during early Beatlemania. While they play original compositions such as "I Saw Her Standing There," "Can't Buy Me Love," and "I'm A Loser," it's their gritty covers of both well-known and obscure soul chestnuts that really make this set special. Arthur Alexander's "Soldier of Love," Smokey Robinson and the Miracles's "You Really Got A Hold on Me," and Larry Williams's "Slow Down" represent just a few of the standout cuts.

The Beatles Anthology Volumes 1-3: Released to coincide with the *Anthology* TV documentary, these double-CD sets lift the curtain on their Abbey Road recording sessions. Volume One excited longtime fans because of four tracks: "That'll Be the Day" and "In Spite of All the Danger," the first tracks Beatles Version 1.0, The Quarrymen, ever recorded; "Leave My Kitten Alone," an outtake from Beatles for Sale, featuring a blistering vocal performance by John Lennon; and "Free as a Bird," the virtual reunion single.

Volume Two incorporates mainly studio outtakes, such as "I

Am the Walrus" minus the sound effects, and the second reunion track, "Real Love." Volume Three includes tracks later released as solo singles like "Teddy Boy" (which later surfaced on McCartney, Paul McCartney's first solo album) and "All Things Must Pass" (subsequently from George Harrison's debut opus).

Let It Be…Naked: After the tension-filed *Get Back* sessions, the fed-up Beatles and their equally exasperated producer, George Martin, handed over the tracks to producer Phil Spector. The resulting album, Let It Be, remained a thorn in McCartney's side for decades. Believing Spector's production too heavy-handed, particularly on the strings-laden "The Long and Winding Road," McCartney wished to erase all traces of Spector from the tracks, restoring the "getting back to their roots" spirit of the intended album, *Get Back*.

Let It Be…Naked remains controversial — some fans prefer the original version — but it makes for fascinating listening, bringing an entirely new perspective to classics like "Let It Be" and "The Long and Winding Road," and "Across the Universe" is stripped of its intrusive sound effects, laying bare Lennon's delicate ballad.

*Love***:** Often called a "Beatles mashup album," the CD functions as the soundtrack to the Las Vegas Cirque du Soleil show of the same name. George Martin and son Giles remixed several classic tracks with astounding results, particularly the astounding mashup of "Within You Without You" and "Tomorrow Never Knows." The Martins created a song encapsulating the best of these two lesser-known George Harrison compositions, highlighting their philosophical and mystical elements. A mashup of "Drive My Car," "The Word," and "What You're Doing" demonstrates the Lennon/McCartney craft of creating intelligent pop songs.

For hardcore fans only: *The Capitol Albums, Volumes One and Two:* The 1987 Beatles CDs were the original U.K. versions, with their particular track listings and album art. But many American fans missed the U.S. Editions they grew up with, and preferred the stereo or "fake stereo" effects on some previously mono cuts. By popular demand, Capitol released the American albums on CD — Volume One includes *Meet The Beatles, The Beatles's Second Album, Something New,* and *Beatles '65;* and Volume Two features *The Early Beatles, Beatles VI,* and the U.S. Versions of *Help!* and *Rubber Soul.*

Collectors and fans of the Capitol Beatles albums will enjoy these box sets (and can stop playing well-worn LPs and cassettes).

Originally published September 8, 2009 at http://blogcritics.org/bought-the-beatles-remasters-try-these/

A Fantasy Beatles Compilation: "Beatles Deep Cuts"

Beatlemania is making a comeback with the upcoming release of the Beatles edition of Rock Band and the welcome announcement that the band's remastered catalog (CDs only) set to hit store shelves in the fall. The digitally remastered CDs will enable fans to gain new appreciation for not only the most well-known singles, but some buried album tracks as well. What would a fantasy "deep Beatles cuts" compilation look like? The following list highlights just some of many Beatles songs that deserve more attention. Note that I'm including only original, officially released songs, as their many covers and bootlegs would merit separate columns.

"There's A Place" (*Please Please Me*): This song highlights the Beatles' gorgeous harmonies, again reflecting the Four Freshman and even The Beach Boys. While Ringo Starr's uptempo drums and John Lennon's harmonica keep the tone light, the lyrics suggest quiet introspection. The lyrics suggest that this place exists within the mind, a space where sadness does not exist. When the narrator is "low" and "blue," he can retreat to this special place within his mind. Among relatively conventionally-themed love songs like "Please Please Me," "Love Me Do," and "P.S. I Love You," "There's A Place" definitely stands out for its more psychological subject matter.

"Yes It Is" (*Past Masters Volume One*): Did the Beatles listen to the Four Freshman's complicated harmonies? This little-played track suggests that the answer is yes. Listen to this beautiful ballad with headphones to fully experience the band's harmonizing artistry. Their vocals emphasize the sadness pervading the song, with the narrator begging his new love not to wear red, for his former flame wore that color, reminding him of "all the things we planned." Along with "Baby's in Black," "Yes It Is" may be one of the darkest songs that the Lennon/McCartney team ever penned.

"No Reply" (*Beatles for Sale*): Anguish, anger, feeling betrayed: "No Reply" runs the emotional gamut. This tune kicks off the album, effectively setting the overall sober tone. The song begins on a relatively quiet note, with Lennon crooning over acoustic guitar and a shuffling beat. But a cymbal crash and escalating voices signal emotional turbulence: "I saw the light!" the band exclaims, illustrating the narrator's realization that his girlfriend is seeing another man. Those strong voices emphasize angry sentiments, the volume increasing on lines like "I nearly died" and, of course, the title phrase. Lennon allows some raspiness when singing "that's a lie," dramatizing the narrator's despair. Again, the lyrics exemplify the group's growing sophistication and willingness to explore darker themes in their songwriting.

"When I Get Home" (*A Hard Day's Night*): So many songs from the seminal rock film remain in the national consciousness, but "When I Get Home" is often overlooked. The lyrics possess a raw sexuality not present throughout the soundtrack. His frustration is palpable as he orders people to get out of his way, that he needs to come home to his lover. In other words, "I've got no time for trivialities." He repeats that he has much to tell his her, but seems interested in more than talking: When he comes home, he plans to love her "till the cows come home," or until he must leave. Over a fast tempo Lennon (at times singing with Paul McCartney and George Harrison) announces that he needs to return home immediately, but adds this mysterious line: "I've got no business being here with you this way." Is he speaking to a coworker? Another lover? While the topic stays vague, the romantic intentions ring loud and clear.

"I Need You" (*Help!*): Yes, *With the Beatles* features the first officially released Harrison composition, "Don't Bother Me." *Help!* however marks Harrison's true coming of age, as his interest in Indian music pervades the album. "I Need You" provides a glimpse into Harrison's willingness to experiment with different sounds — the distorted guitar exemplifies this fact — and the interesting chord changes show his increasing musical sophistication.

"The Word" (*Rubber Soul*): Want to hear true foreshadowing of 1967's "Summer of Love"? Look no further than this buried track, which features Lennon/McCartney lyrics that eerily predict the psychedelic era. "Have you heard the word is love?" they sing, once again showing off their perfect harmonizing skills. Over an upbeat track punctuated by sharp guitar riffs, The Beatles demonstrate their interest in exploring deeper human themes, that Lennon wants to teach everyone what he has learned. This song signals a move away from the "I Want to Hold Your Hand" era toward the eventual "All You Need Is Love," and the message retains its relevance.

"Love You To" (*Revolver*): Any doubt that Harrison's infatuation with Indian music was just a passing fancy was answered with this track. The sitar and percussion dominate, but the lyrics wax philosophical on staying true to oneself in a fast-paced world: "You don't get time to hang a sign on me," sings Harrison, his voice complementing the sitar's droning sound. As the tune fades out, the tempo speeds up, emphasizing the world's turbulence. While Harrison would eventually write some of the Beatles' finest songs, "Love You To" announces his arrival as a truly distinctive singer and songwriter. For another example, try "Within You Without You" from *Sgt. Pepper's Lonely Hearts Club Band*.

"I Will" (*The Beatles/White Album*): McCartney possesses a true gift for crafting simple but lovely ballads. One of his finest compositions, "I Will," inexplicably receives little radio airplay to this day. Over a gentle galloping beat, the spare instrumentation stresses the intimacy of the subject matter, which is the sometimes quiet elation of love: "Your song will fill the air," he sings, "Sing it loud so I can hear you." Like "Here, There, and Everywhere," McCartney successfully conveys all-consuming love and devotion in a deceptively simple melody.

"Everybody's Got Something to Hide (Except for Me and My Monkey)" (*The Beatles/White Album*): What better song is there for, to paraphrase Spïnal Tap, cranking up to 11? Hard-charging guitar solos and bass lines power this rocker, with Lennon's always-impressive rock vocals screaming the lyrics. The words' meaning may be debated, but all can agree that the *White Album* track illustrates how hard the Beatles could rock.

"Oh! Darling" (*Abbey Road*): Sure, the sprawling medley comprising the second side of the album (for those of you who remember LPs) is famous, and the album is also remembered for impressive singles like "Something," "Here Comes the Sun," "Come Together," and "Octopus's Garden." But this blues workout receives little attention, which is a shame since McCartney gives one of his finest vocal performances on the track. Normally Lennon would take the lead on such a gritty number, but amazingly McCartney pulls out a nuanced but impassioned vocal. Several books claim that Lennon wished he had sung lead on this song, which is unsurprising. But "Oh! Darling" should put to rest the notion that all McCartney could sing was ballads.

This list represents just a small sample of buried Beatles treasures. I'll revisit this topic in future columns, focusing on lost covers, alternate takes, and live versions. The Beatles catalog contains such a vast amount of work that one can constantly unearth lesser-known cuts. Perhaps that is yet another reason why the group remains popular and hugely influential to this day. Go beyond the Beatles 1 compilation and dig into these deep cuts.

Originally published April 14, 2009 at http://blogcritics.org/a-fantasy-beatles- compilation-beatles-deep/

PART FIVE
BONUS TRACK

Ten Underrated Ringo Starr Drumming Performances

Few other musicians have been as misunderstood and mislabeled as Ringo Starr. George Martin famously doubted Starr's abilities when the Beatles recorded "Love Me Do," bringing in session drummer Andy White to play what the producer believed was a drum part beyond Starr's abilities. Two phrases frequently occur in critics' assessments of the Beatles: "The luckiest man in the world" and "an average drummer." A quote attributed to John Lennon circulated for years in which he supposedly said "he's not even the best drummer in the Beatles," a myth debunked by Mark Lewisohn in his book *Tune In*. While Starr received long overdue recognition through his induction into the 2015 Rock and Roll Hall of Fame, he is still accused of not being a "technically good" drummer.

In reality, Starr brought a new style of drumming to rock and roll. Bernhard Castiglioni, founder of the website *Drummerworld*, explained Starr's unique contributions in a discussion group posted. He gripped both sticks like hammers in the "matched" grip style, unlike the traditional grip favored by many players. During the *Rubber Soul* recording sessions, Starr showed a willingness to experiment with sound by tuning them lower, deadening the sound with towels and other materials, and increasing the tonal impact by having microphones played on each drum. He became famous for keeping perfect time, and possesses an impressive ability to easily transition into odd time signatures. Unlike other rock drummers, his versatility enabled him to play rock R&B, swing, and country equally well.

Another reason Starr is constantly underrated is his lack of flash.

He famously eschewed drum solos (making a rare — and grudging — exception for "The End") and lacked the dramatic, pounding style of Keith Moon. Yet as drummer Patrick Berkery writes in his *Salon* article "Every Snide Joke You've Told about Ringo Is Wrong: The Least-Celebrated Beatle Is Finally Getting the Respect He Deserves," drummers are still told to "play it like Ringo" in the recording studio. In other words, Berkery explains, "they're being tasked with adding to a song the kind of tumbling fills that have a melody of their own . . . give a tune a swinging feel that also rocks . . . attack a number with psychedelic abandon . . . or perhaps apply all three of those elements to one song ('Rain')."

Listening to the 1962 Decca audition illustrates how Starr functioned as the group's engine, propelling George Harrison, Paul McCartney and John Lennon to rock just a little harder, to swing just a little more, and to increase the energy just a little bit. Starr has frequently stated in interviews that "Rain" remains his favorite performance, and the aforementioned "The End," "Come Together," and the hard rocking "Birthday" are two more obvious standouts. But his deft work graces many more Beatles cuts, illustrating how he served as the Beatles' backbone. The following list highlights ten Ringo Starr performances that are too often overlooked.

"All I've Got to Do" (*With the Beatles*, 1963): Starr is known for his hard-charging style, and he uses it to great effect on this Smokey Robinson-inspired tune. While never overpowering Lennon's searing lead vocal, Starr provides a complex arrangement that accentuates the song's stop-start rhythm. He effortlessly changes from the initially off-kilter beat to a slightly faster, pounding style, signaled by Lennon, McCartney, and Harrison's harmonized delivery of the title phrase. As the tone changes from quietly romantic lines like "And when I wanna kiss you, yeah" to excited utterances such as "Call you on the phone / And you'll come running home," Starr increases the volume to heighten the narrator's anticipation. His steady beat drives the song, and the bass pedal provides a "bottom" that emphasizes the Lennon composition's R&B roots.

"I'm Happy Just to Dance with You" (*A Hard Day's Night*, 1964): Lennon and McCartney wrote the song specifically for Harrison's vocal range, and this upbeat, charming tune features lyrics that made teenage girls swoon. Since "I'm Happy Just to Dance with You" concerns dancing as much as the first blush of love, the percussion is paramount. Starr uses a slightly Latin feel, his drum rolls adding to the narrator's dramatic declaration of "Just to dance with you is everything I need." Another tool to stress the beat is what has been described as an African or Arabian drum by various accounts. While this sound may be placed too prominently in the mix, it does add to the song's danceability.

"I Don't Want to Spoil the Party" (*Beatles for Sale*, **1964**): A track with a country flair, this Lennon composition reveals Starr's musical roots. As McCartney reveals in Barry Miles' *Many Years from Now*, he and Lennon originally penned the song for Starr to sing. "Ringo had a great style and delivery," McCartney said, thus they wanted to write one showcase for the drummer on each album. While Starr did not perform the lead vocal, he laid down a steady beat that drove the song, varying the rhythm to great effect during the bridges, such as in the lines describing that he will still love his girlfriend even if she breaks his heart. Starr famously loved country and western music, and he applied his passion to a song that forecast *Rubber Soul's* acoustic sound.

"What You're Doing" (*Beatles for Sale*, **1964**): In 1984, Starr told drummer Max Weinberg in *The Big Beat* that "if I didn't have a hi-hat, I'd be lost . . . I like it tight and I tend to play on the edge. It's a better sound for me." "What You're Doing" is a classic example of Starr's heavy use of the hi-hat. As the bass and snare drum rhythm pattern begins, one can immediately identify the song's identity. Starr is a master at the "drum hook," a distinctive riff that catches the ear. While he would demonstrate this skill most notably on "Revolution," "What You're Doing" is an early example of his rapidly growing abilities. After the beginning, Ringo resumes a steady drum pattern accented with closed hi hats, but effortlessly switches to the hook toward the end.

"Drive My Car" (*Rubber Soul*, **1965**): A multi-percussionist, Starr not only plays drums but hits the tambourine and cowbell at crucial points. He also uses his instrument to dramatic effect, employing a syncopated pattern on the snare and bass drum to accent lines such as the winking lyric "you can do something in between" and of course the ultimate punchline: "But I've got a driver and that's a start." Without his accents and fills, the song's innuendo and twist ending would not be as evident.

"The Word" (*Rubber Soul*, **1965**): In addition to his drums, Starr also contributes an essential element: the maracas. His steady sense of time anchors the song, but in addition he uses his trademark backward drum fills (due to his being left handed) to underscore the lines "It's so fine / It's sunshine." In "The Word" and countless other tracks, Starr proves himself a master at the tasteful fills, accenting key phrases but never overpowering the vocals. He does not specialize in flash, but in tasteful understatement. However, the drums remain a crucial part of the mix. According to Starr, he would not be able to repeat the fills the exact same way. "I can't do it twice the same — ever. I mean, I could do a straight shuffle or something, but fills are never the same, take to take. I couldn't do it that way again the following week, let along twenty years later," he told Weinberg.

"Good Morning Good Morning" (*Sgt. Pepper's Lonely Hearts Club Band*, **1967**): A deceptively straightforward song, "Good Morning" required Starr to execute drum fills (using two bass drums), cymbal crashes, and rhythm pattern changes at specific points. As the song fades out, eventually overtaken by the animal noises, one can hear Starr perform awkward yet effective drum fills, adding to the growing chaos and cacophony. While seemingly chaotic, the beat is always kept in check through Starr's skill. To fully appreciate this masterful performance, listen to the *Anthology 2* version without brass overdubs, backing vocals, and other sound effects.

"Oh! Darling" (*Abbey Road*, **1969**): This *Abbey Road* classic is often praised for McCartney's unhinged blues vocal. While his voice is indeed impressive, "Oh! Darling" also succeeds due to Starr's subtle yet forceful drumming. His fills at the song's emotional high points, such as when McCartney sings phrases like "I'll never do you no harm" that underscore the singer's desperation. Starr particularly shines, however, during the bridge, when McCartney virtually screams "When you told me you didn't need me anymore." Drum rolls, fills, crashing cymbals, and forceful pounding emphasize

McCartney's desire and frustration, and firmly root the song in the blues. This emotional performance exemplifies Starr's technique, namely drumming by feel. "I was into another space in my head in the way I was playing then. I couldn't ever double-track a fill. When I'd do a fill I always felt I went into a blackout. I didn't know what I'd do," he told Weinberg.

"Something" (*Abbey Road*, **1969**): The tender ballad required subtle drumming, which Starr achieves in his own style. His soft drum rolls and fills accent but never overshadow Harrison's tender words. Instead of his typical pounding style, Starr's playing sounds muted, his soft cymbal crashes perfectly accompanying the song's romanticism. His drumming increases in intensity during the bridge, stressing the narrator's uncertainty when crying out "You're asking me will my love grow / I don't know." Changing to a virtual marching tempo, Starr pounds the skins harder, adding drum rolls to heighten the emotional intensity.

"I Me Mine" (*Let It Be...Naked* **version, 1970/2003**): A blues waltz, the Harrison composition "I Me Mine" addresses how LSD can overinflate the ego. The bluesy waltz benefits from Harrison's clear voice and crunching guitars, but Starr's rapidly changing drum patterns keep the song interesting. He begins by playing a waltz time signature, but drum fills signal the song's climax: chanting the title phrase. As Harrison, Lennon, and McCartney repeat the words, Starr uses the high hat and then full drums, his rolls placing the song in the rock/blues canon. In other words, Starr's performance alerts the listener that the track is no charming waltz, but a full-out rock track. To fully experience Starr's skill in "I Me Mine," listen to the clearer *Let It Be...Naked* mix.

Amazingly, critics still feel the need to defend Starr. A July 4, 2015 *Spectator* article went viral on social media, and it featured the blaring headline "Ringo's No Joke. He Was a Genius and the Beatles Were Lucky to Have Him." In the 2008 book *Can't Buy Me Love: The Beatles, Britain, and America*, author Jonathan Gould further defends Starr: "There is little question that the invitation to join the Beatles was the single luckiest thing that ever happened to Ringo Starr. But Ringo's acceptance of that invitation was also one of the luckiest things that ever happened to the Beatles." The time has come to retire the "Ringo was just a lucky guy" cliche and accept reality: Starr set new standards for rock drummers.

As the above songs demonstrate, Starr's beat is steady but inventive, powerful yet subtle. His ability to devise drum "hooks" is unparalleled, and he set a new precedent for drummers in rock bands. Unlike previous stick men who would remain largely anonymous and remain in the background, Starr demanded recognition. Armed with his trademark Ludwig drum kit, he would perch on a riser slightly above the other Beatles, waving his head back and forth with the beat, hair flying in all directions, his cocky but charming grin standing out from Harrison, Lennon, and McCartney.

Overall, Starr elevated the rock drummer's status, and summarized his philosophy to Weinberg: "It's a drummer's back-of-the-bus complex, I guess . . . But you know what else we know? That the band would be shit without us. You have to know that you are as important as they are." Through his unique drumming style, heightened profile, and personality, Starr definitely proved that point.

ACKNOWLEDGMENTS

I am very fortunate to have met some extraordinary people in the Beatles research and the fan communities over the past 20 or so years. In addition to being good friends, they have taught me a great deal about the Beatles and music in general. Many have also advised and mentored me, and words cannot express my gratitude for their support and encouragement.

First, I thank my *Beatlefan* family. Bill, thank you for the opportunity to write for your magazine all those years ago. You gave me my start in the Beatles community, and I will always be grateful. Al Sussman, thank you for your longtime mentorship and for encouraging me to become more active at Fest for Beatle Fans conventions. Brad Hundt, Tom Frangione, and Rip Rense, I feel honored and privileged to be your colleague. Your knowledge and insights continue to inspire me.

Getting started in publishing is no easy task, but Robert Rodriguez urged me to take the step forward. Thank you for your confidence in me and your extremely useful advice — it's no exaggeration to say that you changed my professional life!

I also want to extend my deepest gratitude to Jude Southerland Kessler, my internet radio partner in crime, teacher, and close friend. You gave me the courage to take my writing and public speaking to the next level, and I absolutely love doing the "Kit 'n Kaboodle" show with you. Here's to many more years of successful and enjoyable collaborations! Thank you for everything, my friend, and shine on.

So many authors and scholars have influenced my work, and I am proud to finally join their ranks as Beatles writers. I particularly want to thank David Bedford, Bruce Spizer, Wally

Podrazik, Anthony Robustelli, Candy Leonard, Lanea Stagg, Thom MacFarlane, Walter Everett, Richard Buskin, Dave Morrell, Allan Kozinn, Andrew Jackson, Aaron Krerowicz, Stuart Shea, and Dave Schwensen. I extend a special thank you to Ken Womack, writer of this book's foreword, who is not only a great author and friend but a fellow Northern Illinois University alum. Go Huskies!

In the 20 years I've attended the Fest for Beatles Fans conventions and other Beatles conferences, I've had the great fortune of meeting wonderful people who have become close friends. There are too many to list here, but I'll mention some who embody the lyric "I get by with a little help from my friends": Susan Ryan, Sara Schmidt, Coral Schmidt, Ken Orth, Ivor Davis, Tina Kukla, Vincent Vigil, Jim Demes, Karen Duhaj, Karen Stoessel, and Kathryn Cox.

Further thanks go out to the Lapidos family — Mark, Carol, Michelle, and Jessica — for hosting the best party in the Beatles fandom. It's been certainly a thrill to transition from attendee to guest, and I thank you for the opportunities to serve on panels and give presentations. Greg Alexander, it has been an honor to know you, as I listened to your "Professor Moptop" segments on WXRT-FM for many years. Not only do we have a great deal in common in terms of the Beatles, but we're both Stevie Wonder fanatics! I look forward to more Fest panels together.

Jorie Gracen, you were one of my earliest Beatles teachers in terms of navigating sites through the Internet. Thank you for your support as I started my "Hard Day's Net" column through *Beatlefan*, and I look forward to attending more Michael Nesmith concerts with you and Mario.

Much of this book is composed of "Deep Beatles" columns at *Something Else Reviews*, and you would not be holding this book in your hands without the kindness and encouragement of editors Nick DeRiso and S. Victor Aaron. You both are a pleasure to work with, and I am grateful for the freedom you grant me and other writers on your site. It's a pleasure to work for such passionate music fans (and, in Nick's case, a fellow Beatlesgeek!), and I feel privileged to be a part of the *Something Else Reviews* family. You have my deepest gratitude.

I would also like to acknowledge Josh Hathaway, my editor at his wonderful site *Blinded by Sound*. Thank you for the opportunity to write about my other musical passion — R&B. Your friendship has been a bonus, and I look forward to the day when we write that concert etiquette book! Gordon Miller, I thoroughly enjoy writing for *Cinema Sentries*, and I appreciate your letting me explore my interest in music and film. Thank you very much for asking me to join your terrific site. Donald Gibson, you were my first editor at *Blogcritics*, and I was extremely lucky to work with someone as talented, open-minded, and kind as you. Your encouragement gave me the courage to pursue online music journalism.

Glen Boyd, I also thank you for your early editing and encouragement. I look forward to reading your next book. Other Blogcritics editors I'd like to thank are Connie Phillips and Barbara Barnett — thank you for your advice and support. Finally, I thank Nort Johnson for hiring me as a new writer for *Showcase Chicago* back in the 1990s. I'll always be grateful for his taking a chance on a college kid and giving me my first break.

My sincerest thanks go out to my family, particularly my parents and my cousins Maureen and Colin Morgan. They have never ceased supporting me ever since I was a child, and I will always be grateful to my father for teaching me everything he knows about music.

Thank you to Enoch Doyle Jeter for designing the beautiful cover and for your creative insight. My deepest thanks also go out to Sara Greene, who designed the logo for 12 Bar Publishing and designed the cover and interior for *Songs We Were Singing*.

Finally, I want to acknowledge Mark Lewisohn for inspiring me to pursue Beatles scholarship. His thorough research, attention to detail, and writing convinced me that there was a place for me in music journalism. It was an honor to finally meet him in person and get to know he and his wife Anita as friends as well as colleagues. Mark, thank you for your extraordinary work and sage advice, and thanks for convincing me to pursue what I love.

SELECTED BIBLIOGRAPHY

While countless books about the Beatles exist, the following list includes sources I consult most frequently in my research. Babiuk, Andy. *Beatles Gear: All the Fab Four's Instruments from Stage to Studio.* Milwaukee, WI: Backbeat Books, 2010.

"Beatles '1' Is Fastest Selling Album Ever." *CNN,* December 6, 2000. Accessed July 7, 2015, https://web.archive.org/web/20031012204655/ http://edition.cnn.com/2000/SHOWBIZ/Music/12/06/ beatles.reut/index.html.

Beatles, The. *Beatles Anthology.* San Francisco, CA: Chronicle Books, 2000.

Bedford, David. *The Fab One Hundred and Four.* Deerfield, IL: Dalton Watson, 2014.

Berkery, Patrick. "Every Snide Joke You've Told about Ringo Is Wrong: The Least-Celebrated Beatle Is Finally Getting the Respect He Deserves." *Salon,* April 14, 2015. Accessed June 26, 2015, http://bit.ly/1JGHlNl.

Bosso, Joe. "Geoff Emerick on the Beatles in the Studio." *Music Radar,* February 6, 2014. Accessed July 7, 2015, https://web.archive.org/web/20140402205148/ http://www.musicradar.com/us/news/guitars/beatles-engineer-geoff-emerick-on-abbey-road-219542.

Buskin, Richard. Beatles 101. N.p.: Parading Press, 2014.

—. "Norman Smith: The Beatles' First Engineer." *Sound on Sound*, May 2008. Accessed July 7, 2015, http://www.soundonsound.com/sos/may08/articles/normansmith.htm.

Caro, Mark. "Maniacs Coming Together to Critique The Beatles Reissues: An Easy Day's Night." *Chicago Tribune*, September 6, 2009. Accessed July 7, 2015, http://articles.chicagotribune.com/2009-09-06/news/0909030377_1_beatles-cds-beatles-fans-george-and-ringo.

Castiglioni, Bernhard. "Ringo Starr." July 11, 2005. Accessed June 26, 2015, http://www.drummerworld.com/forums/showthread.php?t=382.

Cohn, Nik. "A Briton Blasts the Beatles." *The New York Times*, December 15, 1968. Accessed July 7, 2015, http://www.nytimes.com/packages/pdf/arts/nikcohn1968.pdf.

Davies, Hunter. *The Beatles: The Authorized Biography*. New York: W. W. Norton, 2010.

Davis, Ivor. *The Beatles and Me on Tour*. N.p.: Cockney Kid Publishing, 2014.

Eccleston, Danny. "Beatles Remasters Reviewed." *Mojo*, August 24, 2009 Accessed July 7, 2015, https://web.archive.org/web/20090828014505/http://www.mojo4music.com/blog/2009/08/beatles_remasters_reviewed.html.

Emerick, Geoff, and Howard Massey. *Here, There, and Everywhere: My Life Recording the Music of the Beatles*. New York: Gotham, 2006.

Erlewine, Stephen Thomas. "The Beatles [White Album]." *AllMusic*. Accessed July 7, 2015, http://www.allmusic.com/album/the-beatles-white-album-mw0000418113.

—. "Beatles for Sale." *AllMusic*. Accessed July 7, 2015,

http://www.allmusic.com/album/beatles-for-sale-mw0000189172.

Everett, Walter. *The Beatles as Musicians: Revolver through the Anthology*. New York: Oxford University Press, 1999.

——. *The Beatles as Musicians: The Quarry Men through Rubber Soul*. New York: Oxford University Press, 2001.

Ewing, Tom. "The Beatles -*Beatles for Sale*." *Pitchfork*, September 8, 2009. Accessed July 7, 2015, http://pitchfork.com/reviews/albums/13424-beatles-for-sale/.

Gendron, Bob. "Beatles' Box in Stereo and Mono…" *TONEAudio*, August 27, 2009. Accessed July 7, 2009, http://www.tonepublications.com/music/beatles-box-in-stereo-and-mono/.

Gould, Jonathan. *Can't Buy Me Love: The Beatles, Britain, and America*. New York: Three Rivers Press, 2007.

Gundersen, Edna. "Remastered Beatles Catalog Comes Together, Real Soon." *USA Today*, September 1, 2009. Accessed July 7, 2015, http://usatoday30.usatoday.com/life/music/news/2009-08-27-beatles-remastered_N.htm.

Gunderson, Chuck. *Some Fun Tonight! The Backstage Story of How the Beatles Rocked America: The Historic Tours of 1964-1966*. N.p.: n.p, 2014.

Harrison, George. *I Me Mine*. San Francisco: Chronicle Books, 2007.

Howlett, Kevin. *The Beatles: The BBC Archives: 1962-1970* New York: Harper Design, 2013.

Hurwitz, Matt. "Young Maestros Helm Beatles Remasters." *Variety*, August 24, 2009. Accessed July 7, 2015, http://variety.com/2009/music/markets-festivals/young-maestros-helm-beatles-remasters-1118007647/.

Inglis, Ian, ed. *The Beatles, Popular Music and Society: A Thousand Voices*. New York: Palgrave Macmillan, 2000.

Jackson, Andrew Grant. *Still the Greatest: The Essential Songs of* the Beatles' Solo Careers. Toronto: Scarecrow Press, 2012.

Kessler, Jude Southerland. *Shoulda Been There*. N.p.: On the Rock Books, 2008.

—. *Shivering Inside*. N.p.: On the Rock Books, 2011.

—. *She Loves You*. N.p.: On the Rock Books, 2013.

Kot, Greg. "Is It Worth the Price?" *Chicago Tribune*, September 6, 2009. Accessed July 7, 2009, http://articles.chicagotribune.com/2009-09-06/news/0909030257_1_beatles-reissues-greatest-album.

Kozinn, Allan. "Original Beatles Albums to Be Reissued." *The New York Times*, April 7, 2009. Accessed July 7, 2015, http://www.nytimes.com/2009/04/08/arts/music/08beat.html?_r=0.

—. *The Beatles*. London: Phaidon, 1995.

Krerowicz, Aaron. *The Beatles & the Avant-Garde*. N.p.: AK Books, 2014.

Levine, Robert. "The Death of High Fidelity." *Rolling Stone*, December 26, 2007. Accessed July 7, 2015, http://www.rollingstone.com/news/story/17777619/the_death_of_high_fidelity.

Lewis, Randy. "Meet (and be) the Beatles." *Los Angeles Times*, August 30, 2009. Accessed July 7, 2015, http://articles.latimes.com/2009/aug/30/entertainment/ca-beatles30.

Lewisohn, Mark. *Beatles Live! The Ultimate Reference Book*. New York: Henry Holt & Co., 1986.

—. *The Complete Beatles Chronicles*. New York: Harmony, 1992.

—. *The Complete Beatles Recording Sessions: The Official Story of the Abbey Road Years 1962-1970*. New York: Sterling, 2013.

—. *Tune In: The Beatles: All These Years*. New York: Crown Archetype, 2013.

McCartney, Paul, and Barry Miles. *Many Years from Now*. New York: Owl Books, 1998.

McDonald, Ian. *Revolution in the Head: The Beatles' Records and the Sixties*. New York: Holt, 1995.

Norman, Phillip. *Shout! The Beatles in Their Generation*. New York: Fireside, 2005.

Robustelli, Anthony. *I Want to Tell You: The Definitive Guide to the Music of the Beatles, Volume 1: 1962-1963*. Brooklyn, New York: Shady Bear Productions, 2014.

Rodriguez, Robert, and Stuart Shea. *Fab Four FAQ: Everything Left to Know about the Beatles…And More!* New York: Hal Leonard, 2007.

Rodriguez, Robert. *Fab Four FAQ 2.0: The Beatles' Solo Years: 1970-1980*. Milwaukee, WI: Backbeat Books, 2010.

—-. *Revolver: How the Beatles Reimagined Rock 'N' Roll*. Milwaukee, WI: Backbeat Books, 2012.

Rowan, Rip. "Over the Limit." *ProRec*, December 2002. Accessed July 7, 2015, http://riprowan.com/over-the-limit/.

Saywers, Jude Skinner , ed. *Read the Beatles: Classic and New Writings on the Beatles, Their Legacy, and Why They Still Matter*. New York: Penguin, 2006.

Schwensen, Dave. *The Beatles at Shea Stadium: The Story Behind Their Greatest Concert*. N.p.: North Shore Publishing, 2013.

Self, Joseph C. "The Beatles vs. Lingasong: The Star Club Litigation." *The 910*, 1995. Accessed July 7, 2015, http://abbeyrd.best.vwh.net/lingsong.htm.

Sheff, David. *All We Are Saying: The Last Major Interview with John Lennon and Yoko Ono*. New York: St. Martin's Press, 2010.

Spizer, Bruce. *The Beatles Story on Capitol Records*, 2 vols. New Orleans: 498 Productions, 2000.

—-. *The Beatles Are Coming!: The Birth of Beatlemania in America*. New Orleans: 498 Productions, 2010.

—-. *Beatles for Sale on Parlophone Records*. New

Orleans: 498 Productions, 2011.

Stark, Stephen. *Meet the Beatles*. New York: Harper Collins, 2009.

The Beatles Anthology. Directed by Bob Smeaton, Geoff Wonfor, and Kevin Godley (1995; Los Angeles, CA: Capitol, 2003). DVD.

Turner, Steve. *A Hard Day's Write: The Stories Behind Every Beatles Song*. London: Carlton, 1999.

Varga, George. "The Beatles Are Hot Again." *San Diego Union-Tribune*, August 30, 2009. Accessed July 7, 2015, http://www.sandiegouniontribune.com/news/2009/aug/30/beatles-are-hot-again/.

Weinberg, Max, and Robert Santelli. *The Big Beat*. New York: Billboard Books, 1984.

Wenner, Jann. *Lennon Remembers*. New York: Verso, 2000.
White, Timothy. "A New 'Yellow Submarine Songtrack' Due in Sept." *Billboard*, June 19, 1999. 1; 76-78.

Womack, Kenneth, ed. *The Cambridge Companion to The Beatles*. New York: Cambridge University Press, 2009.

—-. *The Beatles Encyclopedia: Everything Fab Four*, 2 vols. Santa Barbara, CA: Greenwood, 2014.

—-. *Long and Winding Roads: The Evolving Artistry of the Beatles*. New York: Bloomsbury, 2014.

—-. and Todd F. Davis, eds. *Reading the Beatles: Cultural Studies, Literary Criticism, and the Fab Four*. New York: SUNY Press, 2012.

Woodall, James. "Ringo's No Joke. He Was A Genius And The Beatles Were Lucky To Have Him." *The Spectator*, July 4, 2015. Accessed July 5, 2015. http://www.spectator.co.uk/arts/arts-feature/9571372/ringos-no-joke-he-was-a-genius-and-the-beatles-were-lucky-to-have-him/.

WEBSITES

New Beatles sites surface virtually every day, but the following list includes the websites I find the most reliable, trustworthy, and user-friendly.

Alan W. Pollack's "Notes On" Series:
http://www.icce.rug.nl/~soundscapes/DATABASES/AWP/awp-notes_on.shtml

Beatles Bible:
http://www.beatlesbible.com

Beatles Examiner:
http://www.examiner.com/beatles-in-national/steve-marinucci

Beatles News:
http://www.beatlesnews.com

Beatlefan:
http://www.beatlefan.com

Bootlegzone:
http://bootlegzone.com

Dave Dermon III's Beatles Singles Pages:
http://www.dermon.com/Beatles/Beatles.htm

DM's Beatles Site:
http://dmbeatles.com

The Internet Beatles Album:
http://www.beatlesagain.com

John Lennon Series:
http://www.johnlennonseries.com

The Macca Report:
http://themaccareport.com/news/report.htm

Meet the Beatles…For Real!
http://www.meetthebeatlesforreal.com

Mitch McGeary's Songs, Pictures and Stories of the Beatles:
http://www.rarebeatles.com/nbeatles.htm

Robert Fontenot's About.com Beatles page:
http://oldies.about.com/od/thebeatles

Rock's Backpages:
http://www.rocksbackpages.com
(paid subscription required to access full site)

The Beatles Index:
http://www.norwegianwood.org/beatles/disko/index.html

The Beatles Interviews Database:
http://www.beatlesinterviews.org

The Beatles Rarity:
http://www.thebeatlesrarity.com

What Goes On:
http://www.beatlesnews.com

What Goes On: The Beatles Anomalies List:
http://wgo.signal11.org.uk/wgo.htm

WogBlog:
http://wogew.blogspot.com

OFFICIAL SITES

The Beatles:
http://www.thebeatles.com

Cirque du Soleil's *Beatles LOVE*:
https://www.cirquedusoleil.com/en/shows/love/default.aspx

George Harrison:
http://www.georgeharrison.com

John Lennon:
http://www.johnlennon.com

Paul McCartney:
http://www.paulmccartney.com

Ringo Starr:
http://www.ringostarr.com

ONLINE RADIO AND PODCASTS

Beatles-A-Rama:
http://beatlesarama.com

Fab 4 Free 4 All:
http://www.fab4free4all.com

The John Lennon Hour:
http://www.blogtalkradio.com/thejohnlennonhour

Something About the Beatles:
http://somethingaboutthebeatles.com

Things We Said Today:
http://www.beatlesexaminer.podbean.com

ABOUT THE AUTHOR

Kit O'Toole is a Chicago-based freelance writer and blogger who has written about rock, jazz, and R&B for over 20 years. Her work has appeared in such print publications as *Showcase Chicago* and *Goldmine*, and she is a contributing editor for *Beatlefan* magazine. As a blogger, O'Toole writes reviews as well as the "Deep Beatles" column for *Something Else Reviews*; she maintains the column "Deep Soul" for *Blinded by Sound*; and writes about music in film for *Cinema Sentries*. She is also the author of *Michael Jackson FAQ*, published by Backbeat Books in 2015. She previously served as a music editor for *Blogcritics*, an online culture magazine.

In addition to her music interests, O'Toole has a background in education. She earned an Ed.D. in Instructional Technology from Northern Illinois University, has taught freshman composition, and tutored students as part of NIU's Writing Across the Curriculum program. She currently resides in the Chicago area. For more information, visit the author's site at www.kitotoole.com.

ABOUT THE ARTIST

A native of Louisiana, Enoch Doyle Jeter holds a masters degree in printmaking from New Mexico Highlands university in Las Vegas, New Mexico. He is the artist in residence at the University of Louisiana at Monroe, where he is an instructor of fine arts printmaking. His works are in public and private collections in Ireland, Venezuela, Holland, Bali, Germany, Puerto Rico, Canada and the USA. Along with his wife, Yvette, Jeter is the cofounder of Enoch's Irish Pub and Cafe in Monroe, Louisiana. The establishment is home to the longest running John Lennon birthday celebration in America, started by a small, but lively, group of friends and family on October 9, 1980. He dedicates his work to his children and grandchildren, all of them fans of the Fab Four, of course.

The image on the cover was commissioned by the author, and was originally executed as a stone lithograph. A hand signed *giclee* print of the image is for sale at Jeter's website (www.enochdoylejeterart.com), or he can be reached at his e-mail address (enochspub@aol.com).

Made in the USA
Middletown, DE
09 August 2015